Praise for
WHY CHRISTIANITY MUST CHANGE OR DIE:

"The Ground of All Being created our minds and then created John Shelby Spong to stretch them. He is a man of faith who speaks of God—bravely and honestly—from his heart. To a postmodern world desperate to rediscover some meaning in life, Spong offers a challenging exploration of faith, prayer, ethics, and Christian community for the 21st century. 'Believers in exile' will find comfort in this book; many others will find it dangerous."

—Philip L. Culbertson, director of Pastoral Studies,
St. John's Theological College, Auckland, New Zealand

"For twenty years John Shelby Spong has been in pursuit of truth wherever it might lead. This passionate personal manifesto is an invitation to journey with him into non-theistic exile where the transcending reality of God as Love is found at the heart of a Christ-like humanity. Prophets in exile have a reputation for being disturbingly honest, but only closed minds and faint hearts have anything to fear from this brave challenge to a Christianity that must change or die."

—Rt. Rev. John C. Saxbee, Bishop of Ludlow,
author of *Liberal Evangelism*

"A vigorous account of John Shelby Spong's journey which will inspire you where you agree with him and make you sharpen your arguments where you don't."

—Rt. Rev. Dr. Peter Selby, Bishop of Worcester, England

"Bishop Spong challenges, provokes, amuses, and inspires in good measure in a book which I hope will bring many to re-think their attitudes to Christian believing."

—Keith Ward, Oxford University

"Has the Church got a future? And can a bishop be interesting? Yes—and Bishop Spong is the proof. He is unstoppably energetic and courageous, always in controversy, and always on the side of the angels. He is just what the Church needs."

—Don Cupitt, University of Cambridge

"Here's a bishop who not only reads, studies, and thinks ... but is prepared to tell us what he thinks, even when it's in conflict with traditional Christian dogma. It is for lack of such honest ecclesiastical leadership that the church today is in decline in a world that increasingly finds its teaching irrelevant. This book is a courageous and creative attempt to show how Christian faith can live into the future."

—Lloyd Geering, author of *Tomorrow's God*

"In this remarkable work, the product of a lifetime of reflection on the meaning of Christian belief, Bishop Spong presses beyond doctrinal formulations that seem to him dated and confining and attempts—with triumphant results—to find words to convey the profound experience of the divine that compels this controversial 'heretic' to continue to call himself a Christian. In a society desperate for meaning and for God, and increasingly threatened by the spiritual, intellectual, and moral vacuity of fundamentalism, *Why Christianity Must Change or Die* seems destined to play an extraordinary role in the lives of readers who, rejecting a religion of fear, close-mindedness, and self-deception, seek an honest and living faith."

—Bruce Bawer, author of
Stealing Jesus: How Fundamentalism Betrays Christianity

"Spong pulls no punches. Writing from self-imposed exile, he demolishes the stifling dogma of traditional Christianity in search of the inner core of truth. It is a courageous, passionate attempt to build a credible theology for a skeptical, scientific age."

—Paul Davies, author of *The Mind of God*

"Bishop Spong's book should be required reading for everyone concerned with facing head-on the intellectual and spiritual challenges of late-twentieth-century religious life. By working through his own Christian faith and tradition with honesty, intelligence, and courage, he provides a challenge for others, wherever they are, to do the same. And what is better, he provides hope and guidance for the journey."

—Karen L. King, professor of New Testament studies
and the history of ancient Christianity,
Harvard Divinity School

"Bishop Spong is a singularity among ecclesiastical leaders in the twentieth century. His candor, courage, and acumen are unparalleled. He aspires to bring a dying church back to life by fearlessly confronting the anomalies that have driven all too many Christians into exile. In his new book, no Christian shibboleth is spared in his penetrating analysis and confession. He takes refuge in no vestiges of Christian orthodoxy. He gathers the anachronisms of traditional faith and nails them to the cross."

—Robert W. Funk, chair,
The Jesus Seminar

"This is an important contribution to the Christian dilemma of our time. With reverence, courage, and compassion, Bishop Spong helps his readers to articulate their difficulties with the conception of God and, in so doing, to take the first step toward a creative resolution."

—Karen Armstrong,
author of *A History of God*

WHY CHRISTIANITY
MUST CHANGE OR DIE

A NEW REFORMATION
OF THE CHURCH'S
FAITH AND PRACTICE

WHY CHRISTIANITY MUST CHANGE OR DIE

A Bishop Speaks to Believers in Exile

JOHN SHELBY SPONG

HarperSanFrancisco
A Division of HarperCollinsPublishers

For further educational resources exploring the ideas and issues addressed in this and other books by John Shelby Spong, please contact:

Christianity for the Third Millennium
P.O. Box 69
Morristown, NJ 07963–0069
Fax: 973–540–9584
E-mail: CMSCTM@AOL.com
Telephone: 908–813–2954

Bible quotations, unless otherwise noted, are from the New Revised Standard Version of the Bible, copyright © 1946, 1952, 1971 by the Division of Christian Education of the National Council of Churches of Christ in the U.S.A. Used by permission.

HarperCollins Web Site: http://www.harpercollins.com

HarperCollins®, 📖 ®, and HarperSanFrancisco™ are trademarks of HarperCollins Publishers Inc.

FIRST HARPERCOLLINS PAPERBACK EDITION PUBLISHED IN 1999

Library of Congress Cataloging-in-Publication Data
Spong, John Shelby.
    Why Christianity must change or die: a bishop speaks to believers in exile: a new reformation of the church's faith and practice / John Shelby Spong.—1ˢᵗ ed.
    Includes bibliographical references and index.
    ISBN 0–06–067532–2 (cloth)
    ISBN 0–06–067536–5 (pbk.)
    ISBN 0–06–060500–6 (international pbk.)
    1. Christianity.   2. Christianity—Controversial literature.   3. Spong, John Shelby.   I. Title.
    BR124.S67 1998
    230—dc21   97–44975

01 02 03 ❖RRD 20 19 18 17 16 15 14

For
Brian Yancy Barney
and
Rachel Elizabeth Barney,
whose mother brought new joy to my life and who made being a
stepfather a privilege and a delight.

Contents

Contents

Preface

THIS BOOK HAS BEEN in progress for more than twenty years. It is a work of faith and conviction. It is my witness as one who desires to worship as a citizen of the modern world and to be able to think as I worship. I write it as a person to whom the Christian Church has accorded honor, rank, and the privilege of leadership in the episcopal office. It comes thus from the life of a bishop whose vows at the time of my consecration included both a promise to defend the faith and to guard the unity of the church. The vocation of doing just that in a rapidly changing world has been my privilege for almost a quarter of a century.

As the author of these pages, I am aware that I can hardly be mentioned in the public press without the adjective *controversial* being attached to my name. That word has almost become a part of my identity.

The first occasion for this acquired reputation came in 1974, when as a priest in Richmond, Virginia, I had the pleasure of conducting an extensive public dialogue with Dr. Jack Daniel Spiro, the rabbi of Richmond's Reformed Temple Beth Ahabah.

This dialogue developed because of a book I had published in 1974 entitled *This Hebrew Lord.*[1] The rabbi, intrigued by this title, read the book and invited me to debate its content with him at the synagogue on three successive Sabbath eve services. As we talked together to plan this event, the format grew to include three Sunday mornings at St. Paul's Episcopal Church, the parish where I was serving located in downtown Richmond. This dialogue excited the public, and both synagogue and church were crowded for each session. It also caught the attention of the newspapers, radio, and television in the Richmond area and was covered extensively.

On one Friday evening during this dialogue, the rabbi asked me to explain to his Jewish audience just how God, the "Holy Other," could be said to have become particular and concrete in the person of Jesus of Nazareth, which was his understanding of the Jesus claim made by Christians.

Seeking in my response to avoid some ideas from popular Christian theology that border on the heresy of monophysitism,[2] I sought to portray the Christ figure in the familiar Jewish terms of "word" and "will," derived from the Hebrew scriptures. The Jews believed that the word of God had been spoken and that the will of God had been lived in particular times and places within human history. So if I could present the person of Jesus in these biblical categories, perhaps my Jewish audience could hear some things in a way different from what they had traditionally thought Christians were saying about Jesus. Throughout Jewish sacred sources, particularly in the postexilic writings, there appeared the concept of messiah. In Hebrew the word for messiah was *mashiach,* which was translated into Greek with the word *christos* and into English with the word *Christ*. "You are the Christ" was the Christian affirmation uttered by Peter at Caesarea Philippi (Mark 8:29). But *mashiach* meant not some abstract belief about Jesus' essence but rather the belief that Jesus was the life through whom the word of God had been spoken and the will of God had been lived out, a life in which the reality of God was experienced as present in history. In a striking way, the Jews had broadened their concept of messiah so that even Cyrus of the Persians was called *mashiach* in the book of Isaiah (45:1),[3] because the Jewish people discerned that the will of God was being accomplished in history through the life of this man who knew neither the Torah nor even the name of Yahweh.

In response to the rabbi's questions on that Sabbath eve, I asserted, "The Bible never says in a simplistic way that Jesus is God. Jesus prays to God in the Gospels. He is not talking to himself. Jesus dies on the cross. It makes no sense to say that the holy God died. The Bible only says that what God is, Jesus is; that God is met in Jesus; that to see Jesus is in some sense to see God." I was pleased with both my answer and with the response of my Jewish audience. It was, however, a theological distinction far too subtle for the secular press to grasp.

"Jesus Is Not God, Rector Asserts" was the headline greeting readers of the *Richmond Times Dispatch* the next day, and the debate was on. Letters to the editor defending Jesus' divinity against this heretical priest flooded that newspaper for at least six weeks. St. Paul's Church was picketed by placard-carrying members of the Janke Road Baptist Church, protesting Jesus' demotion. The conservative church press, led by the crusty editor of *The Living Church*, Carroll Simcox, and Perry Laukhuff, the right-wing editor of a now-defunct newsletter entitled *The Certain Trumpet*, took up the challenge.

This event occurred during a time of great upheaval in the Episcopal Church, when women were demanding access to ordination. In protest against the slow bureaucratic church decision-making process, women had been ordained "irregularly" in Philadelphia in 1974 and in Washington in 1975. An enormous amount of anger against these changes was flowing from conservative advocates, who wished to purge the church of those who broke rank with "the historic faith and practice" of an all-male Christian priesthood. The bishop of the Diocese of Virginia, Robert B. Hall, was known to be sympathetic to ordaining women. When one of the irregularly ordained women concelebrated the Eucharist in a church of that diocese with Bishop Hall in the congregation, he responded to his critics by claiming that his eyes were closed in prayer so that he did not see the presence of the offending woman. Conservatives were not pleased. So the combination of this liberal bishop, who would not uphold the church's ban against women, with this liberal priest in dialogue with Jewish people caused the right-wing religious press to refer to conservative Virginia as "a disaster area." The Diocese of Virginia had never been so significantly honored before.

This debate had just begun to cool down when I was elected Bishop of Newark on March 6, 1976. Now the rector who "denied that Jesus was God" would be one of the ruling bishops of the church. It was more than the likes of Simcox and Laukhuff could manage. So they mounted a national campaign to prevent my election from being confirmed. Quotations from *This Hebrew Lord* were lifted from its pages and circulated widely to every bishop and to the members of every diocesan standing committee in the United States. Assisted by the Reverend Dr. Philip Cato, I wrote a careful and reasoned response to these rather reckless charges. It did not help. "A new Bishop Pike is being born," the press asserted. One diocese, West Virginia, where I had declined a year earlier to be a candidate for bishop, now decided I was not fit to be a bishop anywhere. Yet, when the votes were cast, I was overwhelmingly confirmed, with only seven standing committees actually voting no. The effect of that campaign, however, was, first, that the sales of *This Hebrew Lord* spiked and, second, that I entered the House of Bishops better known than bishops who had been in that house for decades. The reputation as controversial, heretical, even as a nonbeliever, has never departed from the minds of my critics.

A book that I published in 1983, entitled *Into the Whirlwind: The Future of the Church,*[4] contained all of the seeds of my future work. I called on the Christian Church to enter the knowledge revolution, the sexual revolution, and the revolution against tribal identity and prejudices in a radically interdependent modern world. But because this volume was still in the realm of the theoretical and the speculative, it did not fan the embers of the dormant controversy. It also sold fewer than twenty thousand copies and so was little noticed.

All of that changed in the late eighties when the issue of the church's discrimination against gay and lesbian people came to a head. In 1987 the Diocese of Newark became the first diocese in the Anglican Communion to call on the church officially to end its homophobic practices and to be honest about ordaining qualified gay and lesbian candidates to the priesthood. This diocese also asked the church to take whatever action might be necessary to free its clergy to bless publicly the sacred commitments of gay and lesbian couples. In 1988 I published a book designed to call the church to a new awareness of these sexual issues. It was entitled *Living in Sin?: A Bishop Rethinks Human Sexuality.* On December 16, 1989, responding to my own study and to the recommendation of the decision-making bodies of the Diocese of Newark, I proceeded to ordain to the priesthood a man who for about five years had lived in a publicly acknowledged, committed relationship with his male partner. He was a seminary graduate who also possessed the glowing endorsement of his theological faculty. The issue was theoretical no longer.

Once again the fury of the religious right was loosed. The catalyst was, of course, this gay ordination, but in the attempt to discredit me in any way possible, the old theological issues were raised over and over again. The implication was that this kind of action should be expected from one who is theologically suspect. From that day to this, the drumbeat of hostility from conservative, fundamentalist, and evangelical circles has been my daily bread. It reached a climax when the assistant bishop of the Diocese of Newark and thus my partner in the episcopal office, the Right Reverend Walter Righter, was officially charged with heresy in 1996. His crime was that, in 1990, acting on my behalf and with my authority, he had ordained to the diaconate the Reverend Barry Stopfel, an openly gay man who lived with his life partner, the Reverend Will Leckie. I had ordained this man to the priesthood a year after his diaconal ordination in a very public ceremony. But when the heresy charge was aimed, it was my associate and not me who was picked to receive it. Perhaps they felt that he would be an easier target or they simply did not want to give me so large a public forum.

During the years that separated that first gay ordination and the heresy trial for Bishop Righter, I continued my writing career and pressed the theological boundaries of the traditional understanding of Christianity. In 1990 I published what is still my best-selling book, *Rescuing the Bible from Fundamentalism* in which, among many other significant positions, I suggested that perhaps the "thorn in the flesh" that plagued Paul, that power to which his body said yes even when his mind said no, was that he was himself a deeply repressed, self-rejecting gay man. In 1992 I published *Born of a Woman,* in which I raised the possibility that the birth narratives of Jesus found in Matthew and Luke were created to cover the charge, surely raised by first-century critics of Christianity, that Jesus was illegitimate. There are hints of that charge scattered throughout the Gospel texts like unexploded land mines, if one knows how to read those texts. I also speculated on the possibility that Jesus might have been married to Mary Magdalene. A significant amount of New Testament data certainly points to the reality of that theory. The deepest resistance to such a suggestion, I discovered, also comes from those whose image of a woman is so negative that they cannot imagine that a divine Christ would ever associate intimately with a polluting woman. My speculation was thus an exercise in consciousness-raising.

In 1994 when *Resurrection: Myth or Reality?* came out, I faced the fact that viewing the resurrection of Jesus as a physical resuscitation was a late developing tradition in early Christianity. I sought to demonstrate that primitive Christianity as represented by Paul, Mark, and I would also argue, Matthew[5] made no such claims and that the original burst of life that accompanied the birth of Christianity was not dependent on this "orthodox" theory.

In 1996, in *Liberating the Gospels,*[6] I contended that the authors of the synoptic Gospels, Matthew, Mark, and Luke, were not eyewitnesses, nor were these Gospels even based primarily on eyewitness memories of the life of Jesus. Rather, these Gospels were liturgical works organized against the background of the Jewish liturgical year. Therefore, they must not be literalized, but their meaning must be probed from within that Jewish context.

The publication of each book resurrected anew the theological debates. Newspaper journalists returned to the common information pool and rewrote the stories of previous controversies with a particular twist. My suggestion that Paul might have been a repressed gay man became a dogmatic assertion. My question about why the birth narratives were originally written was turned into a statement that Mary had been raped. My attempt to probe the origins of the resurrection narratives was changed into the accusation that I denied the truth of the resurrection. My analysis of the organizing principle behind the synoptic tradition was turned into the charge that I did not believe the Bible at all. The culmination of this kind of journalism came in 1997 when the *Edinburgh* (Scotland) *Evening Newspaper,* in a long feature article, called me "the most radical bishop in the world."

Each of these books, however, found an enthusiastic audience of seeking lay people, who were willing to be carried far beyond the distortions of these scare headlines. Invitations to speak on these themes came from across the United States and throughout the world. The reception I was accorded lifted me into being one of the better-known religious authors in the English-speaking world. But I also found an increasing and unremitting hostility among certain groups of ordained people and among their fellow lay travelers in conservative, evangelical, and fundamentalist circles.

I have had a "truth squad" based at an evangelical theological college in Sydney follow me throughout Australia wherever I lectured, handing out their tracts and publications designed to mute my witness. I have lectured with guards protecting me in Calgary, Alberta. I have walked through shouting picket lines in San Diego, California, to deliver a lecture. I have endured a bomb threat at Catholic University in Brisbane, Queensland. I have been the recipient of sixteen death threats, all of which came from Bible-quoting "true believers." Finally, I have been attacked in books from the religious right by such people as Alistair MacGrath, N. T. (Tom) Wright, and Luke Timothy Johnson and in a proposed monograph of essays called *Can A Bishop Be Wrong?,* edited by Peter Moore of the Trinity School for Ministry, an evangelical seminary in western Pennsylvania.

All of these efforts had an effect. When the attacking books were published, which were revealingly hostile and without saving academic merit, my controversial reputation was solidified. I do not even seek to deny it any longer.

Actually, I am grateful for each of my critics. What they unwittingly did was to identify me as a resource for the religious seekers of our world who yearn to believe in God but who are also repelled by the premodern literalizations that so frequently masquerade as Christianity. My mail from these people has been unbelievable. I have tried to answer each letter, and in the process I have built an audience that has journeyed with me in my search for a way to be an honest and deeply committed believer in our day. I write this book for that audience. Like me, they are believers in exile.

As I pause to recognize those to whom I am indebted for this book, I think back especially to the influence of three of my chief mentors and teachers. The first was John Elbridge Hines, the presiding bishop of the Episcopal (Anglican) Church in the United States from 1964 to 1973, who exhibited the courage of his convictions sufficient to lead Christianity to places it had never been before and who had the grace and integrity to undergo vilification without responding in negativity. John Hines was an institutional man, and though he possessed a brilliant mind, he did not have the time to pursue biblical and theological issues in great depth. However, more than any ecclesiastical figure in my knowledge, he pushed his church into real dialogue with the real world.

The second was John A. T. Robinson, the English bishop of the 1960s and 1970s who was the author of the surprise bestseller *Honest to God*. This man forged the rare path that I have walked by trying to combine his career as a bishop with his career as a scholar and a writer. He also inspired me through our personal relationship to take up this task as he was laying it down. I am grateful that my wife, Christine, and I have been able to stay in touch with John Robinson's widow, Ruth, and with his brother, Edward, over the years. As a matter of fact, I sat at John Robinson's desk at Arncliffe in North Yorkshire in June of 1997 to work out the chapter on prayer in this book while Chris and I were Ruth's guests in the Robinsons' home. That experience brought to me a new realization of how deep my debt to John Robinson really is as I continue his honest quest to reconcile authentic Christian faith with knowledge and awareness.

The final mentor that I must mention is Michael D. Goulder, retired professor from the University of Birmingham in the United Kingdom. He is also the only New Testament scholar I know who now claims to be an atheist and who resigned both his priesthood and his membership in the church when he felt that he could no longer be part of that faith community whose god was too small to be God for him and his world. Michael stands as a symbol of those people whom the church can never seem to stretch its boundaries wide enough to include. But more than perhaps he has realized, he has opened windows to new vistas of God for me.

I have also spent some quality time with Don Cupitt of Emmanuel College, Cambridge; Keith Ward, of Christ Church, Oxford; the various members of the Jesus Seminar; English/Australian physicist Paul Davies; world-renowned author Karen Armstrong; the New Zealand Presbyterian "heretic" and professor Lloyd Geering; as well as many others whose thought and work have moved me to explore the areas that I discuss in this book. Surprisingly, to some of my mentors, like Cupitt and Goulder, I am a hopeless conservative for remaining committed to the church and the Christian faith. To others, like Robinson, Armstrong, and Ward, I am a fellow pilgrim. None of them, however, will be surprised when I call myself "a believer in exile."

When all is said and done, I write out of my faith commitment as a Christian and not in an attempt to create controversy. But where this faith has been corrupted into literalized propositional statements, I have become its exposer and its critic. I have come to see the controversy that ensues not as negative and not even as destructive to the church. I regard it rather as a positive sign of health and vitality. It represents a faith tradition in ferment, simultaneously dying and being resurrected. It reveals the willingness to explore the truth of God without seeking to protect God from the disturbance of new insights. It arises out of the sense that God must be worshiped with the mind as well as the heart. It also reveals that any god who is threatened by new truth from any source is clearly dead already. Such a deceased god needs to be snatched away from threatened believers so that the anxiety of "a god vacuum" at the heart of some peoples' lives will drive them into honesty and integrity as either believers or nonbelievers. There is no hope for the revival of worship so long as an idol lives undisturbed in the place reserved for a living God.

Clifford L. Stanley, one of my theology professors almost forty-five years ago, was fond of saying, "Any god who can be killed ought to be killed." The theological seminary in which I was trained had as its motto, "Seek the truth come whence it may, cost what it will."[7] I have tried to follow both the words of my teacher and the motto of my seminary quite closely. So I speak today to my audience of seekers and searchers, to those who are either members of the church alumni association or who still hang onto their Christian identity by the skin of their teeth. I also speak to those lay people who have come to believe that their own sense of honesty requires them to close their minds to most of what they hear in church on Sunday mornings.

I speak to those who have been taught that to engage in worship requires that they never raise questions. These are my companions on this journey, the ones with whom I seek dialogue. To them I issue the biblical invitation: "Come now, let us reason together, says the Lord" (Isa. 1:18). They are the ones who seem to understand that Christianity must change or die.

I am grateful to many people who assisted me in the preparation of this manuscript. First, I express my thanks to the clergy and people of the Diocese of Newark, who have undergirded, encouraged, and supported my writing vocation within the context of my episcopal career, now in its twenty-third year of life. The content of this book first appeared in public in a series of diocesan lectures given at Christ Church, Ridgewood, New Jersey, where the Reverend Margaret Gunness is rector and the Reverend David Ware was the associate on the first occasion and the Reverend John Thompson-Quartey is presently the associate; at Grace Church in Madison, New Jersey, where the Reverend Lauren Ackland is rector and the Reverend Wesley Wubbenhorst was the assistant; and at St. Luke's Church in Montclair, New Jersey, where the Reverend Robert Schiesler is rector and the Reverend Jill McNish is the assistant. It was also made public in Edmonton and Calgary in a series of lectures sponsored by the United Church of Canada, a faith community I greatly admire.

Much of this book's final form was written while on sabbatical leave, which was a great gift given to me by my wonderful diocese. I spent part of that sabbatical in the library of the University of Edinburgh in Scotland and was greatly assisted in that endeavor by the library staff as well as by the primus of the Episcopal Church in Scotland, the Most Reverend Richard Holloway, his assistant, Ms. Pat McBryde, and one of his clergy, the Reverend James Wynn-Evans.

The other part of that sabbatical I spent as a visiting scholar at Oxford University, where the Bodleian Library was made available to me, and again the kindness of the staff was greatly appreciated. That Oxford stay was made possible by Keith and Marian Ward of Christ Church in Oxford. Keith is Regius Professor of Divinity at Oxford and was especially helpful to me in checking original sources. Talking to Keith Ward is like encountering an encyclopedia of knowledge. Marian's academic credentials are also impressive.

I am much in debt to two other people: first to Christine Mary Spong, who is far more to me than just a very special wife. She is also an outstanding editor. She travels with me everywhere I go. In the lectures that I am privileged to give around the world, she hears my thoughts being born and then witnesses them maturing and becoming a permanent part of who I am. She listens to the reactions of my various audiences and helps me to clarify my concepts. She edits my monthly newspaper column. When my lectures have been videotaped for public use as educational aids, she has been the primary editor and producer of those videos.[8] Better than anyone else, she knows when my material "sings" and when it does not. She also has a special gift with words and a sense of how a sentence can be transformed from the mundane to the exciting. Christine seeks to bring the written word into an approximate correspondence with the verbal word so that the excitement present in a speech can also leap off a page. I love her beyond measure, and I also admire her enormously as a coworker and a partner in ministry. She is a rare and wonderful combination. I salute her with gratitude.

The second person is Lyn Conrad, my executive secretary, whose word processor accomplished miracles while this book evolved from lectures into chapters. This is the second book on which Lyn has worked with me, and her patience with endless revisions, her ability to check out factual details, and her encouragement as each chapter has unfolded have given me the ability to forge ahead. I am also grateful to her husband, David, who must receive her home some evenings exhausted and frazzled.

The members of the core staff of our diocese also have had their work increased because of my second career as an author. I am grateful that they seem to think that the pluses in this have outweighed the minuses. This small and wonderful group of colleagues, each of whom is also a good friend, includes my partner in the episcopal office, our bishop suffragan, the Right Reverend Jack Marston McKelvey; our chief financial officer, Mr. John George Zinn; our administrative officer, Mr. Michael Francaviglia; our personnel, congregational development, and public relations officer, Ms. Dale Gruner, and our dean, the Very Reverend Petero Sabune.

The other members of our staff who share our building at 31 Mulberry Street in downtown Newark include the Reverend Richard Bardusch, Cecil Broner, Sandonna Bryant, Rupert Cole, Gail Deckenbach, the Reverend Larry Falkowski, David Farrand, Charles Hayes, Barbara Haynesworth, the Reverend Elizabeth Kaeton, Mary Knight, Carla Lerman, Barbara Lescota, Dennis Morterud, William Quinlan, Joyce Riley, Tim Russo, Lucy Sprague, Elizabeth Stone, Peter VanBrunt, and Johanna Young.

Finally, I am grateful to my family. Beyond my wife, Christine, there are our married children: Ellen Spong and her husband, Gus Epps; Katharine Spong and her husband, Jack Catlett; Jaquelin Spong and her husband, Todd Hylton; as well as the four wonderful grandchildren that they have presented to us: Shelby Catlett and John (Jay) Catlett, John Lanier Hylton, and Lydia Ann Hylton. Then there are our unmarried son and daughter, Brian and Rachel Barney, to whom this book is dedicated. Brian is preparing to enter medical school, and Rachel is an officer and a pilot in the United States Marine Corps. All of these family members contribute to making our lives very blessed and happy. Lastly, I salute our mothers, Doolie Boyce Griffith Spong, who is in the ninety-second year of her life, and Ina Chase Bridger, who is afraid someone might suggest that she is approaching ninety. She isn't! She is a sprightly seventy-plus and is a delight. I sometimes marvel at just how much love surrounds my life. It is centered in this incredible family.

John Shelby Spong
Newark, 1998

WHY CHRISTIANITY
MUST CHANGE OR DIE

ONE

✳

On Saying the Christian Creed with Honesty

"We believe in God ... "

Beginning with these words, the corporate faith of the Christian Church finds expression in the phrases of what it calls the Apostles' Creed. That "we" who "believe in God" is made up of many individuals. I am one of them.

I define myself above all other things as a believer. I am indeed a passionate believer. God is the ultimate reality in my life. I live in a constant and almost mystical awareness of the divine presence. I sometimes think of myself as one who breathes the very air of God or, to borrow an image from the East, as one who swims in the infinite depths of the sea of God. Like the psalmist of old, I have the sense of God's inescapableness.[1] I am what I would call a God-intoxicated human being.

Yet, when I seek to put my understanding of this God into human words, my certainty all but disappears. Human words always contract and diminish my God awareness. They never expand it.

The God I know is not concrete or specific. This God is rather shrouded in mystery, wonder, and awe. The deeper I journey into this divine presence, the less any literalized phrases, including the phrases of the Christian creed, seem relevant. The God I know can only be pointed to; this God can never be enclosed by propositional statements.

The words of the Apostles' Creed, and its later expansion known as the Nicene Creed, were fashioned inside a worldview that no longer exists. Indeed, it is quite alien to the world in which I live. The way reality was perceived when the Christian creeds were formulated has been obliterated by the expansion of knowledge. That fact is so obvious that it hardly needs to be spoken. If the God I worship must be identified with these ancient creedal words in any literal sense, God would become for me not just unbelievable, but in fact no longer worthy of being the subject of my devotion. I am not alone in this conclusion. Indeed, I am one of a countless host of modern men and women for whom traditional religious understandings have lost most of their ancient power. We are that silent majority of believers who find it increasingly difficult to remain members of the Church and still be thinking people. The Church does not encourage us in this task. That institution seems increasingly brittle and therefore not eager to relate to its creeds as a set of symbols that must be broken open so that the concept of God can be embraced by new possibilities.

Institutional Christianity seems fearful of inquiry, fearful of freedom, fearful of knowledge—indeed, fearful of anything except its own repetitious propaganda, which has its origins in a world that none of us any longer inhabits. The Church historically has been willing to criticize, marginalize, or even expel its most creative thinkers. The list would stretch from Origen through Erasmus to Hans Küng. This institution seems far more eager to expend its energy defending its limited truth than to see its holy words for what they are—mere pointers toward the reality that limited words always distort and can never finally capture. This simple conclusion becomes inescapable as soon as the creeds themselves begin to spell out their affirmations and our questions shout to be heard.

The opening phrase of the Apostles' Creed speaks first of God as the "Father Almighty." Both of these words offend me deeply. Here the mystery that I treasure in God begins to be filled with limiting cultural definitions. The word *Father* is such a human word—so male, so dated.[2] It elicits the traditional God images of the old man who lives just beyond the sky. It shouts of the masculinity of the deity, a concept that has been used for thousands of years to justify the oppression of women by religious institutions. That history and that practice repel me today. The Christian Church at times has gone so far as to debate whether women actually had souls and whether girl babies ought to be baptized. That Church universally relegated women to clearly defined secondary roles until the latter years of the twentieth century, when that sexist prejudice began to dissipate. Even the recent ecclesiastical breakthrough in some faith communities, which has allowed women to be pastors, priests, and bishops, is embraced by only a small minority of the Christians of the world. The Church dedicated to the worship of a God who was called "Father" has consistently justified its rampant discrimination against women as the will of this patriarchal deity or, at the very least, as something idolatrously called the "unchanging sacred tradition of the Church." I do not care to worship a God defined by masculinity. I am no longer tolerant of gatherings where all the participants are men, sitting in a solemn assembly, clothed in their ecclesiastical dress, and acting as if they can determine what a woman may do morally with her own body. I have no interest in being part of an institution that is so deeply biased against women and intends to stay that way.

The word *Almighty* is equally troubling. *Almighty* has been translated theologically by the Church into such concepts as omnipotence (all-powerful) and omniscience (all-knowing). These two understandings constitute a provocative and disturbing claim. By attributing omnipotence to God, one also attributes to the deity the power to remedy any wrong or to prevent any disaster. Yet wrongs and disasters continue to be a part of life. Religious thinkers have danced around these realities since the dawn of time. The traditional arguments about free will and the virtues developed through suffering are today so weak and so unconvincing. To attribute to God omnipotent power in our world is thus logically to assert that the God who possesses this power must have chosen not to use it. The only real alternatives to this conclusion are found in asserting that God is limited, uncaring, malevolent, or nonexistent. None of these alternatives is very satisfactory. It was the playwright Archibald MacLeish who said, "If God is God, he is not good. If God is good, he is not God!"[3] The problem of evil simply cannot be solved by those pious claims of antiquity. Yet people continue to use this creedal language and to call God "Almighty." Perhaps they simply do not raise these real but difficult questions.

When we define God's almighty nature in terms of being all-knowing or omniscient, other equally difficult issues arise. The Bible, the Church's sacred textbook, portrays the God of antiquity as acting in ways that violate both our knowledge and our sensibilities today. If an all-knowing God had really made many of the assumptions that the Bible makes, then this God would be revealed as hopelessly ignorant. For many biblical assumptions are today dismissed as quite simply wrong. Sickness, for example, does not result from sin being punished. Nor does a cure result from our prayers for God's intervention or from the sense that we have been sufficiently chastised so that the punishment of our sickness might cease. In the disciplines of medicine, we deal today with viruses, bacteria, leukemia,[4] and tumors. God, called in the creeds "almighty," appears in our time to have little or nothing to do with either our sicknesses or our cures. In our generation, we attack viruses, germs, leukemia, and tumors not with appeals to an almighty God, but with drugs, chemotherapy, and surgery. To appeal only to the almighty power of our God in the face of these crises of the human experience would be regarded as naive in the world that we inhabit. That is just one of the vast changes in the perception of reality that separates our world from the world in which the creeds were written.

Epilepsy and mental illness also are no longer understood to result from demon possession, even though Jesus was portrayed in the Bible as believing that they did (Mark 5:8 and 9:25). Once again, honesty requires that we confront the Bible's limited grasp on truth. No doctor would treat an epileptic child today by ordering the demon out of him or her in the name of God. Religious people defend these tenets of creedal orthodoxy by saying that God expects us today to use our brains and the new knowledge that is available to us. But it is the very newness of that knowledge that the Church has resisted, fought against, and condemned through the centuries. Almost every medical breakthrough has been opposed by Christian leaders as a diminishment of God's power or as an attack on the divine capacity to control life by being able to punish sin with sickness.

Timothy Dwight, a Presbyterian divine and the president of Yale University from 1795 to 1817, was one of the acknowledged religious and intellectual leaders in the United States in his era. He preached passionately against the newly developing medical invention called vaccination. "If God had decreed from all eternity,"

President Dwight asserted, "that a certain person should die of smallpox, it would be a frightful sin to avoid and annul that decree by the trick of vaccination."[5] Such words amaze us today, but they arose out of the same mentality that created the creeds. When cures for disease began to be found in drugs and surgery, power was immediately drained from the Church and from the status of the clergy. No longer could either church leaders or clergy pretend that they alone possessed the divine ability to interpret every event in life as either a deserved blessing or a curse. In retrospect, the almighty quality of God, interpreted in terms of God's all-knowing capacity, has been successfully challenged. So what then does the creedal word *almighty* mean? Is it still a usable concept to apply to God?

What is true in the area of human disease is equally true in our understanding of those things we once named "acts of God" but that we now tend to call "natural disasters" (except in insurance policies). I refer to such phenomena as hurricanes, tornadoes, earthquakes, volcanoes, floods, and drought. Today we predict and chart these occurrences with remarkable efficiency and with absolutely no reference to God whatsoever. The almighty power that we once attributed to God no longer seems to be responsible for these disasters, nor is that divine power invoked in this generation to bring them to an end. Hurricanes and earthquakes, floods and droughts all seem to follow natural patterns until their fury is exhausted. If the Almighty One is not deemed capable by modern people of stopping these phenomena, then once again we need to ask about the meaning of the word *almighty* when it is applied to God. Does it have some poetic meaning that we no longer understand? It is true that a popular televangelist once claimed credit for praying a hurricane away from a path that would have threatened his television empire. Aside from the self-serving nature of such an incredible claim, one wonders how those people into whose path the evangelist supposedly directed the hurricane felt about the efficacy of this man's prayers and about the implied sense of God's valuation of them. I would have been more impressed if the purpose of those prayers had been to still the violent winds. It seems that this option did not occur to the evangelical showman. The fact remains that so much of what was once attributed to divine power we now explain with no reference to God whatsoever, and any understanding that linked these natural phenomena with human behavior and thus with human deserving has been totally broken.

Other aspects of the almightyness of God found in the Bible are also notably missing from the expectations of people living in this modern world. The Bible suggested that this almighty God had the ability to rain bread called "manna" from heaven upon the favored people to save them from starvation in the wilderness (Exod. 16). But there appears to be no such divine rescue of starving people in our time; at least no heavenly bread falls upon them. In our generation starving people in Somalia, Rwanda, and in the region of the world known as the sub-Sahara simply die, unless human relief operations are mounted.

This "almighty" deity also appeared, in the sacred text, to have had a not-so-noble political and moral agenda. The biblical God is portrayed as having had the power to split the Red Sea to allow the chosen ones to walk through on dry land (Exod. 14:1–22) and as stopping the sun in the sky to allow the people of Israel more time to achieve a military victory over the Amorites (Josh. 10:12). But in this same sacred text, that Red Sea was also closed by this God just in time to drown the hated Egyptians (Exod. 14:23–31), and that sun was finally allowed to set as soon as the slaughter of the wicked Amorites was complete (Josh. 10:13). What kind of almighty power is this? Is it even ethical? Is one capable of worshiping so capricious a deity who appears to embody the worst of our human tribal and political hatreds? So what do we mean, then, when we call God "almighty" in the Christian creed? Does any one of us really believe that? Yet can a God who is not capable of acting in this world in either of these traditional ways be more than a pale shadow of what God was once thought to be? Could anyone worship a God dismissed as impotent?

As awesome as these issues are, our problems with the creed do not stop there. Next, this statement of faith calls God "the creator of heaven and earth." What is heaven? Where is heaven? It is clear that in this ancient world the heaven that God created was thought of as God's home, and it was located beyond the sky. But those of us in this generation know that the sky is neither the roof of the world nor the floor of heaven. So what are we referring to when we assert that this almighty God created heaven? Are we talking about that almost infinite universe that no one living knew anything about when the Bible was written?

To ascribe to God the power to have created the earth also presents modern men and women with difficulties. We can now date the birth of this planet, rather accurately, by radioactive particles to be four and one-half to five billion years old. The biblical understanding of creation placed the birth of this world at a point a little more than six thousand years ago. That was the calculation arrived at by Bishop James Ussher of Ireland from biblical data. We now know that this biblical estimate represents only .00000012 of our known geological age. If the history of this planet were to be put on a twenty-four-hour clock from its beginning to the present, human life would appear only in the last few milliseconds or nanoseconds before midnight. There is also no scientific confidence today that human life was either the purpose or is the end of the creative process. Human beings feel so fragile and so accidental as these insights cascade in upon us. A world brought into being almost five billion years ago, and in which human life did not appear until almost yesterday, makes the creator seem distant and unreachable, indeed perhaps unreal. At the very least, whatever understanding we might have of creation today is surely different from the ideas of those who wrote the book that the Christians continue to call "the word of God." So inevitably, when members of this generation think about the origins of our universe, we do not bring biblical content, at least in any literal way, to our understanding of that universe. In what sense, then, is God the creator of heaven or the creator of the earth? Is that simply metaphoric? Yet these words still appear in this creed. So what do they mean to us, and can we still use them with integrity?

"We believe in Jesus Christ, his only Son, our Lord."

A sense of relief comes over our questioning souls when we arrive at this part of the creed. At least Jesus is more historically specific than God. We can imagine him, embrace him, and describe him in the words of our world. He is real. He lived in history at a particular time and place. Historical people, like Herod and Pontius Pilate, who can be documented from other sources, appear in his story. His name was Jesus of Nazareth. One can visit that village even today. Yet this relief at the specificity of Jesus is quickly tempered when the other creedal affirmations about this Jesus begin to be heard. He is first called God's "only son." Does that mean that none of the rest of us is or can be the son or the daughter of God? That kind of exclusive claim has been made throughout the ages with great power by the Christian Church. It is part of our religious mentality, no matter how limited and ungodlike it makes God seem to be. This phrase also seems to suggest that none of the other religious systems of the world can offer its people a point of connection with the divine. Many Christians have also made exactly that claim, and its effect for centuries has been to fuel a quite unholy attitude of religious imperialism. This arrogant claim also denies our own modern experience. I have surely met holiness in Jews,

Muslims, Hindus, and Buddhists, which I am not willing either to deny or to denigrate. So what does the phrase "God's only son" mean to those of us who cannot and will not be bound by the religious prejudices of the past?

"He was conceived by the power of the Holy Spirit and born of the Virgin Mary." Certainly if that phrase is to be understood literally, it violates everything we know about biology. Do we not yet recognize that all virgin birth tales—and there have been many in human history—are legendary? They are human attempts to suggest that humanity alone did not have the ability to produce a life like the one being described. All virgin birth stories, including the ones about Jesus, were fully discredited as biological truths by the discovery in 1724 of the existence of an egg cell. That discovery meant that the woman could no longer be regarded simply as the passive receptacle for the seed of the male, which is the implication of these narratives. Divinity thus could no longer be said to enter her offspring as a divine gift without being compromised by her own humanity. The woman from that moment on had to be recognized as a cocreator, an equal genetic participant in the procreation of every life. The primary assumption in the biblical story of the virgin birth— namely, that Jesus' divine nature came to him directly from God through his mother's impregnation by the Holy Spirit—is a hopelessly sexist idea born in a totally patriarchal world that denied the woman's contribution to every new life. The story of Jesus' birth, when literalized, is now seen to be filled with the stuff of legends. Yet classical theology has placed the content of these legends into the basic Christian creed and for most of the years of the Church's life has treated these phrases as literally true. In our day, the advances in our knowledge have rendered these phrases nonsensical whenever the assumption is made that they describe some objective truth. So how do we continue to say those words with integrity? Or do we?

Not only was the entry of Jesus into this world held to be abnormal by the biblical writers, but the creed goes on to suggest that his exit was abnormal as well. He ascended into heaven, we say, making the cycle of the divine round trip from Jesus' original home in heaven complete. Like the stories of his virgin birth, the stories of Jesus' literal ascension have been equally discredited by the expansion of knowledge. The biblical account of Jesus' return to heaven was based upon the ancient idea that the sky was the abode of God and that it was "up." A literal ascension makes no sense to those of us who live on this side of Copernicus, Galileo, and the space age. Indeed, the very word *up* is a meaningless concept in our time. When citizens of China and the United States point upward, they are pointing in diametrically opposite directions. "Up" is a spatial image. It reflects the assumption that the flat earth is the center of the universe, and, as such, it is incomprehensible to the modern mind. Today, if one could rise from this earth in an upward trajectory and go far enough, that person would not arrive in heaven but would rather achieve an orbit or, by escaping the gravitational pull of the earth, would journey into the infinite depths of space. Those up and down images are irrelevant in our space-comprehending world. A Jesus who came from heaven above to earth below by way of a virgin birth and who journeyed back to the presence of God by way of a cosmic ascension is not made of the same stuff of which you and I are made. How, for example, could such a life be one who "in every respect has been tempted as we are, yet without sin," as the Epistle to the Hebrews claims (Heb. 4:15)? What kind of temptation would that be? Thus, Jesus' humanity, so essential to traditional Christian theology, is instantly compromised. If we take these texts literally, he becomes not the incarnate one, "the perfect God and perfect man," but a kind of celestial visitor from another planet, not unlike Superman or Captain Marvel!

Yet if we can no longer speak of him in this ancient theological language, then are there some other words that we can employ that will do justice to the Christ experience or to the God that Christians claim he represented, revealed, or manifested? When those entry and departure adventures of Jesus are accompanied, as they are in the literal biblical texts, by a series of other wonders, which include both a star set in the sky, presumably by God, to mark the birthplace of this Jesus (Matt. 2:1–12) and talking angels who inform us that Jesus will return in the same manner that the disciples had seen him depart (Acts 1:10, 11), it is impossible for me to find a believable faith. I suspect that this is also true for other citizens of this century.

Between those two phrases in the creed that describe Jesus' legendary and miraculous entry into and his equally legendary and miraculous exit from this world, history does, however, enter the creed, for we say, "He suffered under Pontius Pilate, was crucified, died, and was buried." That is objective, measurable, and literal data.

Pontius Pilate was real. He served as the Roman governor in Judea from 26 C.E. to 36 C.E. Crucifixion was the way that the ancient Roman empire carried out the sentence of capital punishment. History, indeed a rather cruel history, is clearly present at this point in the creed.

Yet when one reads the dramatic narratives in the Gospels that accompany the story of Jesus' crucifixion, they do not appear to be historical at all. These treasured biblical tales describe some dramatic events that supposedly accompanied Jesus' actual death, such as darkness covering the earth (Mark 15:33; Matt. 27:45; Luke 23:44). Our ability today, by the use of computers, to recreate the exact locations of heavenly bodies in the sky on any day in the past or the future, precludes the possibility of an eclipse in Palestine anywhere near that time. So what was this darkness? The biblical story also says that earthquakes accompanied Jesus' death (Matt. 27:51). If that were not incredulous enough, the Gospels go on to assert that in this critical moment of salvation history, the curtain in the temple was split from top to bottom (Mark 15:38; Matt. 27:51; Luke 23:45), the graves of the dead were opened, and bodies long deceased emerged from those graves to walk around Jerusalem (Matt. 27:52, 53). We also read of Jesus' burial in a new tomb provided by a ruler of the Jews named Joseph of Arimathea (Mark 15:42–47; Matt. 27:57–61; Luke 23:50–56; John 19:38–42). That is hardly the way the body of an executed felon in conquered first-century Judea would have been handled.[6] Clearly, history has been interpreted in rather dramatic and fanciful ways in these narratives, and one has trouble deciding where history stops and interpretive storytelling begins.

When we move on to the biblical narrative of Jesus' resurrection, we discover another series of problems present in the contradictions found in the Gospel texts. Almost every detail of the resurrection of Jesus appearing in one Gospel is contradicted in another Gospel.[7] Yet Christianity was born in whatever the experience of that Easter moment was, and if no ultimate reality resides in that experience, then, in Paul's words, our "faith is in vain" (1 Cor. 15:14). Such a faith is also probably destined not to be eternal.

But what was that experience that has come to be called the resurrection? Did its reality differ from the description of it given in the Gospel narratives? Can we get beyond those biblical words to a place where we can touch the uninterpreted essence of Easter? Is the truth of Easter bound in time, or is it beyond time and therefore beyond history? Since the experience of resurrection is absolutely essential to the rise of Christianity, this creedal phrase becomes the great divide for the modern man or woman who yearns to be a believer. Where each of us stands in relation to this issue will determine more than most any other whether or not we can still be defined as Christians.

The text of this creed moves on, driving us next into what the church has traditionally called "the second coming" and "the final judgment." What meaning can the phrase "He will come again to judge the living and the dead" have as the third millennium of the common era takes center stage? The New Testament clearly expected the almost momentary return of Jesus to this earth (John 14:3; Matt 16:27; Mark 9:1). Yet that return has not yet occurred. Was that Gospel anticipation another example of inaccuracies in the biblical account?

Beyond that problem, however, we need to ask what the judgment of God means in the light of the way life is now understood. What is the basis on which what the Bible calls the final judgment will be conducted? When the Bible was written, the people knew little or nothing about social and psychological interdependence. Can anyone be judged today simply as an individual who is solely responsible for who he or she is or for what he or she has done? Postmodern people who know the depths of human interconnectedness, who understand psychological wounding and blessing, cannot be moralistic in the way that these traditional creedal images of judgment have always assumed. So if we continue to say these creedal phrases and claim to be believers still, we are forced to ask what these words mean when they emerge from our lips. Can any of us still say these phrases literally with honesty? Do we still believe what they have traditionally been interpreted to assert?

This creed concludes with a paragraph dedicated to the Holy Spirit, who was said to have created the church at Pentecost and who, it is suggested, continues to fill the Church today with a "God presence." First, we need to note that all of these Pentecost symbols come out of the same three-tiered skies into which Jesus was said to have ascended. The assumption lying behind the story of the sending of the Holy Spirit is that the earth is the center of the universe and that onto it the heavenly gifts of the God who lives above the sky can be poured. Second, the creed asserts that this Spirit will issue in the communion of saints, which will continually renew the "holy catholic Church." The Church, throughout its history, has indeed had moments when it certainly looked like saints living in communion. Many lives have been enriched and transformed by their associations with Christian worship and fellowship. But the Church has also had in its history some rather dreadful moments marked by such things as "holy" wars, "sacred" crusades, inquisitions, inhumane anti-Semitism, and an overt, killing racism, sexism, and homophobia. In these episodes incredible violence has been unleashed upon both God's people and God's creation by those who counted themselves as believers. These horrors have even been inflicted in the name of the God of love. Where was the communion of saints during those episodes? What do we do with this known history when we recite these words of this creed?

Next we say that the Holy Spirit gives us the forgiveness of sins, the resurrection of the body, and the life everlasting. It is a great creedal crescendo. Is there a divine source of forgiveness for our guilt and acceptance for our inadequacy? If so, how do we appropriate it? Is there an ultimate hope that transcends our mortality? If so, how are we to understand and articulate that hope today? When we examine the history of the Church, it appears that guilt, not forgiveness, has been the great lever of ecclesiastical control. Guilt has also been the source of so much of the Church's power. The Church's faith in life after death has been predicated on that guilt being alleviated, purged, or punished eternally. How do these realities fit into this great creedal crescendo?

Many believers cannot recite the Christian creed in our generation without having these questions arise. Creedal language comes out of another time. It reflects assumptions that this generation can no longer make. It thus employs a language that is not native to us. If we could just cease being believers, these problems would disappear. But some of us cannot cease believing. God is too real for us. We also cannot resign from our modern world or close our minds to its insights. We cannot pretend that we live in the first century. We cannot park our brains at the door of our places of worship in order to accept as real the words that were used to interpret God in years past but that can no longer today illumine our understanding of God.

Many of us can continue to be believers only if we are able to be honest believers. We want to be people of faith, not people drugged on the narcotic of religion. We are not able to endure the mental lobotomy that one suspects is the fate of those who project themselves as the unquestioning religious citizens of our age. We do not want to be among those who fear that if we think about what we say about God, either our minds will close down or our faith will explode. We are not drawn to those increasingly defensive religious answers of our generation. Nor are we willing to pretend that these ancient words still have power and meaning for us if they do not. We wonder if it is still possible to be a believer and a citizen of our century at the same time.

Perhaps before we can proceed in this inquiry, we need to embrace the idea that the creeds did not drop from heaven fully written. These familiar liturgical words were not even part of the original Christian understanding of the God revealed in Jesus. What we call the Apostles' Creed of the Christian Church did not begin to be formulated until the latter years of the third century and was not adopted until the fourth century of this common era. Even after adoption, its claim to being the literal and final truth of God was compromised when it was later modified by the Nicene Creed and still later by the Athanasian Creed. The purpose of every written creed historically was not to clarify the truth of God. It was, rather, to rule out some contending point of view. The adoption and expansion of these creeds took place in church councils amid raucous debates and politically motivated compromises. I see no reason to believe that the people who participated in these councils of the church in that distant time were any more brilliant, insightful, or knowledge-able than are the Christians of today. I do not, therefore, believe that the Christological formula was set for all time at Chalcedon in 451 C.E.[8] I believe that we Christians must inevitably revisit Chalcedon and once again do the hard work of rethinking and redefining the Christ experience for our time and in words and concepts appropriate to our world. I even favor the reopening of the debate between Arius and Athanasius on the nature of the Christ.[9] I also support efforts to reexamine and perhaps even to transcend the trinitarian compromise, if those now-literalized words prove to be no longer capable of leading us into the expe-rience of God toward which they originally pointed. I am increasingly unimpressed with what people call "orthodox" Christianity. It has become a kind of religious straitjacket into which all Christians must be bound or face expulsion from the faith community by those who think of themselves as the true believers. To be called an orthodox Christian does not mean that one's point of view is right. It only means that this point of view won out in the ancient debate. I am convinced that the future of the Christian faith rests not on reasserting those words of antiq-uity, but on our ability to refashion the symbols by which Christianity is to be understood in our time. This would include rethinking its creedal patterns in the light of contemporary understandings of the world. I hasten to recognize that any and all contemporary reformulations of the Christian faith will still be but the products of yet another age in human history. As such, they will inevitably reflect our levels of knowledge and our prejudices. So any recasting of the creeds that we might produce today will be no more eternal than those formulations of the fourth and fifth centuries proved to be, nor should they be.

What I am requesting, however, is that modern believers be allowed, and even encouraged, to recognize that the words employed in the theological debate that formed the creeds so long ago have become empty and meaningless to this generation because the way we perceive the shape of reality has changed so dramatically. Our task is neither to literalize nor to worship the words of yesterday's theological consensus. It is, rather, to return to the experience that created these creedal words in the first place and then to seek to incorporate that experience in the words that we today can use, without compromising its truth or our integrity as citizens of this century. As a believer, I am not prepared to deny the reality of the underlying Christian experience. Yet I do recognize that the future understanding and the very shape of Christianity will inevitably be different, profoundly different, from that which has come down to us from the past. The real issue for me is whether or not that developing future is or still can be adequately attached to its Christian past.

So while claiming to be a believer, and still asserting my deeply held commitment to Jesus as Lord and Christ, I also recognize that I live in a state of exile from the presuppositions of my own religious past. I am exiled from the literal understandings that shaped the creed at its creation. I am exiled from the worldview in which the creed was formed.

The only thing I know to do in this moment of Christian history is to enter this exile, to feel its anxiety and discomfort, but to continue to be a believer. That is now my self-definition. I am a believer who increasingly lives in exile from the traditional way in which Christianity has heretofore been proclaimed. "A believer in exile" is a new status in religious circles, but I am convinced that countless numbers of people who either still inhabit religious institutions or who once did will resonate with that designation.

I see in this moment of Christian history a new vocation for me as a religious leader and a new vocation for the Christian Church in all of its manifestations. That vocation is to legitimize the questions, the probings, and, in whatever form, the faith of the believer in exile. I believe that a conversation and a dialogue must be opened with those who cannot any longer give their assent to those premodern theological concepts that continue to mark the life of our increasingly irrelevant ecclesiastical institution. I think the time has come for the Church to invite its people into a frightening journey into the mystery of God and to stop proclaiming that somehow the truth of God is still bound by either our literal scriptures or our literal creeds.

The hunger for God is deep and pervasive in our society today. We need to recognize that this is not the same thing as hunger for the answers the church has traditionally given. Indeed, many seekers today do not act as if the Church will ever be a place where God can be fruitfully sought.

I hope there will be among those who will read or hear these words a significant group of people who are willing to walk by the side of those of us who yearn to be believers but who find ourselves in exile from the forms in which that faith has been proclaimed by the Church through the ages.

TWO

✳

The Meaning of Exile and How We Got There

CLAIMING THE IDENTITY of a believer in exile forces us to ask certain questions. What does exile mean? How does one recognize it? What were the forces that compelled us in this direction? Is exile a transitional state on our journey into God, or is it the dawning recognition that God is no more? These are not easy questions for believers to raise. They elicit fear and what theologians call existential angst. But belief will have no integrity, and faith no honesty, if the real questions are avoided.

I begin by stating the obvious. Exile is never a voluntary experience. It is always something forced upon a person or a people by things or circumstances over which the affected ones have no control. One does not leave one's values, one's way of life, or one's defining beliefs voluntarily.

The second fact is that exile is not a wilderness through which one journeys to arrive at a promised land. Exile is an enforced dislocation into which one enters without any verifiable hope of either a return to the past or an arrival at some future desired place.

I have quite specifically chosen this exile image to describe the state of faith in our postmodern world. I do so because the concept of exile is a familiar word in the sacred history of the Jewish and Christian people. Our spiritual ancestors have been there before. They indeed called a specific and defining moment in their faith journey "the Exile." An examination of that critical time in our religious past might help us to embrace our present situation. It might also provide us with insight into our own religious future, if there is to be a future. So let me bring that exile into focus.

THE EXILE OF THE PAST

Around the year 598 B.C.E. the little nation of Judah found itself under attack at the hands of a powerful enemy. Out of the north, the Babylonian army, commanded by a general named Nebuchadnezzar, swept down across the land, conquering everything in its path. In the time-honored military maneuver of the Jewish people, they retreated into Jerusalem, sacrificing the countryside in the process. Jerusalem was an all-but-impenetrable fortress. It was built high upon a hill. It was surrounded by thick exterior walls, behind which a small Jewish army could successfully hold off a vastly superior opponent. Jerusalem was equipped with a sufficient interior source of water that could not be cut off by its foes. It was the Jewish defensive custom at all times to store adequate provisions inside the city walls to enable the people to survive the siege of their enemies for a considerable time.

Long sieges were difficult to maintain in the ancient world. The attacking army grew restless if progress toward conquest was not achieved within reasonable limits. The spoils of victory available in a single city were not so great that enemy forces were tempted to remain for too long or pay too high a military price if other fields remained to conquer. The normal siege might last for a few weeks or even months before either surrender or a negotiated settlement would be worked out. If the defenses were formidable, the negotiated settlement was all but guaranteed. This would usually mean that a tribute would be paid and the defeated nation might agree to a certain vassal status. The conquerors would settle for being enriched, if not totally victorious. Then the army would move on, leaving the conquered people poorer and less free but still possessing a modicum of independence and the ability to keep their way of life and their values intact.

When the army of the Babylonians appeared on the Jewish horizon in those early years of the sixth century B.C.E., the city of Jerusalem had not been conquered by an external enemy for over four hundred years. Standing within its protective walls was the sacred Temple of Yahweh that Solomon had built. That temple was believed by the Jews, quite literally, to be the earthly dwelling place of their God. Jerusalem's elevation enabled it to catch the rays of the western sun, which transformed its sandstone construction into a lustrous hue. Looking toward this city from the south made it visually easy for people to conclude that this was not only a "golden city," but also the very place where heaven and earth came together. These qualities even led to the creation of a sense of invincibility, which encouraged a certain mythology to gather about this special place. It was called the City of God. The Jewish people came to assume that Jerusalem's centuries of freedom from conquest were neither accidental nor the result of its natural defenses alone. This city, they believed, was protected by nothing less than the holy God. An almost giddy confidence surrounded Jerusalem in the minds of its citizens. It found expression in the writings of an eighth-century prophet named Micah, who warned the people that such assumptions might well turn out to be a false hope (Mic. 3:9–12). Nonetheless, the idea that Jerusalem was divinely protected came to be understood as possessing even the authority of sacred scripture.

In the seventh century B.C.E., some two or three decades before the arrival of these Babylonian forces, the Deuteronomic reforms under a king named Josiah had centralized Jewish worship in Jerusalem. Three great festivals—Passover, Pentecost, and Tabernacles—were required to be celebrated exclusively inside the holy city, making it the liturgical center of Jewish life and thus adding greatly to its reputation.

Despite these inflated expectations, on this particular occasion things did not work out according to plan. The Babylonian army was immense, both in numbers and power. Jehoiachin, the king of Judah, surveying the military odds, finally decided to seek a negotiated settlement. He offered to surrender in the hope of gaining favorable terms. But this was a cruel enemy, and the price of surrender turned out to be the king's own capture and removal to Babylon along with his princes, his mighty men of valor, and a substantial number of the craftsmen and artisans of Judah. The Babylonians would leave no one in the land except, as the Bible said, "the poor people." The Babylonians then set up a vassal king named Zedekiah, the uncle of Jehoiachin, to rule in his stead. The Jewish nation had secured but the tiniest vestige of freedom. Yet, in this pitifully weakened state, Judah did still exist.

About ten years later, in 588 B.C.E., tiring of this vassal status, the people of Judah rebelled against their Babylonian conquerors and declared their independence. The Babylonian army responded by moving down once more into siege positions. This time, having learned their lesson, the Jews, who had retreated inside the walls of fortress Jerusalem, were determined to outlast their enemy no matter how long it took. It was to be the ultimate test of wills in Jewish history. And so it was that weeks faded into months. Months faded into the first year and then moved on toward the end of the second year. No army of antiquity had ever been this persistent for so small a prize. Eventually the Jewish food supplies were gone. People inside Jerusalem were starving. Cannibalism threatened to become a way of life. Weapons were in short supply. Once arrows, spears, and even rocks had been hurled at the enemy outside the city walls, they could not be retrieved.

Finally, in 586 B.C.E., the end came. With the morale of the defenders at rock bottom, the desperate Jewish army tried to escape from the city by night in search of supplies. However, they were spotted, pursued, defeated, and captured by the Babylonians. Then, without opposition, the enemy soldiers poured into Jerusalem. The few remaining Jewish resisters were massacred. The buildings of the city were razed to the ground, the houses were burned, and, most appalling of all to the Jews, the Temple of Solomon, God's dwelling place, was destroyed. The Babylonians next executed the sons of King Zedekiah in his sight and then proceeded to gouge out the king's eyes. The murder of his sons was to be his final vision. The remaining living citizens of Jerusalem and Judea were ordered to prepare for the long march into Babylon. It was the second and final deportation. None of the Jews from either deportation would ever see their homeland again, nor would they ever worship in their holy city again. The Jewish nation had come to an end (2 Kings 24, 25).

Everything these people valued, everything that defined them to themselves, was gone. Their nation was no more. Jerusalem, God's special city, was a pile of stones. The Temple, God's earthly dwelling place, was laid waste. The priesthood, their sacred customs, their creedal statements, the social fabric that gave order to Jewish life—all were lost.

The God the Jews worshiped had been identified with this land. Their sacred story had proclaimed that occupying this land was their God-given destiny. Their life inside Judah was organized according to the laws of this God. The calendar that they followed each year was punctuated by the great festivals and fasts of their religious life, which bound these Jewish people to their sacred soil and even helped them count and mark the passage of time.

Now the Jewish population was to be totally transported to Babylon, and, according to the pacification program of the Babylonians, foreigners would be imported to resettle their land. These foreigners knew neither Yahweh nor the Torah. This land would no longer be known as "the land of the Jews." These descendants of Abraham, Isaac, Jacob, Judah, and Joseph were once again to be aliens, homeless wanderers on the face of the earth. Since the Jews were convinced that the Torah could not be lived or obeyed in any other place save Judah, even the Torah lost its meaning. The festivals, which required a Jerusalem setting for their observance, could never be celebrated again. The very context out of which both their beliefs and their religious practices had emerged was now destroyed.

In the despair of meaninglessness, these Jewish people were forced to leave everything they knew and everything they valued to begin their journey into a Babylonian captivity. There was no hope of return. On one of these journeys into the exile, the book of Psalms recounted how the Babylonian soldiers taunted the defeated Jews. "Sing us one of the songs of Zion," their conquerors urged. But the Jews could not sing. They could weep and they could remember, but they could not sing. The God to whom their songs were directed was in Jerusalem. "How shall we sing the Lord's song in a foreign land?" was their response (Ps. 137:1–4). There appeared to be no hope for their return. They were in exile.

In this final defeat, the God of the Jews appeared to have been violated and laid waste. Perhaps these Jewish people assumed that their God, like their nation, was also now dead. A deity who was revealed to be too weak to protect the people was not a deity they could continue to worship. They were now compelled to live in a land that belonged to another deity. It was quite impossible in their minds to be a Jew outside of Judah. God, who dwelled in Jerusalem, could not hear the prayers of those who were exiles in Babylon. They could not act out the demands of the law beyond the boundaries of their nation. The Jerusalem high priesthood could no longer interpret the law, for the priesthood was no more. Since the law governed both their religious and their civic lives, this governing principle was no more. They were subjected rather to the customs and values of a foreign God whom they did not know and, perhaps more important, who did not know them. The God they had once worshiped was no longer able to hear their cries. The faith they once knew no longer existed. It had been obliterated in this violent act of war, defeat, and dislocation.

These Jews had once believed that God fought at their side against their enemies. They could believe that no longer. They once believed that God might punish them for their waywardness but that God would not destroy them. They could believe that no longer. They once believed that they were a specially chosen people. They could believe that no longer. They once believed that God had instructed them on where to live and how to worship. They could believe that no longer. They once believed that God dwelled in Jerusalem and ruled over Judah. They could believe that no longer. They once believed that God could hear their prayers. They could believe that no longer. They once believed that they had a destiny and a future. They could believe that no longer. They once believed that God could and would care for them. They could believe that no longer.

They could not sing the Lord's song again, for they were in a strange and devastating exile, and in that exile the God they had once served lost all meaning. This God, quite frankly, could no longer be God for them. It is traumatic to watch the God who has given shape, definition, and meaning to life be removed from a people's awareness. There are but two alternatives for such a displaced deity. This God must either grow or die. That is what being in a spiritual exile is all about.

THE EXILE OF THE PRESENT

In this postmodern world, those who still claim allegiance to the Christian religion find themselves, I believe, living in a similar kind of exile. Our God has also been taken away from us. For us, however, that removal of God did not occur in a single moment of violent defeat. It rather happened over a period of centuries as the steady and relentless advances in knowledge altered forever our ability to believe in the God content that stood at the heart of our sacred tradition.

The Christian faith came into existence in a world radically different from the one it now seeks to inhabit. According to the ancient work of a Greek astronomer named Hipparchus, the universe was assumed to consist of three tiers. Later a man named Ptolemy would develop this theory to a fine point and stamp his name upon it.[1] But at the time the Gospels were written, it was common wisdom that the earth was flat and was located directly beneath the sky. Beyond that sky was the realm in which the all-seeing holy God was believed to live. Thus human life was thought to bask in the ready and constant attention of this personal deity. Hell was the third tier of this universe and was assumed to be located beneath the earth. In this cozy three-tiered world everything that was not understood or that seemed either irrational or inconvenient was assumed to be a manifestation of this heavenly God's specific divine intervention. Concepts like miracle and magic abounded. When bad things occurred in people's lives, they were interpreted to be divine punishment, the just deservings for errant human behavior.

The God of the biblical story was assumed to be not only intensely personal, but also intimately involved in human affairs. This God was almost universally envisioned as male and was also thought of after the analogy of a mighty warrior who validated warfare as a noble and even a divine enterprise. The biblical phrase "Lord God of Sabaoth" meant "God of the Military Forces."[2] This God had a deep tribal identity; indeed, God's foreign policy in the biblical narrative was clearly pro-Jewish. God had freed the Jews from slavery in Egypt by visiting great violence on the Egyptians. God had led the marauding Israelites in their conquest of the land of Canaan. God had championed his people in their continuing conflict with the Philistines. One can only imagine that such a view of God was wildly popular among the Jews. It was not, however, a very pleasant view of God if you happened to be an Egyptian, a Canaanite, or a Philistine. A universal God of love this deity was not.

The Christian God evolved from these tribal roots and played the role of a quite similar tribal power throughout most of Christian history. In 312 C.E., for example, this God was said to have favored Constantine over Maxentius in the battle of Milvian Bridge, which was fought for the control of the Roman Empire. It was said that on the night prior to the battle God had posted the sign of the cross in the sky with the words "In This Sign Conquer" inscribed beneath it. This sign was designed to inform Constantine that he was God's chosen one. Such signs in the sky were thought to be appropriate in an era when the divine dwelling place was believed to be, quite literally, just beyond that blue barrier. In such a view, the sky was regarded as a veritable stage on which heavenly messages could be displayed regularly for all earthlings to ponder.

As Christian history unfolded, the power of the Church to control knowledge and public opinion increased exponentially, and so these views of God as both an external power and an invasive deity became dominant in all of Western civilization. When the Spanish armada, sailing for England in 1588, was destroyed at sea by a storm, it was widely interpreted by the English as a defeat for the Spanish Catholic deity at the hands of the English Protestant deity. God had sent that storm out of the sky to destroy the Spaniards and thus to shape English history with a new version of the biblical favored-nation status.

These ideas of God were firmly set and universally believed, and they formed the essence of the faith of Christians for the first sixteen hundred years or so of their history. The language of the Christian creeds took form in this period of time. But when the modern age began to dawn, a new understanding of the shape of the universe began to grow and God's place as the heavenly director of human affairs began to totter.

This revolution in Western thought began first, perhaps, with the work of Nicolaus Copernicus (1473–1573), who with relatively primitive astronomical tools began to study the sun, the moon, the stars, and the heavens in a new way. He came to some startling conclusions, which changed forever the way we would think about the skies and the God who presumably inhabited them. In this time before mass communications, the insights of Copernicus went almost unnoticed, however, until a disciple named Galileo Galilei (1564–1642), building on those Copernican insights, began to revise in a public way the perception of the universe and the place of the planet Earth within that universe. Galileo concluded that the sun did not rotate around the earth but rather that the earth rotated around the sun. It was a revolutionary idea and represented a major shift in human consciousness. This meant that the Earth could no longer be envisioned as the center of the universe and thus that God might not be quite so involved in the day-to-day affairs of human beings. This idea sent shivers down the spines of the ecclesiastical power brokers of the day, whose understanding of God depended on these heretofore unquestioned assumptions. Galileo was condemned to death as a heretic. In order to save his life, he was given the opportunity to recant, which he, not very courageously, decided to accept. His recantation, however, changed nothing. The ancient worldview against which the Christian story had been framed had been dealt a mighty blow. In time it would even be seen by some as a fatal blow. At that moment, however, it was only the first step toward our exile.

The process of adjusting to this new understanding of the world produced a long-term but inevitable trauma. The biblical view of the universe was slowly and quietly discarded. Perhaps the full acceptance of this idea was not complete until December 28, 1991, when the Vatican finally admitted officially that Galileo had been right and that the Church, as well as the Bible, had been wrong about the shape of the universe and the place of human beings and this world within that universe.

That Vatican admission came far too late. The world had for some centuries already assumed that truth. Air travel, satellite communications, and space exploration were all built on the insights of Copernicus and Galileo. When those insights became the working assumptions of human beings, the power of the Church to control life, or even to interpret it, began to fade perceptibly. That lost ecclesiastical power would never be recovered.

People began to grasp the fact that God did not sit on a throne beyond the sky looking down. Divine intervention became a problematic concept. As the knowledge of the universe grew, the religious community tried to adjust. Christianity began to shift the location of God from "up there" to "out there," as if somehow that new spatial image made God more believable. Finally, however, distances overwhelmed even this concept of God's dwelling place. The nearest star to our sun, Alpha Centauri, is about 4.3 light-years away. The large Magellanic cloud, the nearest galaxy to our galaxy, is about 150,000 light-years away. Andromeda, the nearest clearly defined galaxy, is 2,000,000 light-years away. What is a light-year? The distance light will journey in a year traveling at the approximate rate of 186,000 miles per second. One light-year equals almost six trillion miles. Our embrace of the vastness of space had the effect, finally, of removing God from the sky and then increasingly even from our human consciousness.

God was no longer either up there or out there. The heavens began to seem empty of that protecting, judging, and even caring divine presence. Yet the ancient world could envision God in no other way; neither can most of the religious systems of our contemporary world. So when believers faced the shock of an empty sky, the content that once filled the word *God* began a slow but certain retreat into oblivion. The modern consciousness was on the way to becoming godless, at least by traditional religious definitions. The Church began to wonder how it could continue to talk about a God beyond the sky who, according to the biblical story, had once sent fire from those same heavens to burn up the sacrifices offered by Elijah on Mount Carmel and thus to defeat the priests of an alien deity known as Baal (1 Kings 18:20–46). How could the story of Jesus ascending into the sky to return to God after his death (Acts 2) still be proclaimed with intellectual integrity? The stories of Jesus appearing out of the sky to his disciples on a mountaintop in Galilee (Matt. 28:16–20) or of Paul seeing a heavenly Jesus in that same sky on the road to Damascus (Acts 9) became increasingly problematic. Those biblical accounts were so obviously shaped by the ancient three-tiered worldview that no long existed. People living in the new world, whose shape Copernicus and Galileo and countless others had delineated, began to awaken to the fact that they could no longer use any of the traditional language about God and a heaven "out there" that so deeply filled our ancient faith system. That language had lost its meaning.

Beyond the time of Galileo, but still within the same century, an English physicist named Isaac Newton (1643–1727) applied his brilliant mathematical mind to this growing body of scientific data first suggested by the insights of Copernicus and Galileo. Newton was determined to demonstrate in intimate detail just how the world worked and, not coincidentally, how God worked within this world. So he began to assert that there were natural explanations for many of the things that in generations past had been considered mysteries attributed solely to the power of God. At that moment the need for God as the explanation for things that previously had been inexplicable began to fade, and with it also faded the previously powerful religious categories of miracle and magic.

This second cataclysmic revolution in theological thought also was not immediately recognized during Newton's day, primarily because Newton, who was a closeted Arian theologically, was also an effective ecclesiastical politician. Recognizing the lingering power of the Church, he wooed church leaders by filling his language with traditional holy words. He referred to the world of nature that he was exploring as a second book containing "the word of God." His task as a scientist, he wrote, was to discern God's message in the book of nature, just as it was the Church's task to discern God's message in the sacred scriptures. It was an effective and applauded political stance.

Yet, when Newton's work was complete, once again the arena in which God language operated had shrunk perceptibly. The view of God as an intervening divine power had been even more seriously undermined. Increasingly human beings learned that their world operated according to fixed laws, which brooked no interference from any external source, divine or otherwise. The explanation of sickness as a divine affliction began to be questioned. The weather patterns began to be seen as morally neutral, expressing no divine opinion about anyone's goodness or lack thereof. After a while even the members of those congregations who continued to gather during a drought to pray for rain did not trust their work sufficiently to bring raincoats and umbrellas.

After Newton, the God understood as either the cause of sickness or the personal director of weather patterns joined the God "up there" or "out there" as a vanished image. When this new loss of a sense of the divine was joined to the growing fear that perhaps no intervening power capable of or eager to respond to our deep yearnings inhabited the heavens, we suddenly began to fear that self-conscious human beings like us just might be alone in this universe. As modern men and women edged toward that conclusion, the lump developing in our throats accompanied the emptiness growing in our souls. One modern poet and playwright even suggested that when God died, human beings began to gather nightly around the divine grave to howl and weep.[3] But even so radical a revolution in the human perception of the world as the one that was accomplished by Isaac Newton did not end the relentless and traumatic march of believers into our modern exile.

A century or so after Newton, an English biologist named Charles R. Darwin (1809–1882) added enormously to the body of breathtaking modern knowledge and to the development of what today is called the secular spirit. The same frightened human beings who once thought that the earth was the center of the universe, and who once believed that they basked continuously in the center of God's heavenly gaze, had consoled themselves after Galileo and Newton with the comforting thought that at least human beings were the crown of God's creation and the purpose for which God had made the world. They even bore within themselves, it was said, the divine image. People living in the pre-Darwinian world simply could not imagine a time before human life, and in their worldview all of nature was believed to exist only for human benefit. They also made the assumption that a great gap separated the human from the subhuman forms of life and that an even greater gap separated the animate world from the inanimate world. The myth of creation with which the Bible opened had long been treated as if it were literally true both geologically and biologically. That myth suggested that the man and the woman were made on the final day of God's busy first week. God finished the perfect creation with this majestic act and proceeded to take the divine rest on the seventh day, thus creating the Sabbath. In the common mind so obviously true were these tales that few people in that believing age conceived of any other possibility—few people, that is, until the writings of Charles Darwin appeared.

In 1859 Darwin's masterpiece, entitled *The Origin of Species,* was published. That book caused most of the remaining principles by which human life was understood in religious terms to go up in smoke. Darwin suggested, for example, that the world of God's creation was not yet finished, directly contradicting the literal biblical text. The world, he said, was still evolving, still being created. Even Darwin had not yet embraced the true age of this planet, but his work opened the door to vastly expanding the timeline. Darwin's insights also caused the distance between human and subhuman life to shrink perceptibly. In the book of Psalms (Ps. 8), it had been suggested that human beings were just a little lower than the angels. But now we began to recognize that we were just a little higher than the animals. Apes and monkeys came to be viewed as our cousins, and defining the moment when human beings first appeared on this earth became problematic. Guesses still range from fifty thousand to two million years ago, depending on which definition of human life one is using.[4] There was much talk in that era about something called "the missing link," as if the various species of life were separated by a single link rather than by centuries of tiny adaptations. Pinpointing mutations in the eons of evolutionary time was difficult. Slowly but surely it dawned upon people that human beings are, in fact, highly evolved animals with superior brains. But since no ultimate worth or eternal destiny had yet been attributed to any animal, questions and doubts about the status that had been claimed previously for Homo sapiens began to be raised. Darwin's insights posed those questions and doubts in an unavoidable way so they began to rattle around in our psyches, to echo in our inner chambers, and to challenge our inflated self-perceptions. Increasingly, human beings felt themselves bound to this earth. "Dust thou art and to dust thou shalt return" became not just a Lenten note of penitence, but a statement of this newly understood reality of human life.

The Christian Church resisted Darwin with vigor, but the ecclesiastical power of antiquity had already been broken, and the Church's ability to threaten Darwin with execution as a heretic no longer existed. Besides, truth can never be deterred just because it is inconvenient. Today, whether his critics like it or not, Charles Darwin's thought organizes the biological sciences of the Western world. His work has made possible such once-unimaginable things as organ transplants using organs derived from subhuman species. They work because Darwin was right. That strange thing called "creation science" is nothing more than ignorant rantings reflecting a frightened and dying religious mentality.

After Darwin, the concept of life after death began to wobble visibly. It had never occurred to people to believe that animals possessed immortal souls and now they began to suspect that human beings might simply be highly developed animals. Most

Christian thought about life after death was based almost intuitively on the concept of a special creation, the sense that human beings bear God's eternal image. It began to be questionable that an immortal soul was in fact attached to every unborn child by God while that person was still in the womb. Another devastating blow had fallen on the religious ideas of antiquity, and the effect was to destabilize believers' lives and empty them of the religious content of the past. The thought of Charles Darwin had continued the relentless assault upon the believability of things that had once been included in the religious system of Christianity. The reality of the exile was becoming unavoidable, but it was destined to become more intense yet.

While Darwin was working on what might be called a secular understanding of biology, an Austrian doctor named Sigmund Freud (1856–1939) was beginning his probe into the inner recesses of the human psyche. In time Freud's thought would be added to the forces destroying the premodern understanding of life that had shaped the religious systems of the Western world. Freud brought to consciousness the infantile nature of so much of the language of the Christian religion, which had portrayed believers as children dependent upon the good favor of the divine heavenly father figure. He exposed the neurotic elements in religion, the childlike desire to win divine reward and to avoid divine punishment. He laid bare the oedipal nature of much of traditional theological thought, and he exposed the cannibalistic aspects of some forms of our eucharistic thinking. Freud's analysis was yet another devastating attack upon the credibility of traditional religious thinking, and Freud, like Galileo before him, was condemned, vilified, and opposed by Christian figures.

Carl G. Jung (1875–1961), Freud's disciple and later his rival, tempered Freud's attack a bit by seeing religious symbols far more positively than Freud had seen them. Jung was quickly embraced as an ally by the beleaguered religious leaders. But even Jung's thought included little, if any, credence for those classical religious concepts of our Christian past. Indeed, Jung saw the Christian religion as part of a historic process necessary for the development of consciousness, but only the fading shadows of religion remained available to the Western world. These shadows were, not unlike the smile of the Cheshire cat, which lingered awhile after the cat had disappeared, quite simply doomed. After the deaths of Freud and Jung, their insights entered the awareness of the Western mind slowly but surely. Today, even those who have never read a word of Freud will talk about a Freudian slip. But when the weight of the insights of Freud and Jung did settle into the thinking of the world, the content that filled most traditional Christian concepts was made to shrink once again. There was indeed almost nothing left. The exile was all but total.

Many other developments in Western thought furthered the squeezing of Christian content into increasingly irrelevant ghettos. Albert Einstein (1879–1955) destabilized both time and space by seeing them not as external properties, but as significantly related aspects of existence. He also introduced relativity as something present in all things, including that which religious human beings had once called "eternal and unchanging truth."

The twentieth century, following Einstein, brought the world of subatomic physics to the fore, and radical randomness and quantum weirdness entered our consciousness. Many religious people grasped eagerly at these fascinating insights, for they seemed to provide a place within our increasingly closed system where a divine power could reinvade our lives. It did not work, however. In subatomic physics, predictability was battered, and the mechanical world of Isaac Newton opened to such things as the impact of the observer and the recognition of an interrelatedness in all of life. God, understood as an external invasive personal being, received little support.

Acting on the insights of the astrophysicists, those engaged in space exploration brought to our awareness a new sense of how empty were the skies and how lonely was human life. Scholars such as Carl Sagan (1934–1997)[5] began to tell us just how much of the traditional religious meaning of the past was no longer valid. The list included almost everything that once had been called the content of our faith.

The understanding of God as a theistic supernatural parent figure in the sky was finally rendered no longer operative. God was simply drained out of existence as a working premise in our society. Rewards and punishments, either in this life or in the life to come, ceased to be the primary motivators of our behavior. The exile was complete.

The God of our traditional past, who was the source of our values, the definer of our sense of right and wrong, was simply no more. We, like the Jews of old, had been forcefully removed from all that had previously given life meaning The God we once worshiped had been obliterated before our eyes. We no longer knew who God was or indeed who we were. We knew that we were in the exile, even if we did not yet possess the words to describe that state of life. That is, I am convinced, where the formerly Christian western world lives today.[6] Some will surely deny it. Others will try to ignore it. None, however, will escape it. No way out of this exile is either visible or guaranteed. We are forced to recognize that other gods have died in human history before this generation. No altars are today erected anywhere to Baal, Astarte, Molech, Re, Jupiter, Zeus, Mars, or Mithra. We wonder if deicide is happening again, only now to our God.

Is it possible in this exile for us to remain believers? Some clearly do not think so. Many citizens of our century have given up believing and have assumed citizenship in the secular city. They no longer call themselves Christians or religious people or even believers. Others, reeling in the face of these pressures, have tried to dismiss all the data derived from the explosion of knowledge in the last few centuries as if it were false or evil or even as if it did not exist. These people maintain their premodern convictions with hostile vigor while asserting that everyone must be wrong but them. With great vehemence, they deny the realities that have produced the exile. They refuse to engage in the debate. They even produce bumper stickers, designed to defend their biblical source of authority, which say, "God wrote it! I believe it! That does it!"

Still others, like me and perhaps the audience to which I have some appeal, have begun to define themselves as believers in exile. They refuse to abandon the reality of God, yet they have been driven by forces over which they have no control to sacrifice much of the content of that God reality. So they are left with an almost contentless concept, which must be allowed to find new meaning or it will die.

In exile the Jewish people in the sixth century B.C.E. were forced to abandon all of the preconceptions and definitions that they had held about God. Our exile has done the same for us. The Jewish people could not return to the good old days. Neither can believers in this generation. Christianity now has arrived in this postmodern world. The God content of the past no longer sustains the contemporary spirit. We sense that our only hope is to journey past those definitions of a God who is external, supernatural, and invasive, which previously defined our belief. We must discover whether or not the death of the God we worshiped yesterday is the same thing as the death of God. Our first hurdle in our new spiritual journey is, however, simply to recognize the reality of the exile. We know the thought processes that have separated us from the God of yesterday and that have forced our entry into the exile. We also recognize how deeply the question of the psalmist, penned during the exile of the Jews, has become the question believers face in our generation.

"Sing us one of the songs of Zion," their tormentors demanded.

"How can we sing the Lord's song in a strange land?" the believers responded.

How indeed? To answer that question for our day is now our task.

THREE

✳

In Search of God:
Is Atheism the Only Alternative
to Theism?

SOME PEOPLE WHOM I greatly respect have decided that the Lord's Song can no longer be sung in this world with integrity. Among this number is a man I mentioned in the preface as one of my great mentors. He is an English scholar named Michael Donald Goulder, the author of some of the most provocative books on the Gospels that I have ever read.[1] Michael has now retired from his post as professor of biblical studies at the University of Birmingham in the United Kingdom.

As a young man, Michael was ordained to the priesthood of the Anglican Church. Because of his superior intellect and gentle spirit, his career developed rapidly. On one occasion he was even seriously considered for the position of Anglican bishop of Hong Kong.

His life, however, increasingly turned away from the institutional aspects of religion and toward an academic career, where his brilliance brought his ideas to an ever-widening audience at home and, through an increasing number of invitations to fill endowed lectureships, to a significant audience abroad. He had become one of the shapers of the Christian message for the future.

In 1981, however, Goulder startled his church associates and his reading public by resigning from both the priesthood and the Christian Church. Today he refers to himself as "a nonaggressive atheist."

Shortly after this resignation, Goulder defended his newly minted atheist position in a public dialogue with another English theologian named John Hick. The dialogue was published under the title *Why Believe in God?* Goulder rested his case for atheism primarily on the argument that the God of the past "no longer had any real work to do." The tasks assigned to this God by traditional wisdom, he suggested, have been slowly but surely stripped from the divine side. This God no longer fights wars and defeats enemies. This God no longer chooses a special people and works through them. This God no longer sends the storms, heals the sick, spares the dying, or even judges the sinner. This God no longer rewards goodness and punishes evil. Yet this virtually unemployed deity is still the primary object and substance of the Christian Church's faith. Goulder felt he no longer could or wanted to be identified with that understanding. In his penetrating analysis of what has happened to the concept of God, Goulder forced a new awareness into theological thinking. Unknowingly, he was calling the church to recognize that it had entered an exile. He concluded that as far as he could see the God of the past had died. He could envision no other alternative.

Goulder made a powerful case and issued a mighty challenge. Institutionally, the church did not know quite how to respond. It was clearly not ready to give up its doctrine of God, and so, after seeking to caricature Goulder's ideas, it went about its business as usual, took up its position behind a veritable Maginot Line of theological defense, and hoped the challenge would simply go away.

However, Goulder had touched a nerve in many of us. Deep in the conscious minds of countless believers is the knowledge that most of the traditional God images have lost both their meaning and their power. Many who still claim to be believers know in the depths of their being that they, too, have rejected these images. The narratives in the Bible, which undergird the superstructure of doctrine and dogma, have had their literal power cut to the bone by the advent of critical scholarship. The hymns and prayers of the church use images and make assumptions that most of us can no longer make. There is an increasing sense even among believers that the word *God* now rings with a hollow emptiness. Clergy in the exercise of their pastoral duties discover that the pious phrases they have dispensed so frequently are increasingly empty. They are received by the people without either enthusiasm or comment, as meaningless clichés. With every passing day, the ties that once bound traditional believers so tightly to these supernatural, supreme-being concepts of God are becoming dramatically loosened. "You will be in my thoughts" or maybe "in my prayers," people say, without really expecting either to do anything or that what they do will have any effect whatsoever. Since such words and phrases once brought comfort, it is assumed, perhaps that they still can, even if we no longer know quite what they mean.

But these clichés are simply regarded as the final weak defenses against an overwhelming sense of the loss of God. The conclusion is more assumed than spoken in our society. Michael

Goulder, once a priest, and still a biblical scholar of world rank, spoke that private assumption in a very public way. He was convinced that the God he once had worshiped was real no more, and he wanted his life to match that conviction with both honesty and integrity.

But the question for us must be, who or what is the God that Goulder has rejected? The answer seems overwhelmingly obvious. He has rejected the idea of God defined as a supernatural person who invades life periodically to accomplish the divine will. This deity is an intensely human figure who does grandiose and expanded, but nonetheless, human things. This is a God clearly defined in what we might call the language of theism. The shorter Oxford English Dictionary defines theism as "belief in one God as creator and supreme ruler of the universe." The *Encyclopedia Britannica* goes a bit further to describe theism as "the view that all limited or finite things are dependent in some way on one supreme or ultimate reality which one may also speak of in personal terms." It goes on to say that the theist "considers the world quite distinct from the author or creator." Richard Swinburne, an English theologian, defines theism as a view of God that is "something like a person without a body, who is eternal, free, able to do anything, knows everything, is perfectly good, is the proper object of human worship and obedience, the creator and sustainer of the universe."[2] Assuming these uses of the word, for the purposes of this book I will define theism as belief in an external, personal, supernatural, and potentially invasive Being. That is the definition of God literally present in the Hebrew scripture. That is, indeed, the definition that has so captured the popular concept of God that no possibility for God seems to exist beyond the scope of theism. Even our language draws that conclusion. For if a person is not a theist, acknowledging the existence of a being called God, then our language suggests that the only alternative is to be an a-theist.

Goulder accepted that logical conclusion, and he had the courage to act upon it.

But theism and God are not the same. Theism is but one human definition of God. Can any human definition ever exhaust the meaning of God? Are we not aware of that ancient bit of folk wisdom suggesting that "if horses had gods they would look like horses"? No creature can finally conceptualize beyond its own limits or its own being. A horse cannot think or imagine beyond the experience of a horse. Despite our human pretensions, that is also true of human beings. If human beings have gods, they will look and act remarkably like human beings. None of us can ever get beyond that. If we are going to speak of God at all, we must begin by acknowledging that limitation. Even if we admit revelation as a source of knowledge, that revelation will be received and understood within the limits of the human experience.

Indeed, a closer look at these gods we human beings have worshiped historically will reveal that they were recorded as having acted not just humanly, but sometimes in the very worst manner of human behavior. The Jewish God in the Hebrew scriptures was assumed to hate anyone that the nation of Israel hated. The gods of the Olympus, served by both Greek and Roman civilizations, were portrayed in a wide variety of what we today would call "compromised" sexual activities. Such a picture of the predilections of the gods makes it easy to understand just why these gods died.

The familiar Christian God acknowledged by almost all of our European ancestors not only blessed the imperialistic and colonial expansion of those nations in the seventeenth, eighteenth, and nineteenth centuries but also declared that this colonialist domination of the underdeveloped peoples of the world was the very will of the Christian deity. So under the banner of Christ, native populations in what we today call the third world were subjugated and converted, while the resources of those conquered nations were being extracted from their soil to bring wealth to the Europeans. That old lament of those we now call Native Americans that "when the Europeans came, we had the land and they had the Bible, but now we have the Bible and they have the land," rings with sardonic but real truth.

It becomes so clear that the God most of us have worshiped during human history has looked and acted in a very human manner. In view of this fact, my first discovery in the exile is that I can no longer approach this subject by asking, "Who is God?" Nor can I be limited to personal images for God. The "who" question and the personal images of God slide quickly together, and theology becomes an exercise not unlike staring into a mirror. The fact is that the God of Thomas Aquinas looked and acted very much like Thomas Aquinas. So, too, did the God of Martin Luther, John Calvin, and Thomas Cranmer look and act like each of these theologians. Definitions of God that are personal or that come as responses to the question "who?" are therefore quite dangerous. Some would say they are also increasingly quite inadequate. Hence, in my search for a new way to speak about God in the exile, I have come to see that I must abandon both personal images and "who?" questions and seek a different starting place.

But to reach this conclusion means that I must be prepared to dismiss most of the God content of the ages. That is what Michael Goulder did. If there is no other way to speak of God, then his path might have to become the path for all of us. For that reason, the enormity of that dismissal becomes a step not taken lightly. It is in recognizing exile, however, that we see the traditional pathway to God to be no longer open to us. Exile people know that there can be no return to the past, so they must be prepared either to give up or to look in some other direction. If exile from all religious systems is not our final destination, then only one alternative is open to us, and that is to go forward into we know not what. That is where the talk of God must now be located. The future may contain no answer either, but we do not know that yet. We do know, however, that the answer surely is not contained in the theistic God concept of yesterday. The believer in exile bets his or her faith on the possibility of a new insight emerging out of a new direction.

As theism begins to crack and die, we can see ever more clearly the process of "God creation" that we human beings have always pursued. The attributes we have claimed for God are nothing but human qualities expanded beyond human limits. Human life is mortal. God, we said, was not mortal. Stating it positively, we claimed God was *immortal*. Human life is finite. God, we said, is not finite. When we stated it positively, God became *infinite*. Human life is limited in power. God is not limited. *Omnipotent* then became our positive word. Human life does not know all things. God is not bound by that limitation. *Omniscient* then became our positive word. Human life is bound to a particular space or by immutable natural laws. God is conceived of as being not so bound. *Omnipresent* and *supernatural* then became our God words.

When we unravel the theological tomes of the ages, the makeup of God becomes quite clear. God is a human being without human limitations who is read into the heavens. We disguised this process by suggesting that the reason God was so much like a human being was that the human beings were in fact created in God's image. However, we now recognize that it was the other way around. The God of theism came into being as a human creation. As such, this God, too, was mortal and is now dying.

Once we have moved beyond our rhetoric and know what it is that we are seeing, then the fingerprints, revealing theism's human creation, become almost amusingly obvious. An illustration of this is in the Noah story in Genesis (9:8–17). God was a great warrior, it was said, and occasionally the wrath of this warrior deity turned against human life. The great flood was interpreted as one such incidence of God's warfare against the sinful creation. When the rains ceased and the floodwaters began to recede, the scriptures suggested that what had actually occurred was that God had laid aside his weapon of war. In that era where the bow, together with its projectiles called arrows, was the primary weapon with which to attack an enemy at some distance, God, the distant heavenly warrior, was said to have laid the divine bow aside. Since God was conceived of as a Being of enormous size, this divine bow had to be large enough to cover the heavens. Since God was magnificent in splendor beyond human imagining, this bow had to include all of the brilliant colors of the spectrum. So when God laid down the divine weapon and ended the warfare designed to punish the sinfulness of humankind, the sign was the divine bow, called the rainbow, that covered the sky. It was an ingenious interpretation, and it lasted until scientists figured out how rain reflects and refracts the rays of the sun into the colors present in a beam of light.

Pressing this inquiry into the sources of theism further, we now need to ask, "What was the human need that caused us to create God in our own image in the first place?" When and why did theism actually emerge? Our deepening probe suggests that theistic religion was born at the exact moment when human self-consciousness first emerged out of the evolutionary process. Indeed, I would suggest that what we might call human history has never existed without both self-consciousness and theistic religion. I would go further and say that it was the emergence of self-consciousness that demanded the creation of theistic religion. Since religion was conceived in theistic terms at the very moment of the rise of self-consciousness, at the dawn of human history, theism was able to develop its powerful and exclusive lock on the definition of God. That is why the death of theism feels like the death of God. The two have never been separated before. So looking still for clues to help us into some new approach to the divine, we seek to understand what happened at the dawn of human life to make this combination so intense.

We are helped in this pursuit of insight by the great father of the psychoanalytic discipline, Sigmund Freud. In 1927 he sketched out his thoughts on this subject in a book entitled *The Future of an Illusion*. Here Freud probed the origins of human life and the various human creations that enabled human beings to cope with their existence. Religion was, he argued, a major one of those human creations.

The birth of theistic religion, Freud argued, grew out of the trauma of self-consciousness. For billions of years, Freud observed, the creatures who inhabited this earth did not have a sufficient intellectual capacity to raise questions about the meaning of their lives or indeed to ask whether life possessed any ultimate meaning. They simply lived and died in an endless pattern without knowing that this was either their reality or their destiny.

Finally, however, a creature evolved with a brain sufficient to be self-aware, self-conscious, and to have the capacity for self-transcendence. The shock of mortality and meaninglessness entered history at that moment, Freud contended. Now the world possessed a creature who could anticipate dying, who could understand disaster, and who could view its destiny to be nothing more than decay. This was a traumatic realization, and with that realization, definable human existence was born.

If trauma is sufficiently intense, and if it cannot be dealt with adequately in any other way, then the inevitable human response is hysteria. Religion, Freud contended, was the coping mechanism, the human response to the trauma of self-consciousness, and it was designed above all else to keep hysteria under control and to manage for these self-conscious creatures the shock of existence.

The first tenet in all human religion, he observed, was that the powers that threatened human beings were assumed to be personal. This meant that the sun, the heat, the cold, the wind, the water, and the storm were defined as the manifestations of supernatural beings or a supernatural being. If this were so, then human beings were not victims of a blind impersonal force unresponsive to their needs. As manifestations of the personal deity, these powers could be related to and controlled in the same way that human beings had always been able to deal with those who possessed authority. These powerful divine figures could also be placated, bargained with, flattered, or appeased. Frail and frightened human beings thus could ingratiate themselves with these external personal powers so that instead of being victimized by them, they could move the deity to protect or spare them instead. So it was that natural disasters were routinely interpreted to be the angry expressions of the supernatural beings or being who lived beyond this world. Those natural forces all emerged from the sky, where God was presumed to live. Therefore, they must have been designed by this deity to reward, punish, or warn according to what humans deserved. Keeping the laws of God, which were understood not as the creation of society but as the revealed will of the deity, then became of paramount importance. It was the way to keep the deity satisfied. Worshiping properly and faithfully also became the first line of defense against possible human disaster. It was a powerful system, against which few people chose to rebel. The one who had broken the rule, therefore, had to be quick to confess it, to promise amends, and even to offer sacrifices if necessary to make up for the offense. If he or she did not, the whole people might perish.

The member of the tribe who was called the shaman, the medicine man or woman, or the high priest claimed the right to speak for this God, to reveal God's rules and to be able to carry out God's plan for proper worship. When this holy figure was also believed to be able to turn away the wrath of a storm or the fury of sickness by prayers, incantations, or sacrifices or to be able to interpret the meaning of that storm or that sickness in a convincing way, then the power of the priesthood was established and the authority of such religious figures was secure.

Freud found in all of these theistic manifestations the suppressed hysteria of a newly self-conscious creature. Defense against hysteria requires that nothing occur that would destabilize the system, for only thus can the angst of self-consciousness be kept in check. The presence of that defense system in human religion was for Freud the sure sign that he had discovered in religion not the manifestation of truth but the manifestation of trauma. Religious truth was said to have been revealed by God and thus its content was not subject to debate. The community authorized to receive this revelation was said to have understood it perfectly and to be able to define it infallibly. Therefore, no one was allowed to debate their interpretations. Religious truth was thus protected by a double immunity.

Real truth, Freud suggested, does not need to be surrounded by such impenetrable barriers. Truth in its objective form can compete and win in debate in the public arena. Religious truth and theistic understandings were shielded from that debate. Religion itself was not an activity in pursuit of truth; it was rather born to be a significant part of the security system of human life.

Only when we recognize this defense mechanism in religion can we grasp the meaning of the constant presence in primitive religion, and certainly still present in Western religion, of an intense, even a killing, anger. Irrational hostility is a symptom of hysteria. Anger has always marked the religious establishment. This is why so many Christian leaders historically have justified

such things as the stifling of debate with ex cathedra pronounce-
ments, the persecution of dissenters, the excommunication of
nonconformists, the execution of heretics, and the engagement
in religious wars. This is also why anger is always just beneath
the surface of organized religion in almost every one of its
Western manifestations. The preaching of evangelists is
marked by finger pointing and face-contorting expressions of
hostility while they talk about the wrath of God. Anger lies
underneath the glee expressed by the preachers of Christian history when they assign unbelievers to hell. Anger is the reason
why many religious people act as if they will not enjoy the bliss
of heaven if they are not simultaneously allowed to view those
not so fortunate writhing before their eyes in the fires of hell.
Anger is the reason why the Church throughout its history kept
writing creed after creed to clarify just who is in and who is out
of this religious enterprise so that religious people would know
who their enemies were and could act appropriately against
them.

It was Freud's contention that theistic religion was born as
the means of dealing with the trauma of self-conscious existence.
It was born as a tool designed to keep our hysteria in check. The
theistic definition of God as a personal being with expanded
supernatural, human, and parental qualities, which has shaped
every religious idea of the Western world, came into existence
not through divine revelation, Freud argued, but out of human
need. Today this theism is collapsing. The theistic God has no
work to do. The power once assigned to this God is now
explained in countless other ways. The theistic God is all but
unemployed. I am convinced that this powerful and provocative
Freudian analysis is correct. That is one reason why human life
in the theistic world has arrived in an exile. Human beings have
evolved to the place where the theistic God concept can be and
must be cast aside. It has become an inoperative premise. If there

is no other possible understanding of God, then surely God has died.

It was when I reached this conclusion but still could not dismiss what seemed to me to be an experience of something other, transcendent, and beyond all of my limits that I knew I had to find another God language. Theism was no more.

FOUR

*

Beyond Theism to New God Images

I T WAS FOR ME a most unusual moment. While I was busily
going about my duties in one of the churches of our diocese, a
lay woman walked up to me and asked, "Bishop, is it possible to
be a Christian without being a theist?"

Her question stopped me cold. Church people do not normally ask this kind of question. More often than not they frame a
question in such a way that the answer will strengthen or affirm
what they already believe. This woman, however, was pressing
the edges of the institutional consensus, apparently ready to move
into some different possibilities. She was also framing for me in a
public setting the very issue that my study was forcing me to
examine.

If we could only succeed in moving theism aside, then other

avenues for exploring God might open up before our eyes. If the "who" question as a means of entering a God inquiry has hit a stone wall, then perhaps we could try a "what" question. If human analogies projected heavenward have become bankrupt, then perhaps we should examine those aspects of human experience where we feel compelled to venture beyond normal limits or into new horizons. Perhaps we can cast the Christian experience in nontheistic images. It is certainly worth a try.

Many sources in human history encourage us to explore this new avenue. The Buddhist tradition, for example, is not a theistic religion. Nowhere in classical Buddhism do the Buddhists posit the existence of an external deity. When Buddhists experience bliss or transcendence in meditation, they do not attribute this to contact with the supernatural. They assume that such states are natural to humanity and can be learned by anyone who lives right and who learns the proper spiritual techniques. Experiencing bliss involves emptying the self so as to transcend the limits of both subjectivity and objectivity to be one with Being itself, which Buddhists describe as timeless and uncreated. However, it hardly would be proper to assert that the Buddhists of the world are atheists, unless atheism can be called profoundly religious.

While visiting in China some years ago, I had the experience of conducting an interfaith dialogue in a Buddhist temple with a Buddhist monk and holy man named the Venerable Kok Kwong. It was a moving and deeply real spiritual experience to roam the terrain of another person's sources of holiness and to allow him to roam over mine. Following the dialogue, I stayed to pray in that temple with its statues of Buddha and its magnificent and striking colors, which called one into an intensity of consciousness. Of course I prayed to the God of my Christian experience, but in the calm of that place, surrounded by the grace of welcome from the Venerable Kok Kwong, I was sure that I was on holy ground. Buddhists clearly believe in God, but not in a deity who is defined in theistic terms. Exploring the levels of meaning that can be found in an Eastern faith tradition can help us learn to see through such limited words as *theism*. It also reveals that our ancient Western definitions of God do not exhaust the reality of God.

We also recall that Socrates was made to drink the hemlock until death came upon him because he, too, was judged guilty of being an atheist. Anyone who reads Socrates today knows how profoundly ignorant that judgment was and is. Socrates had a different vision. He viewed the reality of God through a different lens, which the lesser minds of his day could not embrace. The popular gods of the Olympus simply were not big enough or true enough to survive the transition from one age of humankind to another. So Socrates said no to these deities and moved to explore new possibilities. It cost him his life. But today, some 2400 years later,[1] he becomes another role model for believers who reject the traditional content of God without rejecting God.

Karen Armstrong, in her insightful book *A History of God,* has demonstrated that Jews, Christians, and Muslims were all at one time accused of being atheists when their ideas began to challenge the popular religious wisdom of their day. It is almost typical of religious people to make idols out of their religious words. Perhaps in their quest for security, they identify their concept of God with God. When that concept is challenged, they think God is being challenged. That is why no concept of God can ever be more than a limited human construct, and personal words about God, we must learn to admit, reveal not God but our own yearning. So believers in exile are forced to face the fact today that all Bibles, creeds, doctrines, prayers, and hymns are nothing but religious artifacts created to allow us to speak of our God experience at an earlier point in our history. But history has moved us to a place where the literal content of these artifacts is all but meaningless, the traditional definitions inoperative, and the symbols no longer competent pointers to reality. Part of the nature of the exile experience is that it is a death watch for God as we have known that God. The anxiety of the exile is that in human history no dying concept of God has ever yet been resuscitated. Theism, as a way of conceiving of God, has become demonstrably inadequate, and the God of theism not only is dying but is also probably not revivable. If the religion of the future depends on keeping alive the definitions of theism, then the human phenomenon that we call religion will have come to an end. If Christianity depends on a theistic definition of God, then we must face the fact that we are watching this noble religious system enter the rigor mortis of its own death throes. "Can one be a Christian without being a theist?" thus becomes a powerful question.

The God worshiped by the Jews before their Babylonian exile was not the same God who emerged from the exile. Much later a longer-range view of Jewish history reconnected the two, but that was not the sense of the people who lived at the time of the exile. Similarly, the God worshiped in the Christian West will not survive the thought revolution that has produced our exile, though we, too, might hope for some future reconnection. The Jews came out of Babylon as a people of faith with a God who had been transformed from the tribal deity of Israel's past. Can we come out of our exile with a God who has been transformed from the theistic concepts of antiquity? That appears to be our only path forward. Can God be real and yet not be located in an external place as a supernatural being? Can God be real if there is no divine entity that can be invoked to come to us in our moments of need? Can God be real if all images of God as a superparent, and thus as a personalistic deity, are dismissed?

To get beyond these definitions, it is necessary to pose the religious questions not by pretending we have a source of divine revelation, but by looking at the human experience in a different way. That is why the word *what* instead of *who* becomes important as our guide. Is there, we now inquire, a depth dimension to life that is ultimately spiritual? If so, what is it? Is there a core to both our life and the life of the world that somehow links us to a presence that we call "transcendent" and "beyond" and that yet is never apart from who we are or what the world is? If so, what is it? Is there a presence in the heart of our life that could never be invoked as a being but nonetheless might be entered as a divine and infinite reality? If so, what is it? If we could open ourselves to such a reality, become intensely aware of it, and have both our being and our consciousness expanded by it, could we use the word *God* to describe that state of being? Could that still be a profound presence even if it were not defined as an external presence? Some will surely charge that this is nothing but a word game, since it is so at odds with traditional religious concepts, but I hold rather that these questions might well open for us a pathway into a God experience beyond the exile. I believe that this is at least an avenue worthy of exploration. It is also an avenue that has always been present as a kind of minority report in religious history if one knows how to search for it.

One ancient Hebrew word for God, for example, was *ruach*. Literally, that word meant "wind," a natural and even an impersonal concept. The wind or *ruach* was observed not as a being, but as a vitalizing force. It had no boundaries and no recognizable destination. Among the Hebrews the *ruach* or wind of God was said to have brooded over the chaos in the story of creation in order to bring forth life. Slowly this *ruach* then evolved and became personalized and was called Spirit. But it is important to note that at its origin *ruach* was an impersonal life force, an experienced "what," not a "who." The *ruach* or wind of God was not external. It rather emerged from within the world and was understood as its very ground, its life-giving reality.

This *ruach* was also thought to be connected in some way to human *nephesh* or breath. That also was and is an impersonal concept. Breath was a force that wells up from within each of us and was thought in some sense to be identical with our life.

Still another impersonal image for God found in the Hebrew scriptures was contained in the word *rock*. Surely one cannot imagine an image less personal than a rock. Yet we find in the book of Samuel the phrase, "There is no rock like our God" (1 Sam. 2:2), and the rocklike aspect of God was celebrated in the Hebrew scriptures. The Psalter proclaims, "The Lord is my rock and my salvation" (Ps. 18:2) and later, "Who is a rock except our God?" (Ps. 18:31) Paul even called Christ the rock from which the Hebrews drank water during the wilderness years (1 Cor. 10:4).

If something as impersonal as the wind, one's breath, or a rock could be used by our forbears to conceive of God, then surely we might be more courageous and break out of our personalistic images and begin to contemplate new meanings and radically different figures of speech in our quest for God.

In other ways ancient people almost intuitively recognized the severe limitations of their theistic concepts of God. It was as if they knew them to be inadequate or even improper but did not quite know what to do about it. Jews were forbidden, for example, to pronounce the sacred name of God. Somehow that made God an object rather than a subject, an embraceable entity rather than an ultimate mystery. Muslims for the same reason were not allowed to depict the Divine One in any visual way. Such depictions were thought to be too limiting.

The mystics of every religious tradition have always cried out against every specific definition of God. The Western mystics appear to have assumed that a personal God was only a stage, and an inferior one at that, in human religious development. The mystical portrait of God was first imaginative, and then it became quickly ineffable. It involved an interior journey, not an exterior one. This inward probe ultimately resulted in a transfigured humanity. It thus enabled the mystic to escape human limits without violating human integrity. At the same time, this wondrous, mystical God experience did not reduce human beings to the status of powerless, dependent children, subject to the will of an external authoritative deity. Rather, it called human life beyond every boundary until that life itself was seen as a revelation of the God who emerged out of life's very depths. Mysticism assumes that all of creation is finally capable of revealing this divine one at the very depths of its own being. So to the mystic, the God of one person is never quite the same as the God of another person. Idolatry is thus countered. In the mystical tradition no one can claim objectivity for his or her insight. Each person is called to journey into the mystery of God along the pathway of his or her own expanding personhood. Every person is thus believed to be capable of being a theophany, a sign of God's presence, but no one person, institution, or way of life can exhaust this revelation.

Critics within the traditional ecclesiastical systems of the Western world today are quick to define and dismiss these almost universal mystical ideas as "pantheism," the assertion that God is nothing but the sum of all that is. If they are a bit more sophisticated, they will call it "panentheism," the assertion that God is in, but not necessarily the sum of, all things. Many theologians, revealing their own limitations, seem to believe that if they can name an idea, they can dismiss it. To the mystic, however, God is not to be identified with what is; rather all that is becomes the source through which the ultimately real God can be seen. God, for the mystics, is found at the depths of life, working in and through the being of this world, calling the whole creation into the transcendence that reveals our deepest potential. It is a God concept better approached, I believe, if we move first from a "who" question to a "what" question and then from what we perceive God to be to what our experience of God is.

The world of professional academic theology has become aware of its own enslavement to those theistic concepts of the past, which no longer have power or meaning. Since at least the nineteenth century the frontier Christian theologians have sought deliverance from this dying theistic God. One does not have to look far into the past to discern this awareness.

The demise of theism began in the breakdown of a biblical literalism in Germany in the early 1800s.[2] From biblical studies, it moved to theological writings, as it became apparent that the theological doctrines of antiquity could no longer be based on the literal texts that once undergirded them. Rudolf Bultmann, probably the dominant New Testament scholar of this century, carried this study to a new intensity by making us aware that all of the Gospel material was encased inside the mythology of antiquity and therefore could not be literalized.[3] The theistic understanding of God was part of that mythology. But Bultmann suggested that if we could demythologize those texts, the insights of a saving truth could still be found.

Alfred North Whitehead, who began his professional life as a mathematician, laid out the theological framework for perceiving of God not just as an external being, but as a divine process coming into being within the life of this world.[4] He conceived of God as existing with all of reality, not prior to it, and as growing by absorbing and transforming what is done in the temporal world. This God was, for Whitehead, the abiding source of all new possibilities. The school of thought known as process theology owes Whitehead credit for this radical idea, on which it is based.

Dietrich Bonhoeffer called the world to something he named "religionless Christianity," and he suggested from his prison cell in Nazi Germany, waiting for his execution as a traitor to the

Third Reich, that we needed to live in this world "as if there were no God."[5] Perhaps the beauty and power of Bonhoeffer's witness as a martyr willing to die to oppose the inhumanity of the Nazi Führer blinded the world to the radical nature of his theological ideas, at least for a season. But a religionless, perhaps even a godless or at least a nontheistic, Christianity appeared on the horizon in the writings of this great Christian thinker.

Paul Tillich, my own teacher and himself a refugee from Nazi Germany, writing as far back as the 1930s and 1940s, suggested that we must abandon the external height images in which the theistic God has historically been perceived and replace them with internal depth images of a deity who is not apart from us but who is the very core and ground of all that is.[6] This God would not be a theistic power, a being among beings, whose existence we could debate. This God would not be the traditional divine worker of miracles and magic, the dispenser of rewards and punishments, blessings and curses. Nor would this God be the capricious heavenly superparent who comforted us, heard our cries, and became the terrestrial Mr. Fix-It for some while allowing others to endure their pain to the bitter end in a radically unfair world.

The God to whom Tillich pointed was the infinite center of life. This God was not a person, but, rather like the insights of the mystics, this God was the mystical presence in which all personhood could flourish. This God was not a being but rather the power that called being forth in all creatures. This God was not an external, personal force that could be invoked but rather an internal reality that, when confronted, opened us to the meaning of life itself.

For Tillich there was no imploring an external power to serve our needs. One rather experienced a growing awareness of the Ground of Being and of one's relationship with all those who also shared that infinite and inexhaustible ground.

Tillich believed that the word *God* had been captured, corrupted, and distorted by the dying external images of yesterday's theistic theological consensus. He was convinced that those images must die before the word *God* could ever be used again with meaning. He urged a moratorium on the use of the word *God* for at least a hundred years. But that urging has not prevailed. God talk abounds, and most of it is still theistic. But there is something distinctively different about speaking of God when one is in the exile. In this exile period all ideas of God are open for debate. The definitions of God are not consistent; they invite exploration. There is no body of agreed-upon data that fills this word and no coercive attempt to impose. Objective truth has disappeared. The language of an ever-changing journey has replaced it.[7]

God has always been identified with that which gives life. This religious understanding has sometimes manifested itself in fertility cults and in agricultural deities. Frequently, the sun received the worship of those who recognized that without its warming rays, there would be no life. Sometimes it was the sky, the rain, the earth, or even the power of fire that became the symbol for the life that was derived from God. Sometimes it was the creator, distant and powerful, even called "The Father almighty, creator of heaven and earth." But behind the content of every image of God was the meaning of God as life giver, source of vitality itself. So Tillich urged his readers to examine existence and to discover that which calls people into life and, once that was found, to acknowledge it as a manifestation of the divine if not the divine source itself.

Feeding this theological point of view also have been insights from the newly developed psychological sciences. Among those insights is the realization that love is also the source and the creator of life. Without love we human beings shrivel. The unloved child, the uncared-for infant, will almost surely die. That is equally true of most higher mammals. Love opens the whole creation up to life and calls all things into being. On the human level, love is the essential power that deepens our relationships and simultaneously expands our own humanity. The more we are freed by love to be ourselves, the more we are enabled to give our lives away to others. The more we know of life-giving love, the more we find the courage to risk exposing ourselves, not in some frenzy of exhibitionism, but as a way of expressing and revealing the Ground of our Being. The more we explore the depths of life, the more we discover that life is interdependent, interconnected, and indivisible. At the core of the human being there is no such thing as separateness and aloneness. Each one of us is an integral participant in a complex living organism, the constituent parts of which die and are born in every instant of time. Yet each part of that living whole participates in the eternity of being united to an ultimate ground of what slowly but surely we may someday learn to call God.

So the call of this internal God found in our depths becomes primarily a call into being. It is a call that has nothing to do with religion per se. It is a call that refocuses what has been known as the religious dimension. The task of the church, for example, becomes less that of indoctrinating or relating people to an external divine power and more that of providing opportunities for people to touch the infinite center of all things and to grow into all that they are destined to be. In this manner they might discover that in their personhood itself the Holy God, who is the Ground of their Being, is revealed as something different from the theistic God of the past. This task is a long way from the typical activities of a religious institution, which usually involve debating proper liturgies and imposing a version of orthodoxy on the minds of worshipers. This understanding of God places a premium on the church's vocation to oppose any tie that binds us to something less than the fullest expression of our humanity.

The definitions of yesterday, which no longer fit, the stereotypes of the past, which prevent us from observing the splendid diversity of God's creation, the prejudices of bygone eras by which we seek to preserve our privileged autonomy all become alien to the Ground of all Being, which is constantly calling our potential into reality. A new agenda for the religious life thus appears with this new way of envisioning God.

This agenda is not a comfortable one for everyone. The question always posed by those who cannot envision God except in superhuman theistic categories is whether a view of God as the Ground of all Being is not impersonal, an "it" instead of a "thou." It seems to them to be a downgrading of the holy. Certainly so much of the comforting nature of the theistic God of the past does not appear present in this concept. It is difficult to pray in any traditional way to "the Ground of all Being." There is in this new way of thinking about God none of the external motivation for goodness or faithfulness in worship that was part of the God of the past. Institutional Christianity loses the power it derived from an external God who judged and who imposed motivating rewards and punishments on the basis of that judgment. All of the theological understandings of the past that were designed primarily to separate those inside the Church from those outside of it sink into irrelevance. That includes most of the creedal language of Christendom, at least as that creedal language was understood to be a literal description of our faith. This realization might well serve to drive us back to the original creed of the Christians. It was a simple three words, "Jesus is Lord." All other creeds are but a commentary on those three words and were designed to serve the institutional power needs of the Church, which defined itself as the source of all truth, and were intended to exclude those who refused to be subject to the ecclesiastical authority.

Above all else, this view of God raises an ultimate question even for believers in exile. Is the Ground of Being real, or is it a philosophical abstraction serving merely to cushion our awakening into the radical aloneness of living in a godless world? Certainly that objection will be raised by the frightened defenders of theism. They will also wonder if meaning can be found in life apart from the theological apparatus of the past. They will question whether there is any basis for moral behavior in such a view of God. Without a behavior-controlling religious institution, they will believe that civilization will sink into moral anarchy, where might becomes the final arbiter of right. That anarchy is always perceived to start when people act outside the defining sexual stereotypes of antiquity.

These are powerful anxiety-filled questions, which ultimately can be answered not by those who ask them in fear, but rather by those for whom the theistic images of yesterday are not revivable. They can be answered only by those living in exile. All others will rush either to defend the dying embers of yesterday's fading convictions or to give up all religious systems as worthless prattle, an expression of the immaturity of humankind who needed a heavenly parent figure in order to endure the trauma of existence.

But let us be clear. If God is no longer to be conceived of as a "personal other," does that mean that the core and ground of all life is impersonal? Does this make God less than personal or mysteriously even more than personal yet still beyond our limited human categories and understandings? Such questions ultimately cannot be answered. They do, however, elicit a series of other questions. Does not the being of God manifest itself in intense personhood? Can one worship the Ground of Being in any other way than by daring to be all that one can be? Can one worship the Source of Life in any other way than by daring to live fully? Can one worship the Source of Love in any other way than by daring to love wastefully and abundantly? Are there any categories that could be said to be more personal than those calling each of us into being, into living, and into loving? Would a

ctured as able to violate all of the natural laws
He could walk on water (Mark 6:45–54). He
loaves to feed a multitude (Mark 6:30–44). He
r into wine (John 2:1–11) and even raise to life
d Lazarus (John 11).

of this same Christian Church relive and cele-
atural life Sunday by Sunday. The content of
d the major cultural holidays of Western civi-
some other way to understand these Jesus sto-
rines that are said to have been based on them?
dern person take these literal, premodern claims
Christianity continue without them? The stakes
igh as we begin our probe of the place, the mean-
e of one Jesus of Nazareth.

these issues properly, it is necessary first to get
perstitious and mystical aura that believers have
her around the Gospels through the centuries. At
he problem lies in the excessive claims made for
es. The Bible is not the word of God in any literal
se. It never has been! The Gospels are not inerrant
ely authored. They were written by communities of
ney express even the biases of those communities.
s are not without significant internal contradictions
ssing moral and intellectual concepts. The Gospels
tic. They reveal changing, evolving theological per-
They are not even original. They lean far more than
n realized on the work of Paul and on the inspiration
brew scriptures.[1] They are not the words of eyewit-
so often has been claimed. Most eyewitnesses to the life
ere long dead before the Gospels entered history. The
vere also shaped by the events of their own time, per-
more dramatically than they were by the events of the
vhich Jesus actually lived. For example, the capture and

life that reflected these qualities not be seen to reveal the image of God that is within that person? Does this reality not reflect a new way to view and to understand that biblical dictum that "in the image of God, created God him. Male and female created God them?"[8] Is it possible that we bear God's image because we are part of who God is? Those are the concepts that beckon our consideration as believers in exile.

Yes, it is frightening to think that there is no heavenly parent in the sky who will take care of us. We recall that moment in our human maturing process when we realized that we had become adults and that we, therefore, had to be responsible for ourselves. No earthly parents could protect us any longer. Perhaps we cushioned that experience with the theistic God premise. It was the common wisdom of the church that young adults who had left the church as teenagers would, after marriage, mortgage, and parenthood, come back to worship. But now the underpinnings of the God to whom those young adults were to return are no longer secure. The realization is dawning that we human beings are alone and therefore are responsible for ourselves, that there is no appeal to a higher power for protection. We are learning that meaning is not external to life but must be discovered in our own depths and imposed on life by an act of our own will. We are being made aware that life is not fair and will not necessarily be made fair either in this life or in any other. So we have to decide how we will live now with this reality. Will the well-being of the social order temper our internal drive toward greed and selfishness? In our personal relationships we will need to face such issues as the place of character and the validity of our most sacred commitments when they are in opposition to the drive for pleasure and personal fulfillment. We will wonder whether there is any longer a need for corporate worship and if so, what form will it take. Can a view of God other than the divine theistic being beyond the world ever sustain the ecclesiastical structure we now call the church?

We walk into every one of these questions when we enter the exile. There are no readily apparent answers. There never are in exile. The only thing that is certain is that one must go forward. There is no return to the now-abandoned security systems of the past. No adult can return to his or her parent's house once maturity has been achieved. When the human spirit has come of age, it cannot return to the image of God as a heavenly parent. The gate to the past is barred, if not by angels with flaming swords (Gen. 3:24), at least by the realization that the theistic God of yesterday is no longer there.

When the Jews were carried into exile in Babylon in the early years of the sixth century B.C.E., they knew they could never sing the Lord's song again, at least not the songs of Zion. They knew that God could never be worshiped in the future the way God had been worshiped in the past. They had to learn a new song or never sing again. That, I believe, is exactly the fate of the modern Christian. I believe the new song is developing, and I want to be part of the generation that will sing it. The replacement of the theistic God of the past with the inescapable God who is the Ground of Being is, in my opinion, the prerequisite to sounding forth the mighty chorus of the future.

So I start here. There is no God external to life. God, rather, is the inescapable depth and center of all that is. God is not a being superior to all other beings. God is the Ground of Being itself. And much flows from this starting place. The artifacts of the faith of the past must be understood in a new way if they are to accompany us beyond the exile, and those that cannot be understood differently will have to be laid aside. Time will inform us as to which is which.

(Acts 2). He was pi[...]
of the universe. H[...]
could expand five [...]
could change wat[...]
the four-days-dea[...]

The liturgies [...]
brate this supern[...]
his life has shap[...]
lization. Is there [...]
ries and the doc[...]

Can any postmo[...]
seriously? Can [...]
are thus quite h[...]
ing, and the ro[...]

To explor[...]
beyond that s[...]
allowed to ga[...]
least part of [...]
these scriptur[...]
or verbal sen[...]
works, divin[...]
faith, and t[...]

The Gospel[...]
or embarra[...]
are not sta[...]
spectives. [...]
has yet bee[...]
of the He[...]
nesses, as [...]
of Jesus w[...]
Gospels [...]
haps eve[...]
time in v[...]

Discove[...]
of the [...]

BUT CAN JESUS BE UND[...]
tive theistic context? Ha[...]
day to set such doctrines as the [...]
very center of its life? Can Jesu[...]
logical context and still be Lor[...]
the Bible have Jesus say, "I and t[...]

Some forty to seventy year[...]
earthly life of Jesus of Nazareth, [...]
book that the Christian Church [...]
inspired. In that book he was portr[...]
power. Angelic beings split open [...]
birth (Luke 2). Out of those same s[...]
his ultimate gift of the Holy Spirit to [...]

destruction of Jerusalem by the Roman army in 70 C.E. is a powerful reality in the background of each of the Gospel narratives. Seeing the Gospels in a proper historical perspective is therefore our first step into biblical knowledge.

Next, we need to be prepared, when we actually read the texts of the New Testament, to discover that there is an enormous gap between the theological claims that have been made for Jesus in the life of institutional Christianity and the record that was actually contained in the Gospels. Most believers, for example, have never been told that there are no camels in the biblical story of the wise men and no stable or stable animals in the story of Jesus' birth, and they have never checked for themselves. (See Matthew 1, 2 and Luke 1, 2.) They do not learn in church that the virgin birth accounts were not original to Christianity and did not appear in Christian history until the ninth decade.[2] The same thing is true of the narratives that speak of a physical bodily resurrection of Jesus. They, too, were ninth-decade additions to the Christian story.[3] Perhaps more important for our present purposes is the fact that the divine nature of Jesus or the interpretations of Jesus as the incarnation of the theistic deity was also a late-developing reality.[4]

By raising these issues, I seek not to disparage these texts, but to begin the process of separating the experience of Jesus from the theological interpretation of that experience found in the New Testament as well as in the doctrinal development of the Church. Such a separation will be essential if we discover, as I suspect we might, that the only way to preserve the Jesus experience is to dismantle and to reject many of the traditional theological interpretations that have held it captive.

I begin this process by tracing the expanding claims made for Jesus in the texts of the Bible itself. The first author of any part of the New Testament was Paul, whose writing career spanned a period of time no earlier than eighteen and no later than thirty-four years after the conclusion of Jesus' earthly life. When we read Paul carefully, not allowing the content of the not-yet-written Gospels to corrupt our understanding, we note some fascinating distinctions. We also become aware that Paul seems far more prone to proclaim Christ than he is to explain Christ, though he does begin the explanatory process. Listen first to Paul's proclamations:

"In Christ God was reconciling the world" (2 Cor. 5:19).

Nothing "in all creation will be able to separate us from the love of God in Christ Jesus our Lord" (Rom. 8:39).

"The free gift of God is eternal life in Christ Jesus Our Lord" (Rom. 6:23).

"We preach Christ crucified ... Christ the power of God and the wisdom of God" (1 Cor. 1:23, 24).

These are ecstatic words. They rise out of one who has been so deeply moved by the Christ experience that he is processing it internally. In these passages he is not yet using the classical theological words designed to enable him to explain to curious and dispassionate observers the meaning that he has found in this Jesus.

But ecstasy of any kind does not remain unexplained for long. It is the nature of us human beings to move from an experience that touches our lives to the ability to speak about that experience rationally. Because we can see that happening in the writings of Paul, we begin this Christ analysis by charting its development.

If one asserts that "God was in this Christ," as Paul does, then the question inevitably arises as to how the holy and distant God happened to be present in that finite and particular life. If that question cannot be answered adequately, the experience comes to be regarded only as a kind of private delusion. So explanation always follows proclamation, but not quite immediately. The ecstasy, early on, defies explanation.

The very moment we move from ecstatic proclamation to explanation, the presuppositions, definitions, and stereotypes of the ages begin to shape our words. That is inescapable. That is also why theological explanations can never be literally true or eternally applicable. Despite institutional religious claims to the contrary, creeds and theology are nothing but explanations. So they are inevitably distorted versions of truth warped by the time in which they were articulated.

This means that our pathway into a proper understanding of the Christ must be to go beneath the explanations found in the New Testament until we can begin to perceive the experience that made those explanations necessary. We start with the earliest records we have, and by moving forward, we will seek to demonstrate how the explanations grew and developed. Then, from the vantage point of that development, we will look backward, hoping to glimpse some of the aspects of that original creating experience.

In his epistle to the Romans, written about the year 58 C.E., or some twenty-eight years after the life of Jesus, Paul began to develop explanations for his Christ experience. He had never visited the church in Rome to which he was writing. The people there were strangers who needed to understand why he was so concerned to come to visit them (Rom. 1:1–15). God, he said to them, had "designated" Jesus "Son of God in power according to the spirit of holiness by his resurrection from the dead" (Rom. 1:4). Please note the strange and, from the point of view of later Christian orthodoxy, the disconcerting elements that are present in this early Pauline statement. "God," by which Paul presumably meant the creator Father, "designated" Jesus to be "son of God." God was the one who was doing the designating. Jesus was the one who was being designated. There was here no sense of divine equality or of what later came to be called incarnation.

Second, Paul declared that God made this declaration "in power" and according to the "spirit of holiness." The Holy Spirit, we need to note, was not yet a separate and distinct aspect of God in the mind of Paul.

Third, this designation of Jesus as God's divine son took place, Paul said, by his "resurrection from the dead." So for Paul it was the Easter experience, which came after the crucifixion, that constituted the basis for the God claim that he was making about Jesus. Paul seemed not to know of miracle stories or of a divinely initiated virgin birth. In this first strata of theological thinking where the God experience in Jesus was being explained, we find a point of view that later came to be called "adoptionism." This means that just some six years before Paul's death it was still his understanding that God had adopted Jesus into the being of God. This was certainly not for Paul an expression that was conducive to later trinitarian thinking. Even this adoptive status was not conferred upon Jesus until the resurrection, Paul was saying. The exaltation of Jesus into heaven, which was Paul's concept of what Easter meant,[5] and the divine designation of Jesus as God's son were thus, in the mind of the earliest New Testament writer, simultaneous experiences. Presumably Jesus was not thought of as God's son prior to that moment. It certainly becomes obvious in this text that the later developing creedal doctrines were far removed from this Pauline understanding. One of the first things that those of us who are believers in exile have to embrace if we want to open Christianity to new possibilities is that there was no body of Christian doctrine that was ever fixed or unchanging. That phrase so often used in religious circles, taken from the relatively late epistle of Jude (Jude 3), suggesting that there was something called "the faith which was once for all delivered to the saints" is quite misleading. No such faith ever existed, at least not as a body of doctrinal statements. Christianity, rather, evolved from simple ecstatic proclamations of faith into more and more complex theological forms with the passage of time. It is not reflected in a set formula, nor has it ever been.

Some ten to fifteen years after Paul had written his epistle to the Romans, the Gospel of Mark came into existence. This represented the first time in Christian history that the biographical details of Jesus' life had been chronicled in a written form. This was some forty years after the conclusion of Jesus' earthly life. Mark quickly informed his reader of his purpose for composing this book. He was writing, he announced in his first verse, "The beginning of the gospel of Jesus Christ—the Son of God."[6] Mark could hardly articulate his conviction in this manner and still accept the Pauline theory that "God designated Jesus Son of God at the time of the resurrection." So he adapted Paul's words to his purpose in an interesting way.

Two parts of Paul's earlier declaration he not only accepted, but gave to them narrative form. Mark took Paul's words, that God had designated Jesus to be God's son, and described just how it was that this designation occurred. The voice of God spoke from heaven, Mark declared, and said of Jesus, "This is my beloved son in whom I am well pleased" (Mark 1:11). Mark has provided for God the actual dialogue to expand this Pauline affirmation. Second, Mark has taken Paul's idea that this designation came by way of the "spirit of holiness" and has given it a specific setting. He wrote that "the heavens opened" and the spirit, descending "like a dove" came upon this Jesus in a very physical way (Mark 1:10). Mark, we begin to recognize, was following the Pauline script closely, and, in the process, he was revealing just how his own definition of Jesus had been dramatically shaped by Paul.

But look at how Mark changed the moment in which this declaration took place. It has been moved rather purposefully. Paul had made the declaration occur at the time of the resurrection. Yet Mark put it into his opening story of Jesus' baptism. He intended to show the power of God constantly at work in the life of Jesus in his Gospel. He could not do that if Jesus had become the Son of God only at the time of the resurrection. So Mark simply moved the Pauline designation from the resurrection to the baptism while keeping every other aspect of the Pauline explanation.

By designating Jesus as God's son as early as the baptism, Mark, however, had to deal with some new difficulties. Since in Mark's scheme of things Jesus' divine status had been declared at his baptism, he had to explain why the disciples, some of whom certainly are portrayed as knowing about the baptism (Mark 1:9–11),[7] had nonetheless been willing to betray him, deny him, forsake him, and flee from him at the time of his arrest and crucifixion. One hardly acts that way toward one who was named God's son by a heavenly voice. Mark solved this question by asserting that Jesus' divine designation, conferred at baptism, was kept secret until it was fully revealed at the time of the resurrection. So with this theory of the messianic secret at work in Mark's text, the first Gospel writer sought to harmonize his baptism declaration of Jesus' divine sonship with Paul's resurrection designation. The tradition was growing.

By the time Matthew wrote, some ten to twenty years after Mark, and perhaps fifty to fifty-five years after the time of Jesus, the story of the proclamation of Jesus' divine origins had moved once again. Matthew began his story of Jesus' life with the narrative of his birth. It was for Matthew an intolerable idea that Jesus became something either at his baptism or at his resurrection that he was not already. So borrowing from Mark's reasoning that resurrection simply revealed fully what God had proclaimed at his baptism, Matthew expanded that to say that both the baptism and the resurrection revealed only that which had been present from the moment of Jesus' conception. With that new point of beginning clear in his narrative, Matthew then proceeded to move all of Paul's original symbols about Jesus' divine designation back into the story of his nativity. God still declared Jesus to be the Son of God, for Matthew. This declaration, however, was now placed into the mouth of the angel who appeared to Joseph in a dream bearing God's message. Matthew went on to say that this divine nature was preordained. Jesus' godly origin had actually fulfilled the words spoken by the prophet Isaiah (Matt. 1:22–23; Isa. 7:14). This status was nonetheless still accomplished, even for Matthew, by the Pauline "spirit of holiness," though by Matthew's time that concept had become the more explicit "Holy Spirit." "That which is conceived in her is of the Holy Spirit," the angel announced (Matt. 1:28). This Spirit was not yet, even for Matthew, fully distinct as a separate part of the triune God, but hints of that developing tradition can be found in this Gospel (Matt. 28:16–20). In Matthew's birth narrative the Spirit actually appeared to function as the male agent in conception. However, we must consistently remind ourselves that, as of this moment in Christian history, no story of the coming of the Holy Spirit as a separate power, either at Pentecost (Luke) or at Easter (John) had yet been written. Nonetheless, by the time Matthew's Gospel was complete, in the ninth decade of the common era, God had declared Jesus to be the Son of God by the spirit of holiness or the Holy Spirit, but the date of that declaration had moved from the resurrection, where it resided first for Paul, to the baptism, where it resided for Mark, to the moment of conception, where Matthew now located it. The virgin birth story, the means through which Matthew accomplished this transition, now entered the tradition.

Luke, writing five to ten years after Matthew, changed Matthew's details around a bit and made his images more concrete and historical, but essentially he left the story line intact. Luke's annunciating angel was, for example, far more specific than the angel had been in Matthew. Luke's angel had a name,

Gabriel (Luke 1:26). This divine creature appeared, according to Luke, in person, not in a dream. Mary, not Joseph, was the recipient of this angelic revelation (Luke 1:28–38). Mary's baby was designated by this angel as both "the Son of God" (Luke 1:30) and "the Son of the Highest" (Luke 1:32). Clearly, Jesus was God's son from conception in this third Gospel, and yet God, speaking through Gabriel, was still declaring Jesus to be God's son by the spirit of holiness. "The Holy Spirit will come upon you" (Luke 1:35), said the angel. Simply put, the original Pauline declaration had been encased in a more and more dramatic narrative as the years rolled by. The "spirit of holiness" was becoming specific. The time of the designation was moving to an earlier and earlier point, from resurrection to baptism to conception. One would think that no point earlier in life than conception could be imagined. But thinking thus would not appreciate fully the ingenuity of the early Christian theological mind.

Jesus' identity with God had become so complete by the tenth decade of the common era that he was said to have shared in that identity prior even to his conception and birth. So preexistence became a category in which Christians began to talk. There are those who suggest that Paul had hinted at preexistence in his later epistles, such as Philippians (2:5–11) and Colossians (2:9),[8] but it clearly remained for the author of the fourth Gospel, writing around the turn of the first century, to give this concept its primary biblical focus.

It is interesting to note that John omitted from his Gospel any narrative about Jesus' birth, though surely by this time that tradition must have been widely discussed. Furthermore, on two occasions John even referred to Jesus as "the son of Joseph" (John 1:45, 6:42). It was as if the author of the fourth Gospel had little use for virgin birth tales, which he may well have regarded as pagan. Virgin birth stories were, in fact, quite popular in the

Mediterranean world at that time. John also seemed to think that two births were necessary for the full spiritual development of every person. One birth was the natural birth according to the flesh. The second birth was the spiritual birth into one's status as God's son or daughter (John 3:4–6). The divine life of Jesus was, for the fourth Gospel, the moment when the logos, or Word of God, which had been part of God's very being since the dawn of creation, was born into the natural order. So, for John, there was no time in all human history when Jesus was not God's son. In this Gospel, Jesus experienced two births. He was born according to the flesh, presumably as the child of Mary and Joseph, but he was also born from above as the incarnation of the eternal logos (John 1:1–14).

The migration of Paul's early affirmation had finally reached its limits. God had designated Jesus as the divine son, indeed as a part of who or what God is. That designation had been accomplished by the spirit of holiness, which had grown rapidly, first into the Holy Spirit and then into the very essence of God. Finally, the time of the designation had journeyed backward in time, from the resurrection to the baptism to the conception to the origins of the creation itself.

New Testament writers faced the same need for interpretation at the other end of the life of Jesus. Once again, a particular definition of God as external to this world was the driving force in those developing explanations. If this theistic deity had entered the life of Jesus through a virgin birth or an incarnation, then there must have been a time when the God present in him would have had to return to that divine abode where God lived beyond this world. Again, we can trace the progress of this theological journey in the biblical narratives.

First Paul, still using a passive verb form to describe the God-Jesus relationship, wrote that Jesus was raised by God from death. For Paul, God did the raising. Jesus was raised; he did not rise, as of his own accord. For Paul, Jesus was raised from the grave into the life of God, not back into life on earth. What we today call resurrection and ascension were apparently, in Paul's mind, a single action.[9] When this divine raising from death into God was later literalized, it was also separated into two steps. First, God raised Jesus from death back into the life of this world. Then God raised Jesus, or more accurately, Jesus simply rose from this world back into the heavenly places where God dwelled.[10] That is when ascension stories began to be told in the later writings of Luke (Luke 24 and Acts 1) and John (20:17). But each of these narratives was built on the assumption that God, by definition, was a Being from beyond this world and that if Jesus was "a God presence" he must have come "down" from God and therefore also must have returned to that place from which he had come. Again, we see the process through which the explanations of the God presence in Jesus developed over the decades.

Once we can establish that biblical interpretations are different from people's original experience of Jesus, then we can begin to explore the deeper question: What was the nature of their experience? What was there about Jesus of Nazareth that made his first-century disciples assert the astonishing claim that "God was in this Christ"? Can we separate the experience from the explanation? Can we reject the explanation without rejecting the experience? Does respecting their experience require us to be committed also to their explanation, which presumed a theistic God? We have taken a first step toward the Jesus reality, but our journey has just begun.

SIX

✳

Jesus as Rescuer:
An Image That Has to Go

SOMETIMES THE DEAD WOOD of the past must be cleared out so that new life has a chance to grow. With regard to the Jesus story, that step becomes vital and urgent. Not every image used to explain Jesus is worthy of survival. The most obvious candidate for dismissal in my mind is also perhaps the oldest of all the interpretations of Jesus. I refer to that image of Jesus as "the divine rescuer."

This image comes in two forms. First, it appears in the rhetoric of the traditional evangelical preacher for whom, given the time limit of a sermon, certain clichés have become all but essential. In the verbal cadences that fall so easily from the preacher's lips, one hears these familiar words: "Jesus died for my sins. He shed his precious blood on the cross of Calvary for my salvation. I have been washed in the blood of the Lamb. Through the sacrifice of Jesus, I have been saved. The stain of sin on my soul has been cleansed."

The words may not be exact, but the themes present in this point of view are familiar. Surely we have heard their echoes thousands of times.

Second, there is the far more sophisticated rhetoric of Christian academic theology through the ages. Thoughtful Christian leaders, working inside the worldview they understand, have spent centuries developing what they call "the theology of the cross" as the essential ingredient in the Jesus story. The process has resulted in many variations on the theme that is regarded as the central tenet of Christianity: the doctrine of the atonement. This doctrine assumes such things as a particular view of the meaning of creation, the fall of human life into something called original sin, and the saving work of Jesus, which resulted in a restoration. This work of Jesus was said to have produced the "at-one-ment" between God and human life that the doctrine of the atonement celebrates.

The language of original sin and atonement has emanated from Christian circles for so long that it has achieved the status of a sacred mantra. This means that it cannot be questioned, nor does its basic structure stand in need of any further explanation. In the light of new circumstances, it is merely adjusted, never reconsidered. Yet, upon closer inspection, these sacred concepts involve us in a view of human life that is no longer operative, a theistic understanding of God articulated in a form that is all but repulsive, a magical view of Jesus that violates our minds, and the practical necessity for the Church to elicit guilt as a prerequisite to conversion. It does not require a genius to discern that this view of both God and Jesus, as well as this understanding of the Church, will never survive the exile.

So pervasive has the Jesus-as-rescuer mentality become in Christianity's self-understanding that one can hardly view Christianity apart from it. Perhaps that is why the near collapse of this religious system now seems so obvious. Most of the content of this faith tradition has been organized in such a way as to serve this rescuer mentality. The service of baptism presupposes the rescue operation. The primary eucharistic worship of the Church, frequently referred to as "the sacrifice of the mass," reenacts liturgically this rescuing view of Jesus. The entire corpus of the Bible traditionally has been read and interpreted in such a way as to undergird this particular understanding of Jesus as the rescuer. The presence of a cross or a crucifix as the central symbol of Christianity proclaims it. It is a circular argument that is difficult to enter, and yet its very circularity has provided the primary cohesiveness for the entire Christian drama as we have known it. The various elements present in this point of view are easy to outline. I will lay them out clearly and thereby raise them to consciousness. Only then do I think it is possible to uproot them so that some new life might emerge, unchoked by this badly dated perspective.

The Bible opens with the story of creation. That text asserts that it was a perfect creation, indeed a completed creation. When God saw all that God had made, this narrative proclaims, God pronounced it good and then rested from the divine labors.

The climax of that originating act came when God made the man and the woman and installed them as the stewards over all of creation. Adam and Eve, the narrative continued, lived inside the perfection of God's world, called the Garden of Eden, where they basked in a perfect relationship with their creator. God provided for their every need. Food and water were abundant. God even walked with these human creatures in the cool of the evening in perfect communion. According to the text, however, boundaries were set in this paradise. The first human family was given access to every single thing present in the garden save one. That was the tree of the knowledge of good and evil, which was found in the center of the garden. The fruit of this tree was "the forbidden fruit." The human creatures were not to eat of the fruit of this tree, for it was said that if they ate, their eyes would be opened and they would know good from evil. This was a fascinating myth, and for most of Christian history it has been treated quite literally (Gen. 2:5–3:24).

Of course, fruit that is forbidden holds tremendous appeal for the human mind. In the biblical narrative Adam and Eve first looked at that tree and its fruit. Next they walked around it and fantasized about this fruit until the desire for it was irresistible. Finally, listening to the voice of temptation incarnate in a wily serpent, and rationalizing what they deeply wanted to do, they disregarded the prohibition and ate of the fruit of the off-limits tree. God had been disobeyed. The perfection of creation had been ruined. Human life had fallen into sin.

The effects of this fall, according to the biblical story, were immediate and permanent. The eyes of Adam and Eve were opened. They saw themselves as individuals separated from God. They felt shame and guilt. They covered their nakedness with fig leaf aprons. When God came to walk with Adam and Eve that evening, they now perceived this God not as their creator, the source of their life, but as their judge, the elicitor of their guilt. So they hid from this deity amid the bushes of the Garden of Eden. Communion was broken. Self-conscious self-centeredness was the inevitable human reaction.

When God found these creatures hiding in the bushes, the reality of the fall became obvious. A divine inquiry commenced, which revealed the human pattern of making excuses and blaming others. Human beings in their fallenness could not even accept responsibility for their own actions. Adam blamed Eve and God. Eve, he said, had been the cause of his downfall, but God had been the fashioner of Eve. It was a fascinating argument. Eve, in turn, blamed the serpent. Punishment quickly ensued.

The first family was banished from the Garden of Eden. Paradise was lost. Life from that moment on, the story asserted, would be a struggle. The snake would crawl on its belly and eat dust through all eternity. The woman would experience pain in childbirth as the human family expanded. The man would have to earn his living by the sweat of his brow in a never-ending struggle to survive. Finally, all of them would die. The immortality that had been theirs as creatures made in God's image was no more. Mortality was to be the universal fate of those who would be tainted by the primal sin of Adam and Eve. An angel with a drawn sword was posted at the entrance to the Garden of Eden to keep the members of the human family forever outside this paradise. Human life was to be lived in struggle, pain, and death somewhere east of Eden. Because of this sin on the part of the first human beings, all human life thereafter, it was asserted, would be born in sin and would suffer death, the ultimate consequence of human sin. The universality of human mortality was interpreted to be a sign of the universality of human sin. It was original sin, all-encompassing sin. All life stood in need of redemption. All life cried out for a savior. This became the central clue to the Christian story as it has been traditionally proclaimed.

According to these arguments, God started the process of redemption by choosing a particular people through whom God would work out the entire divine process of salvation. Just why God needed to do it over a time span of thousands of years was left unaddressed, as if to say that's just the way it is.

The Christian story of redemption has been told in terms of this myth. Salvation began on a very small scale, said the text, with the call of Abraham (Gen. 12:1–3). The descendants of Abraham were ultimately to be a people more numerous than the stars of the heavens or the grains of sand upon the seashore (Gen. 22:17). As that nation developed, however, it was purged with regularity. Isaac was chosen over Ishmael. Jacob was chosen over Esau. Judah and Joseph were chosen over the firstborn Reuben (1 Chron. 5:1, 3). Through Joseph, this people went to dwell in Egypt to avoid a famine. In time they fell into slavery. The story of salvation, however, began again some four hundred years later with Moses and the exodus.

Once free of their bondage, the people were led by God, through Moses, to Mount Sinai, where the law of God, called the Torah, was given to the people (Exod. 19–20). The law was to be a schoolmaster to lead these fallen people back into a state of grace.¹ Hope for ultimate redemption from their fall lay in this process, for the assumption grew that if one special child of Israel could, for the space of twenty-four hours, keep every requirement of the Torah, the Kingdom of God would come and a new Garden of Eden in which God's rule would always be obeyed would be established. The law was thus designed to be Israel's way out of the fallen sinful status of human life. None of the children of Israel did keep the law perfectly for twenty-four hours, and so the search for salvation in history rolled on.

A sacrificial system was developed in the ancient world to help overcome this supposed chasm between the fallen creatures and the Holy God. Israel participated in this sacrificial system. Israel developed in its liturgical life a day called Yom Kippur, dedicated to that sense of human sinfulness and designed to be an occasion to pray for atonement or restoration. Two rituals marked this day. One was the public confession of the people's sins, which were ceremoniously heaped upon the back of a goat. Thus laden with the people's sins, this goat, called the scapegoat, was run out into the wilderness and was believed to have carried the sins of the people with it, thus purging them (Lev. 16).

The second ritual of Yom Kippur was the sacrificial offering of the lamb of the atonement (Lev. 23:26–32). This ritualistic lamb was carefully inspected to make certain it was physically perfect. There could be no scratches, no blemishes, and no broken bones. Human life, so alienated from God, so fallen into sin, had to come before God under the symbol of something that was perfect. A perfect physical specimen met part of that requirement. The lamb was also subhuman and therefore incapable of being immoral, since morality requires the ability to choose evil. So a morally perfect, physically perfect, but still subhuman sacrifice was offered to God to atone for, even to pay for, the sins of the people. The assumption was that to be human was to be sinful. Paul would later put this assumption into writing: "all have sinned and fall short of the glory of God" (Rom. 3:23). So it was that the giving of the law and the process of sacrificial worship were the interim steps that human beings adopted to deal with the presumed hopeless sinfulness of the people. To be human was by definition to be evil, fallen, and in need of rescue.

The prophetic movement of Israel was said by these early Christian leaders to have been but one more aspect in God's never-ending attempt to call the fallen creation back to the perfection that had been the divine purpose of the creative act. The prophets were charismatic voices for God who arose outside the existing power structure to challenge people to return to the way of righteousness. Normally the prophets failed in this mission, but nonetheless they strove after their goal mightily. They were appreciated, as is the fate of most prophets, only long after the fact of their demise. Prophets tended to be either banished or killed, but their messages burned brightly and were recorded to be read and reread over the years (Matt. 23:37; Luke 13:34). When the prophets failed to call the people back to their destiny in the Garden of Eden, they were said at least to point to that coming time when redemption would finally be accomplished and salvation ultimately achieved.

It was the conviction that humans were sinful and in need of redemption that enabled guilt and religion to be so closely tied together in the history of the Western world. The power of Western religion has always rested on the ability of religious people to understand and to manipulate that sense of human inadequacy that expresses itself as guilt. This religious system assumes that the purpose of life is to be whole, free, and at one with one's creator or with the source of life. That is what gives the sense of alienation its power. In this ancient time the source of life was almost universally thought to be an external supernatural being who could see all and who knew all, a heavenly parent, if you will. This was the God who "knows the secrets of the heart" (Ps. 44:21). In the presence of this personal and judging deity, human beings, knowing that they were not what they were created to be, sought to hide, and in time it was assumed that one aspect of our humanity was to be skilled at hiding. We hid from God, from one another, and from ourselves. Since it was human to be evil, it was also human to hide. It was human to pretend. The religious leaders of the ages learned that controlling people's behavior rested upon exacerbating these human feelings of guilt. So religious empires were built on helping people live with and, to some degree, overcome their sense of guilt. Confession, penances, acts of supererogation, and masses for the dead were but a few of the guilt levers built into the Christian enterprise, which dominated the Western world.

The stroke of genius that allowed this ecclesiastical power to succeed was achieved when the pervasive human guilt over inadequacy and failure was connected to the universal human reality of desire, especially sexual desire. That connection was largely a Christian achievement. Now whenever sexual desire emerged, guilt became overwhelming. Holiness was defined as sexlessness. The desire that compelled people in love toward fulfillment in one another was condemned. Women were made to feel guilty because they were women, guilty if they menstruated, guilty if they loved a man, guilty if they got married, guilty if they had children. There was only one virtuous woman, and she was a virgin mother. Men were made to feel guilty for having any sexual desires, guilty for having power, guilty for loving a woman. The system was universal. Sex was evil. Sex was universal. So evil was universal. It was said to be the heritage of Adam. We were fallen creatures in need of rescue. This was the common understanding of life that shaped the message of Western religion in general and Christianity in particular. How could guilt be overcome? How could our broken humanity be repaired? How could human life be rescued from its fall? Those were the questions that Christianity organized itself to answer.

The experience of Jesus was captured by this mind-set. The linkage between our sense of inadequacy and the role of Jesus happened very quickly and was apparent before the first generation of Christians had died. The initial step in this process was to see the death of Jesus in terms of sin and salvation. By the time Paul wrote to the Corinthians in the mid-fifties, that step had been achieved. Christ died, said Paul, "for our sins" (1 Cor. 15:3). Our sins somehow required his death. He was the sacrifice made on our behalf.

In the first Gospel to be written, the word *ransom* was used (Mark 10:45). The life of Jesus was a "ransom" paid for many. This Gospel of Mark, probably following the suggestion of Paul, was the first to set the narrative details of Jesus' death into the context of the Passover so that Jesus was quickly and immediately identified with the paschal lamb who was slain to break the power of death.[2] That story written in the book of Exodus formed the center of the Jewish liturgy of their founding moment. God had enabled their escape from slavery by sending the angel of death to slay the first born in all the land of Egypt. The Jews were spared this slaughter when they killed the paschal lamb and placed the blood of this lamb on the doorposts of their homes. In the Christian reinterpretation of this moment, the blood of the paschal lamb was now replaced by the blood of Jesus. This new paschal lamb had shed his blood on the cross, which came to be thought of as the doorposts of the world, thus breaking the power of the angel of death. All we human beings had to do was to come before the Lord through the blood of this new paschal lamb. The view of Jesus as the rescuer of the fallen human enterprise was off to a rousing start.

By the time the Epistle to the Hebrews was written, probably in the eighties, the cycle was complete. For this work brought firmly into Christian thinking the idea that Jesus, in his death, had been the perfect offering long sought for in the Yom Kippur atonement ritual. Jesus was, first of all, a perfect physical specimen. "He knew all his bones, not one of them was broken" (Exod. 12:46; Ps. 34:20; John 19:36). He was also the sinless one. He was the perfect son of Israel who had kept every requirement of the Torah and had achieved the status of moral perfection. So his sacrifice made all further sacrifices unnecessary. The gaping void separating human life from God had been overcome. God, it was said, had sent his son to "pay the price of sin," to be the perfect sacrifice, to break the hold that sin and/or the devil had over human life. He had overcome the fall and had broken the power of death. "For as in Adam all die, so also in Christ shall all be made alive" (1 Cor. 15:22), Paul said of Jesus.

As this understanding of the redemptive work of Christ was being developed in Christian history, Augustine, the bishop of Hippo (354–430) and one of the premier theological minds of the Western world, set the stage for an interpretation of Christ that would last for more than a thousand years. He solidified the relationship between Jesus and the fallen world by making concrete the theory of the atonement accomplished in Jesus. For Augustine, Adam and Eve were quite literally the first human beings. Their banishment from the garden resulted in death being the price that all human beings had to pay for their sin.

Death was not natural, Augustine argued, it was punitive. The sin of Adam had been passed on through the sex act to every other human being. The connection between sin and sex was clearly established. All human beings were lost, incapable of saving themselves, and destined to die in their sin. That universality of sin was what Christ had broken. He had suffered the consequences of sin, had paid the ransom due to either God or the devil, and had broken the power of death over human life. He had taken away the sting of death, which was sin. He had robbed death of its victory. "O death, where is thy victory. O grave, where is thy sting?" Paul continued by saying, "The sting of death is sin" (1 Cor. 15:55, 56).

As Augustine worked out this theological understanding of life, the virgin birth tradition became very important to him. The virgin birth accounts were literally true for Augustine, and they were absolutely necessary to salvation itself. Indeed, salvation could not have been achieved, for Augustine, apart from the literal virgin birth.[3]

The reasoning behind this was clear. The sin of Adam was passed on sexually from father to son. Human life was born in the sin of Adam, from which no one could escape. A savior required to do the redemptive task could not himself be the victim of Adam's sin. That separating of Jesus from the human sin of the fall was accomplished for Augustine by the virgin birth. The sin of Adam did not corrupt the humanity of Jesus because the Holy Spirit of God was his father. He was thus not a child of Adam at all. At that time it was believed that the woman did not contribute genetically or materially to the birth of the child but merely nurtured the male's "seed" to maturity. So the fallenness of the woman's humanity was not an issue.

In time, however, when the woman's role as genetic cocreator was understood, this issue had to be revisited, lest the savior himself be corrupted with the sin of Adam via his mother, who also was a daughter of Adam. That was handled by the Catholic tradition in the nineteenth century with the doctrine of the Immaculate Conception of the Blessed Virgin. She, too, was miraculously delivered from the corruption of Adam's sin. Her conception was unstained by human sin. By the intervening power of the Holy God, the virgin was prevented by her immaculate conception from passing on to the savior the effects of Adam's sin. Salvation was thus assured. Jesus, the sinless one, was qualified by his origins to make the perfect offering. In doing so he had taken away the sin of the world. His blood had washed us human beings clean. By the blood of Christ we were saved (Rom. 5:9; Heb 9:12; 1 Pet. 1:19). That was the way in which the saving work of Christ was understood among the early Christians.

Religious minds next developed these themes to new levels of understanding. That was when atonement doctrines and theology of the cross books began to come into being.[4] In this developing point of view in the early church, barbaric though it now sounds, the image of God began to include a sense of righteousness that was thought to require a blood sacrifice. A text from the Epistle to the Hebrews (9:22), which stated, "that without the shedding of blood, there is no forgiveness of sins," was employed to justify this point of view. It was then said that God demanded this offering of Jesus. The suffering servant image from Second Isaiah was applied to Jesus: "with his stripes, we are healed." God, the Father, it was said, had laid upon the Son the iniquities of us all (Isa. 53:5, 6). In the evangelical tradition of the nineteenth century these themes would enter the hymnody of Christianity and so we sang of being "washed in the blood" or "saved by the blood of Jesus." We even sang of fountains filled with his cleansing blood. As preachers expounded on these themes it was said "God nailed his son to the cross for our salvation." On and on the variations on this theme have played throughout Christian history.

Seldom did Christians pause to recognize the ogre into which they had turned God. A human father who would nail his son to a cross for any purpose would be arrested for child abuse. Yet that continued to be said of God as if it made God more holy and more worthy of worship.

Behind all of these images, we need to recognize, was that pervasive sense of human life fallen from its purpose in creation. The need to overcome this fall, to restore the world to the perfection intended by God in creation, was the underlying plan of salvation. Jesus, as the God/man, was cast in the role of rescuer. He was of the heavenly God who dwelled beyond the sky, so he "came down" for our salvation. He was also human, so he entered the human arena as the savior, untarnished by the sin of Adam. Yet, innocent though he was, he suffered the consequences of Adam's fall, for it was his role to die. In his death he, like the paschal lamb, broke the power of death, and, like the animals of Yom Kippur, he not only was the perfect sacrifice, but he also took away the sins of the world. Jesus accomplished all of this in his crucifixion, which was understood as the sacrificial moment. The resurrection was, of course, the symbol of the acceptability to God of the sacrifice made on the cross of Calvary. In accepting the offering of this death on the cross, God prepared to overcome that death, via the resurrection. Altogether, it was a neat and clever theological system.

This view of Christianity is increasingly difficult for many of us to accept or believe. I would choose to loathe rather than to worship a deity who required the sacrifice of his son. But on many other levels as well, this entire theological system, with these strange presuppositions, has completely unraveled in our postmodern world. It now needs to be removed quite consciously from Christianity.

The unraveling began with the realization that Adam and Eve were not the primeval human parents and that all life did not stem from these two. The theory of evolution made Adam and Eve legendary at best. Evolution was not easy for the religious establishment to accept, and still voices are raised today in remote areas of the world to resist it. Those voices will never succeed. Human life clearly evolved over a four-and-a-half-to-five-billion-year process. There were no first parents, and so the primeval act of disobedience on the part of the first parents could not possibly have affected the whole human race. The myth was thus dealt a death blow, and the monolithic story of salvation built by Christian apologists over the ages began to totter.

The first line of defense was to move from a literal Adam and Eve to a symbolic Adam and Eve, and from a literal story of life in the Garden of Eden to a symbolic story of human expulsion from the perfection that God had intended for us in creation.

Human beings, it was said, by their very nature were alienated from God. That became the new definition of sin. It was not an act primeval or otherwise. It was rather a description of our being. It was ontological. This made sin the universal human condition. Only human beings were disturbed by sin, for only human beings remembered that for which they were originally intended. "Thou hast made us for thyself alone," wrote Augustine, "and our hearts are restless until they find their rest in you."[5] Animals did not chafe under the conditions of existence. Animals did not resist death unless it came prematurely with violence. For them death was thought to be natural, but not for those created in God's image. The story of Adam and Eve was thus transformed into a parable about the meaning of life destined for God but living in alienation from God. That alienation was the original sin. The fall narrative thus became a story about the dawn of self-consciousness. It was an interesting transition from literalism to symbol, and it saved the myth for, perhaps, another century.

This transition, however, could not save it for all time. In their scramble to transform Adam and Eve from literal history into symbols reflecting human ontology, most folks did not realize that Darwin had raised an even greater difficulty with this premodern mentality than simply deliteralizing Adam and Eve. Darwin had challenged successfully the concept of the goodness of creation.

To ascribe goodness to creation implies that the work of creation is complete. Darwin, however, made us aware that the creation is even now not finished. Galaxies are still being formed. Human life is also still evolving. Suddenly the whole mythological framework in which and by which the Christ figure had been captured came tumbling down. What is sin? It is not and never can be alienation from the perfection for which God in the act of creation had intended us, for there is no such thing as a perfect creation. Thus, there was no fall into sin. Yet there is a sense in which all human beings are still caught in the struggle to become our deepest and truest selves. We human beings have emerged slowly but surely out of the evolutionary soup of billions of years. We were not created in God's image in any literal way. We simply evolved out of lower forms of life and ultimately developed a higher consciousness. The purpose of creation was not necessarily fulfilled in the arrival of human life, for human life, as we know it, did not enter history until very recently.

There is also ample reason today to believe that the species of life known as Homo sapiens is not eternal. We have fouled our environmental nest so thoroughly, we have overpopulated our world so irresponsibly, we have developed weapons of mass destruction so totally that human survival faces, at best, long odds. We human beings appear to be incidental, both to the past life and to the future life of this planet. Life seems quite capable of going on with or without human participation. Yet all of our basic religious understandings and interpretations of life still assume a radically anthropocentric universe. The meaning of human life is thought by all religious systems to be central to every other consideration.

What could the concept of a primal fall of human life into sin possibly mean to those creatures who only recently evolved onto the stage of the world and who give no evidence that their stay will be permanent? How can there be a fall into sin if there has never been a perfection from which to fall? What kind of deity is it who would require of us a sacrificial offering to overcome a chasm that is now understood to be nonexistent? Why would anyone be drawn to the image of a divine rescuer who, with his self-sacrifice, would pay the price of sin? The traditional understanding of salvation history and the various theories of the atonement all come tumbling down at this point, and this includes the interpretation we have traditionally imposed upon the cross of Calvary. All of these interpretations involve us in images of an external deity who acted like a capricious human authority figure who would be displeased with human conduct and who would require some kind of restitution. They involve us in a definition of human life as sinful and fallen. Yet that external deity is quite simply dead today, and those definitions of human life that force us to dream of atoning acts, sacrifices, and stories of divine intervention are nonsensical. So the vast majority of the traditional Christ language has become inoperable. Jesus, as the agent of God's divine rescue operation, is not a Jesus who will appeal to or communicate with the citizens of this century.

We human beings do not live in sin. We are not born in sin. We do not need to have the stain of our original sin washed away in baptism. We are not fallen creatures who will lose salvation if we are not baptized.

We have rather emerged out of our evolutionary past, and we are still being formed. Our lack of wholeness is a sign of the baggage we carry as survivors of that long, difficult past. We are the bearers of what English biologist Richard Dawkins has called "the selfish gene."[6] When any of us gets caught in a battle for survival, even now our higher instincts still collapse and our radical self-centeredness causes us to engage in a tooth-and-claw struggle all over again. That is quite simply a description of our being. That is what it means to be human.

A savior who restores us to our prefallen status is therefore pre-Darwinian superstition and post-Darwinian nonsense. A supernatural redeemer who enters our fallen world to restore creation is a theistic myth. So we must free Jesus from the rescuer role. Yet so totally has he been captured by this understanding that most of us know of no other way to speak of him except to reduce him to a good teacher or a good example. Had the Christ experience been no more than that, I doubt seriously if it would have survived. Yet the Jesus portrayed in the creedal statement "as one who, for us and for our salvation, came down from heaven" simply no longer communicates to our world. Those concepts must be uprooted and dismissed. If the Christ experience is real, then we must find a new way to talk about it.

For now, I say only that this old traditional view of the Christ has died as a viable alternative. We can move no further if that conviction is not accepted. That fact alone announces the dawning of a sweeping change in the theological landscape.

SEVEN

✳

The Christ as Spirit Person

WE CAN DOCUMENT, I believe, that in the beginning of the Christian experience Jesus was portrayed primarily and simply as a "spirit person." At the very least, we can demonstrate that the first references to him include an abundant use of the word *spirit*.

Spirit is a fascinating word. It reflects the limitations found in all human vocabulary. Human vocabulary, we must remember, developed only when it was agreed, in our quest to communicate reality, that certain human sounds mean certain things. Vocabulary replaced a more intuitive, nonverbal way of communicating among primitive people only about 50,000 years ago. When language did develop, people everywhere and in every dialect seemed to use a word like *spirit* whenever they confronted an experience that made all other words seem inadequate, for a word like *spirit* can be found in the vocabulary of every nation and tribe.

Spirit is a nebulous, hard to define, totally subjective concept. It is therefore amenable to a wide variety of interpretive data. This word appears to point to a presence that is assumed to be real but cannot be easily described. It speaks of a discontent rising out of the human situation that compels us to venture into the unknown. It carries within it hints of transcendence or limitlessness, a destiny perceived but never fulfilled or a reality acknowledged but never proved. It is an almost universal human habit to interpret with the language of spirit our holy moments, our God experiences, and our glimpses into that which may be beyond our grasp. Perhaps this word *spirit* is itself a kind of commentary on our humanity. But the fact is that the earliest Christians first referred to Jesus as a "spirit person." So to probe the Jesus experience, we need to focus on why the word *spirit* was the first word applied to him by his original followers.

Sometime around the year 50 or 51 of this common era, within little more than two decades of the actual life of Jesus of Nazareth, the first written record of Jesus that we still possess appeared in Christian history. It was from the pen of a well-trained and articulate Jewish man named Paul of Tarsus. It is found in what most scholars believe was his first epistle, the one we today call 1 Thessalonians. Here, in the opening verses of what is probably the oldest book to be included in the New Testament, Paul speaks of the good news about Jesus who came "in power and in the holy spirit"[1] (1 Thess. 1:5) and who as such inspired joy (1 Thess. 1:6). Through this Jesus, Paul went on to say, God has given the holy spirit to you (1 Thess. 4:8). He further urged that believers be careful lest they "quench the spirit" (1 Thess. 5:19). This spirit, he suggested, was designed to keep their spirits "sound and blameless" (1 Thess. 5:23). These verses must not be read through that later definition of the Holy Spirit and Pentecost described in the book of Acts. Acts was not written until forty or fifty years after these early epistles. Paul appears to be arguing here that the spirit present in this Jesus was able to enhance and even to bring to birth the spirit that was present in each of those to whom he wrote. So here is where Paul began in articulating the meaning of this Christ. That meaning lay inside his understanding of the word *spirit*.

Using his other writings, we seek to discover what that word meant to Paul. A year or so after 1 Thessalonians, Paul, writing in the letter to the Galatians (52–54 C.E.), contrasted the gift of the spirit with the results of keeping the Torah (Gal. 3:2–14), which was for devout Jews the pathway to God. Both the Torah and the spirit were in some sense the gifts of God, thought Paul. Yet, he asked, which produced life? Which gave you wholeness? Did the law enter your hearts and enable you to hear God's call? Did the law issue in your ability to know God as "Abba, Father" (Gal. 4:6)? We read that today as a conflict between Christianity and Judaism. I want us to see it rather as Paul's claim that the spirit issued in life and wholeness and as his invitation to his readers into intimacy with God. Life and wholeness, he was saying, are the gifts of God present in the life of this Christ.

Paul also argued in this same epistle to the Galatians that the spirit created in the disciples of Jesus the hope for "righteousness," which was but another word for that state of wholeness or holiness (Gal. 5:5). In other references in this early epistle, Paul urged the Jesus people to "walk by the spirit" (Gal. 5:16), and he described the fruit of the spirit as love, joy, peace, patience, kindness, goodness, gentleness, and even faith (Gal. 5:22). Faith itself is not proper belief. It is rather a manifestation of the presence of spirit, Paul was saying. The early vocabulary that Paul used to describe Jesus needs to be heard apart from later doctrinal concepts.

Around the middle years of the sixth decade, 54–56, when the material we now call 1 Corinthians was being written, Paul carried his spirit language to new levels.[2] The spirit searches everything, he asserted, even the deep things or "the depths of God" (1 Cor. 2:10). Spirit was the depth dimension of human life, Paul was arguing, and even more, spirit was the depth dimension of God's divine life. It was a breathtaking concept. The same spirit, which is of God, is also within us. Paul was actually suggesting that a unity already exists between God and human life and that this unity is located in that depth of human experience where the word *spirit* appears to be the chosen metaphor. When we human beings are united with God, Paul declared, we become "one spirit with him" (1 Cor. 6:17). Given the supernatural theistic definition of God that was all but universal, this was perhaps the only way Paul could contemplate the possibility that somehow in the Christ experience the external supernatural being could also be found and known to be present in the depths of every life as its center, core, and ultimate meaning. Jesus had made clear this spirit center in every life. So Paul concluded these thoughts by asserting that our human bodies are but "the temple of the holy spirit" (1 Cor. 6:19). The physical Temple in Jerusalem had been created with human hands to provide the external supernatural God with an earthly dwelling place—a home, if you will. Paul was now suggesting that a new dwelling place for God might be not beyond the sky, but within each of us. In these words Paul was groping for a way to make rational sense out of his experience that in the human Jesus, God had been perceived to be dwelling on this earth in a dramatically new way, and the God in this Jesus had somehow made contact with the God who was within Paul. His experience was driving him as far as his traditional theological concepts would allow him to move in his attempt to define this powerful new reality that was for him a God experience that needed to be processed.

It was Paul's radical suggestion that in Jesus, God and human life were now seen to flow together. This startling conclusion revealed how deeply Paul was struggling to find a nontheistic definition for God that would account for what he believed he had met in the Christ.

Paul was aided in this struggle by some impersonal words found in the Jewish vocabulary, which, as we have already noted, were used to speak of God and, more particularly, of the spirit of God without being caught in the language of a personal Being. So once again I pick up the Jewish word for wind, *ruach,* and the Jewish word for breath, *nephesh,* and seek to explore their Jewish meaning. The *ruach* or wind was first of all impersonal. It was conceived of by Jews to be mysterious in both its origin and in its destination. It "blows where it wills and you hear the sound of it, but you do not know whence it comes or whither it goes," said the Johannine Gospel (3:8) written near the end of the first century of the common era. That writer went on to say, "So is everyone who is born of the spirit." The wind is an analogy for the spiritual life. Wind also had an animating power. It vitalized the world, which shook and waved as a sign of the wind's power. To try to capture the wind, or to strive after the wind, or even to define the wind was vanity, said the book of Ecclesiastes (2:17, 26, 4:4). The wind was also assumed by the Jewish mind to have come from God. "Thou didst blow with thy wind," said the book of Exodus (15:10), and "There went forth a wind from the Lord," said the book of Numbers (11:31). God might have been defined by these ancient people as a distant, theistic, personal power who lived beyond the sky, but in the very mysterious wind, which the Jews felt on their own faces, they believed they found themselves touched by God here and now. So the theistic concept of God and the nontheistic experience of God were already in a creative tension. The wind was a symbol of God's vitality, God's incorporeal status, and God's intimacy, and even though the divine one dwelled beyond this world, a God presence in this world forced God's reality upon them. So the Hebrew word for wind, *ruach,* became a synonym for spirit.

The second Jewish word for spirit was *nephesh,* breath. In the ancient Jewish story of creation, God created life in the man, Adam, when God "breathed into Adam's nostrils the breath of life and this creature became a living being" (Gen. 2:7). So the mighty wind, the *ruach,* we discover, was also sometimes understood to be the very breath of God. Hence, God's breath, or the divine *nephesh,* came to be thought of as the very source of all life, and *nephesh* or breath was identified with the vitality and animation found in every living being. Therefore, in Jewish thinking, spirit was conceived of externally as the wind, the *ruach,* and internally as the breath of life itself, the *nephesh.* When *nephesh* was removed from a being, that being became inert and dead. That is how *nephesh,* the breath of God within us, came to be identified with that nonmaterial part of our reality. Thus *nephesh* would later be translated as "soul" or "spirit." But at its inception and at its heart, it referred to the breath of God dwelling within us, calling us to life itself.

Once we have clarified these words and scraped them clean of later doctrinal connotations, we can begin to see the interconnections among wind, breath, and spirit all over the Jewish and Christian story. The task of spirit was always to give life. In this ancient understanding, the spiritual person was not the pious person or the religious person, but the vital, alive, whole, and real person. So the Jewish scriptures tell us that in Ezekiel's vision, when the wind or breath of God blew over the mountain and touched the dead dry bones in the valley, those bones came alive (Ezek. 37:1–10). That is the result of *ruach* spirit. Later in the Christian scriptures, when the Holy Spirit descended upon the gathered Christian community at Pentecost (Acts 2), we note that it came as a mighty rushing wind, a *ruach,* and it resulted in barriers being broken and community being restored.[3] When the Christian Church formulated its creeds in the fourth and fifth centuries of this common era, it had its adherents say, "I believe in the Holy Spirit, *the Lord, the giver of life.*" Spirit as *ruach* and *nephesh* always meant life-giver.

So all of these ancient Jewish meanings were available to Paul, and they shaped his understanding of the word *spirit,* by which he tried to communicate the meaning he found in Jesus. Jesus was a "spirit person." He was alive. He gave life to others. His life was expansive. It was not bound by traditional limits. Thus those who were touched by his spirit also came alive and began the expanding process of entering the limitless dimensions of their own lives. That was the experience to which the word *spirit* pointed. That was the meaning that Paul sought to capture when he used "spirit" words to talk about Jesus of Nazareth whom he called Christ long before Peter was said to have done so in the Gospels.

Paul also wrote that he was not concerned to know the Christ from a human point of view (2 Cor. 5:16). Jesus was a spirit person for him, a God-presence, a mediator who made what Paul called the Holy God accessible in a new way. Jesus had been for Paul the God bearer, the human life through which a new reality of God had been channeled. God was still primarily defined by Paul in theistic terms as an external supernatural deity, yet he had been forced by his experience to see this God present in the heart of a human being named Jesus, and somehow in this Jesus, God was now to be made available to others. Paul had no language big enough to make sense out of this experience. So he struggled with the language he had. Near the end of his life, Paul wrote that this Jesus did not see equality with God as a thing to be grasped, but humbled himself even to death on a cross.[4] God, however, had placed the divine stamp on this life and had exalted him to God's presence so that at the name of Jesus, every knee shall bow (Phil. 2:5–11). Somehow, Paul was suggesting, that God, still defined in terms of the traditional theistic understanding, had come out of the external heights of heaven and had been found in the very depths of human life. This, I believe was the substance of the faith of Christians before any narrative of the historical life of this Jesus had been penned. This was also the substance of the developing mythological life that fed the later theological development of the Christian church. No other word could capture this meaning except the word *spirit,* and so the first Christian writer, Paul, made this word the centerpiece of his attempt to communicate the Christ experience in human words.

When Gospel writing finally did enter the Christian enterprise some four to seven decades after the conclusion of Jesus' earthly life, and some two decades after Paul first began to write, the struggle to articulate the meaning of Christ continued. We can watch it flowing beneath the words chosen by the evangelists, if we know how to read the symbols. The experience of Jesus clearly needed to be narrated. In these Gospel stories the Jesus experience would be explained, interpreted, and rationalized in terms of a first-century Jewish worldview. Inevitably, this meant that the Jesus experience would be distorted.

This point must be heard: the Gospels are first-century narrations based on first-century interpretations. Therefore they are a first-century filtering of the experience of Jesus. They have never been other than that. We must read them today not to discover the literal truth about Jesus, but rather to be led into the Jesus experience they were seeking to convey. That experience always lies behind the distortions, which are inevitable since words are limited. If the Gospels are to be for us revelations of truth, we must enter these texts, go beneath the words, discover the experience that made the words necessary, and in this manner seek the meaning to which the words point. One must never identify the text with the revelation or the messenger with the message. That has been the major error in our two thousand years of Christian history. It is an insight that today is still feared and resisted. But let it be clearly stated, the Gospels are not in any literal sense holy, they are not accurate, and they are not to be confused with reality. They are rather beautiful portraits painted by first-century Jewish artists, designed to point the reader toward that which is in fact holy, accurate, and real. The Gospels represent that stage in the development of the faith story in which ecstatic exclamation begins to be placed into narrative form.

Once we begin to grasp this truth, we can enter the Gospels in a new way. When we do, we discover that, like religious people through the ages, the Gospel writers also fell back on and indeed required the use of this same word *spirit* to tell their story. We looked earlier at the way the interpretive process regarding Jesus grew over the decades of New Testament writing. Now we turn to asking why the word *spirit* always lay at the center of that interpretation process.

Two of the Gospels, Matthew and Luke, begin their story of Jesus with the suggestion that he was conceived by the Holy Spirit. That was a fascinating first century way to suggest that Jesus was a spirit person. Surely this was not biology that was being described. Before the virgin birth stories developed in the ninth decade of this common era, no writer anywhere had so much as hinted at a miraculous birth tradition. Paul never even mentioned Jesus' family of origin, save first to say that like every other human being he was "born of a woman" (Gal. 4:4), and second to suggest that according to the flesh he was descended from the house of David (Rom. 1:3). Mark, the earliest Gospel, also contained no reference whatsoever to Jesus having had a supernatural birth. Mark, however, did speak of the mother of Jesus on two occasions, and neither of them was flattering, to say the least. The first time the name Mary appeared in written Christian literature, and the only time her name was spoken in Mark's Gospel, it came on the lips of a critic of Jesus. "Is not this the carpenter, the son of Mary?" (Mark 6:3) a member of a crowd shouted. That reference was clearly intended to be insulting. To call a grown Jewish man the son of a woman was to cast doubt upon his paternity. In Mark's Gospel, his mother was portrayed as seeking to "put Jesus away," fearing that he was "beside himself" (Mark 3:21). There was no quiet maternal devotion from Mary to Jesus in this first Gospel tradition. There was rather the threatened response of an embarrassed mother who assumed that Jesus' behavior was abnormal and that this abnormality was not regarded positively. That was hardly the stance a woman would take if an angel had told her that she would conceive a special child or if she knew herself to be a virgin mother. Nor is this a stance that would be taken by a mother to whom shepherds had come in wonder or to whom wise men had journeyed with gifts to welcome her child's birth. The first Gospel writer, Mark, could not even have imagined such stories.

The birth stories, when they finally did appear, thus clearly were not intended to be read as history. They were rather interpretive portraits based on Jewish sacred stories being painted by first-century Jews in a language and style that Jews understood. Matthew took the virgin concept out of a mistranslation of Isaiah 7:14 (Matt. 1:18–25), and Luke built on Matthew's mistake. The wise men (Matt. 2:1–12) came out of Isaiah 60, with an additional note drawn from the story of the visit to Solomon by the Queen of Sheba (1 Kings 10). The star was lifted out of the Balaam-Balak story in Numbers 22–24 and out of other popular episodes in the oral tradition of the Jews. The shepherds were suggested by the association of Bethlehem with David, the shepherd boy who became king (Luke 2:1–20). The song of Mary (Luke 1:46–55) was adapted from the song of Hannah in the book of Samuel (1 Sam. 2:1–10). The story of the pregnant Mary's visit to the pregnant Elizabeth (Luke 1:39–45) was an adaptation of the story of Rebekah, pregnant with Esau and

Jacob (Gen. 25:19–26). The whole character of Joseph, the earthly father of Jesus, was drawn and shaped by the ancient story of the patriarch Joseph from Genesis 37–50 (Matt. 1, 2). On and on we could go with this analysis. These stories were designed to be understood as midrashic writing, not literal biography.[5]

When the Gospel stories of Jesus' birth were written, probably in the middle to late years of the ninth decade of the common era, no one knew his parents, much less the details of his birth. These stories were created to help interpret the meaning of his adult life. So our question becomes, what were these Gospel writers seeking to convey when they suggested that Jesus was conceived by the spirit?

Their experience was that in this Jesus, they had met God. That was the reality to which they were responding. But like Paul before them, the Gospel writers were victims of the limits of language and the limits of the prevailing definition of God. Since God had always been conceived of as other, external, unlimited, supernatural, and belonging to the heavenly realm, how could they speak of God as present in Jesus? So birth stories were developed in order to assert that this external God must have come out of the sky to enter him in some supernatural, miraculous way at his conception. Jesus must therefore have been the spirit's child. There was in him a transcendence, a holiness, that only God could have created. They were trying to say that the qualities they had met in him were not within the capability of human beings by themselves to create. Therefore, he must be the product of God's spirit. So these Gospel writers, reflecting their faith communities, mined both their sacred tradition and their vocabulary in order to speak rationally of what they had experienced.

When Jesus reached adulthood, another spirit story was told about him on the occasion of his baptism (Mark 1:1–11), to which we have already referred. Now we look at this story again, but this time from the perspective of the meaning of *spirit*. For Mark, who made no effort to record a birth narrative, the baptism was his first spirit story. For Matthew and Luke, the baptism narrative was the birth story being retold in a new adult context (Matt. 3:1–17; Luke 3:1–22). In this first adult story recorded about Jesus in every Gospel, he approached the Jordan River. The Jordan was a mystical divide whose waters, we learn in the scriptures, had been parted, like the Red Sea, by God's power on three different occasions—once for Joshua (Josh. 2:11–13), once for Elijah (2 Kings 2:8), and once for Elisha (2 Kings 2:14). That Jordan River was also thought to offer a doorway into the promised land where God was believed to reign as king. So in these biblical narratives of his baptism, Jesus was also made to step into this mystical Jordan River. The waters of the Jordan River, however, did not part for him. Rather, Jesus parted the barrier that separated God from the world. Jesus belonged, the tradition was asserting, to the realm of God, which was above. So he was portrayed as splitting that very firmament that the creation story had said separated the waters above from the waters below (Gen. 1:6, 7). Then those heavenly waters flowed down on him as spirit, marking him as a spirit person, a God presence. For Jews, living water was also a synonym for spirit. When the Kingdom of God arrived in Jewish thought as expressed by the prophets, fountains of living water would flow out of Jerusalem (Zech. 14:8). The outpouring of this water was called "spirit" (Isa. 12:3, 44:3, 55:1). In the Johannine Gospel, Jesus was said to have promised the Samaritan woman "living water" which would free her from ever again having to draw from the well (John 4:1–15). Later in this same Gospel, the Christ figure was said to have referred to those who believe in him as able to produce "living water" that he calls spirit (John 7:37–39). In case anyone misunderstood this spirit meaning, the Gospel writers simply added to their story the detail that a heavenly voice offstage proclaimed Jesus' identity as God's son.

Surely this baptism account also was never intended to be a literal story. There never was a roof in the sky above the earth, which could be opened to let spirit from the realm of heaven descend upon an earthly being. The voice of God in this story was lifted as an almost direct quotation from Isaiah 42, from the moment in which Isaiah's mythical servant of God first appeared in human history. The story of Jesus' baptism was nothing but a midrashic "Moses at the Red Sea" story, magnified to heavenly proportions and retold about Jesus. Jews traditionally had asserted that God was with Moses. Now they were asserting that this same God presence had been met in Jesus. Thus it was that by drawing on their sacred history, these first-century Jewish folk found the words to talk about the God presence they had met in Jesus. They knew no God except a God defined as an external being with supernatural power, and so they described the God presence they met in Jesus in the only God language they knew how to use. God had come down by spiritual conception or by an outpouring of heavenly spirit upon him. Jesus was a spirit person, a window into the holy, an incarnation of the divine. Underneath the description, however, lay an experience, and it is that experience that beckons us even as we set the literalness of their description of that experience aside.

The spirit, we are next told, led this Jesus into the wilderness, where he was tested, tempted, or tried. How would a spirit man respond to the typical levers of human compromise? Faced with the promise of food, the promise of magic, the promise of power, how deeply manipulable we human beings seem to be! However, Jesus, we are told, passed the test. A spirit person must know that bread never fills the deepest hunger in our souls for God, that God cannot be put to the test, and that wholeness is never realized when something less than the holy

God is worshiped. After this, Jesus left the wilderness, we are told, and spiritual beings called angels cared for him (Matt. 4:1–11).

Once again we need to face the limits of these words. There was no literal wilderness period of temptation for Jesus of Nazareth. That, too, was a midrashic Moses story, magnified infinitely in a frail human attempt to find words big enough to plumb the God presence known in this spirit person Jesus.[6] What did it mean for these Gospel writers to assert that he was spirit filled, spirit led, and spirit tested? That is the question we must face if we are going to enter the meaning of the God who was perceived to be the ultimate reality met in Jesus of Nazareth.

Next a new Sinai came into focus, and the spirit person Jesus, portrayed as the new Moses, was made to utter, in one Gospel (Matt. 5:1–11), eight blessings or beatitudes, and in another Gospel (Luke 6:20–22) four beatitudes or blessings. Each beatitude represented a sign that the reign of God had begun in the human heart. "Blessed are the poor in spirit," "those who mourn," "the meek," "those who hunger and thirst for righteousness," "the merciful," "the pure in heart," "the peacemaker," and "the persecuted." They belong to the Kingdom of Heaven. They shall see God, obtain mercy, be comforted, and even inherit the earth. It was strange language. One wonders what in their mind's eye they envisioned the reign of God or the seeing of God to be like. Later this spirit person Jesus was portrayed as urging his followers not to be worried when they were dragged before councils for his sake, but rather to let the holy spirit or the "spirit of your Father" speak through them (Mark 13:11; Matt. 10:16–20; Luke 12:11, 12). Jesus was portrayed as possessing a spirit that was accessible also to them. What Jesus was they also could become: that was the hidden message. Later it was even suggested that believers might be capable of doing even greater things than Jesus (John 14:12). This was heady teaching indeed for the disciples.

On another occasion Jesus was made to suggest that even David, who lived a thousand years before Jesus, had called Jesus Lord (Mark 12:37). Was the Gospel writer suggesting that one who was a spirit person was also a participant in timelessness? Is that also what was perceived when Jesus was made to say, "Before Abraham was, I am" (John 8:58)?

When a story was told about Jesus' power to raise one from the dead, the words used were "her spirit returned" (Luke 8:55). So spirit clearly had something to do with life. Jesus, when he was dying, was made to say in one Gospel, "Father, into your hands I commit my spirit" (Luke 23:46). In another it was said of him simply that "he yielded up the spirit" (Matt. 27:50). The ancient Jewish connection between spirit and life was clearly present in the Gospel tradition. So our question becomes, what kind of life was it that came to be identified with spirit? Spirit is the source of life, John's Gospel quoted Jesus as saying (John 7:29). So one who is radically, deeply, and fully alive was called a spirit person. If that person can enable others to come to a similar quality of life, he will be called the God bearer.

Jesus was also portrayed as one who "rejoiced in the spirit" (Luke 10:21), as one who said, "the heavenly Father [will] give the Holy Spirit to those who ask" (Luke 11:13), as one who had defined God as spirit, and as one who suggested that since God is spirit, those who worship him must do so "in spirit and truth" (John 4:24).

Finally, the promise of Jesus was that he would send the spirit to his disciples and that this spirit would teach them all things (John 14:26) and guide them into all truth. When John's Gospel told the story of the resurrection, it presented a portrait of a risen Jesus who "breathed on them," enabling them to receive the Holy Spirit (John 20:22), tying us back once again to the meaning of breath as somehow connected with spirit and life.

What God had done to Adam to begin the creation, Jesus was now said to have done to the disciples to begin the new creation. What God's wind had done to the dead, dry bones of the Jewish people in the book of Ezekiel, so now Luke in his Pentecost story (Acts 2) was suggesting that Jesus' gift of the spirit did for his lifeless and hopeless disciples. A mighty rushing wind came upon them, and they came to life. Jesus' ultimate and final gift to the world was the gift of a life-giving spirit.

Earlier we suggested that the stories of Jesus' miraculous birth were entrance stories. That is, they were the means by which the Gospel writers sought to get the theistic God out of heaven and onto the earth so that their God experience in Jesus would make sense. Now we must look yet again at the exit stories of Jesus' life, but not this time just at his return into the sky, which we have already examined, but specifically at the narratives that came to be called the Easter story.

Reading the resurrection stories, we note first the heightening of the miraculous in a thousand different ways. Resurrection came to mean that the grave was empty. A giant stone had been mysteriously removed from the mouth of Jesus' tomb. Angelic messengers, who earlier had announced his birth, now came from heaven to proclaim him raised from the dead (see Mark 16:1–8; Matt. 28; Luke 24; John 20). On one occasion this risen Jesus was said to have appeared to the disciples out of the clouds of heaven (Matt. 28:16–20). The purpose of this theophany was to commission the disciples to go into all the world to teach and to baptize. Spirit, said this Jesus, was to be part of that baptism formula. Still later the risen Jesus was portrayed as having the power to appear and disappear at will (Luke 24:13–35), as inviting his disciples to handle his body to guarantee that he was not a ghost (Luke 24:39), as able to enter into a locked and barred upper room without opening a door (John 20:19ff.), as inviting Thomas to explore his wounds by hand (John 20:27), and, finally, as rising into the sky of a three-tiered universe (Acts 1:1–11). These physical details accompanying Jesus' departure from this world were clearly enhanced as the years passed. It was another way of saying that God and Jesus had achieved a oneness that transcended his earthly life.

What these writers were trying to say, within their limited concepts, was that in the particular life of the spirit person Jesus, they saw not only God, but also a picture of what each of us might look like in our fulfilled spirit state. They were suggesting that Jesus was the portrait of the destiny available to all who are to be the recipients of the Holy Spirit. They were hinting that the spirit person Jesus could be discovered over and over in each of us as we open ourselves daily to new human heights. These were startling claims. When this incredible life came violently and prematurely to an end, these God qualities, which had been experienced in this Jesus, were thought to have embraced his followers, making them aware that the spirit presence they had known in Jesus was now a reality manifested in them. As the recipients of the spirit from Jesus, they were alive in a new way. It was the same quality of life that they believed they had met in Jesus, and so in the power of that new life they shouted, "Jesus lives!"

In time, literal-minded people would transform that proclamation into stories about his physical resuscitation. That was and is one of the inevitabilities of trying to speak of God and spirit with limited human words. In the power of this spirit-filled experience, these disciples also came to believe that death could not define this Jesus, nor could it contain him. In time this faith assertion also got narrated as a story of a literal tomb that could not physically hold his body in death. As the years rolled by and the stories were told and retold, they obviously grew. In time, narratives describing angels who descended from the sky to roll back the confining stone were added. Next an earthquake was said to have shaken the world to mark the dramatic moment when the disciples recognized that the spirit that had been in Jesus was now the essence of their own lives. Out of the grave in limitless freedom, breaking every barrier that bound human life, the spirit person emerged until he was perceived as having poured God's Holy Spirit personally upon them.

Underneath the prevailing theistic images of God, we see a divine presence called spirit within us and most spectacularly in Jesus of Nazareth. We find our spirits touched by his spirit, our lives enhanced by his life, our being called to a new level by his being. In the limited God vocabulary of the first-century Jewish world, they were driven to assert that a God presence, somehow connected with spirit, had been met in Jesus of Nazareth.

So I start with that insight. I assert that Jesus is a spirit person, a God presence, and this assertion becomes my point of entry into his meaning. Beyond the boundaries of theism, which have limited us for so long, we discover a startling revelation of God at the very center of human life, and Jesus, the spirit person, stands at the heart of that revelation. Perhaps that is why we have seen him as a God bearer. Perhaps that is why we have tended to use the language of incarnation.

With this nontheistic clue pointing toward Jesus as the spirit person, we now are ready to enter the Gospel stories anew and to roam within them beneath their literalness. We are not looking for the external descriptions, the signs of a God who has come down. Instead we are searching for a humanity through which the meaning of God, who is in the midst of life, might be revealed. It promises to be an exciting journey.

EIGHT

✳

What Think Ye of Christ? Where the Human Enters the Divine

WHAT THINK YE OF CHRIST? Who is Christ for you or
for me? Does that first-century life still have some rele-
vance for those of us living today? In what sense, if any, can we
call him savior? Is he an example that we might choose to emu-
late? Is there anything more than that?

Can we, in fact, do what I have proposed? Can we remove
from Christ the theistic framework of the past, which portrayed
him either as a heavenly deity who had come to earth as a kind
of divine visitor or as a human being who somehow possessed
the power of a supernatural God? Can we still speak of him in
any sense as the "only son" of the heavenly father?

If these things are no longer options for our time, is anything left by which to commend the being of this Jesus, not just his teaching, to our postmodern world? How can we today talk about the meaning of his cross apart from seeing his death as some kind of sacrifice? Is something more than just a human tragedy to be found in the symbol of the cross? Does that cross carry with it any salvific meaning, and if so, what is it? Surely, there must be some way a believer in exile can respond meaningfully to these probing questions.

If there is not, then perhaps we should bow to the inevitable and admit that we are not just in a period of exile, but rather that we have entered the death throes of that venerable religious system we once called Christianity.

Despite my protestations to the contrary, it will surely be suggested by my critics that what I have been doing in my career and in this volume is nothing less than trying to create a new religion—and a humanistic one at that. If that is so, they will suggest that I should be courageous and admit that Christianity, like many other human religious systems, has simply faded away, and that I should resign from the life of the Church. Why, they ask, would I or anyone else engage in this tortuous process of recasting, rethinking, reinterpreting, and revisioning? Those are valid concerns.

I enter this process because I can neither dismiss this Christ nor live comfortably with the way he has been traditionally interpreted. I am not prepared to conclude that the traditional way of interpreting Jesus has exhausted the possibilities. I can with no great difficulty set aside those interpretations, but I cannot set aside the Christ experience, which created the necessity for those theistic interpretations of yesterday. I still find the power of the Christ compelling.

I am moved by the generations of believers whose lives have been enriched, even transformed, by this Jesus. My own experience is that time after time my relationship with Jesus has propelled me beyond limiting barrier after limiting barrier. So I will not let him go until I have explored the meaning of his life with a new intensity. I will not be put off from this quest until I have entered a level of truth that is beyond the threatened defensiveness of the present theological establishment. I will entertain openly every possibility that might explain this Jesus more adequately. Perhaps he was just a misunderstood zealot, a hapless victim, or a deluded madman, but I do not think so. Something draws me back to him again and again. He also might have been a God presence, even a continuing God presence, if I could only discern how to communicate that in language free of the theistic God patterns of the past.

The only pathway I know to follow into this exploration is that of examining Jesus' humanity, the presence beneath the theistic explanations. What was there about this man's very being, including his death, that caused him to be understood by his Jewish contemporaries as the paschal lamb of the Passover, who somehow broke the power of death? Why did his earliest Jewish followers view him as the sacrificial lamb of Yom Kippur who overcame the separation between God and human life, or as the scapegoat of ancient Israel who became the sin bearer and who thus took away the sins of the people? What was there about the crucifixion of this Jesus that caused them to speak of him as the innocent victim or the suffering servant, following the image created in the writings of an unknown sixth-century B.C.E. prophet we today call Second Isaiah (Isa. 40–55)? What was it that occurred after the crucifixion that caused these same Jewish people to believe that God had raised him into the very being of God and that he therefore should be identified with the image of the Son of Man from the writings of Daniel (Dan. 7:13, 14), who would someday come again in the clouds of heaven as the final agent of God's judgment? What was there about the totality of his life that caused the writer of John's Gospel to link him to a preexistent logos, or Word of God—a divine outpouring, if you will? That logos image was derived from the writings of a first-century Jewish philosopher named Philo as well as from the more ancient writers of the Jewish book of Proverbs (3:19, 20; 8:22–31), who spoke of "wisdom" in much the same way.

Were all of these images simply applied to Jesus by chance? Did those first believers simply create the Christ story in order to fulfill their own biblical expectations? Was desire the mother of the invention, or was there something in his life that was so real, so timeless, so revelatory, and so transcendent that these images became not just appropriate but inescapable? Why was it unavoidable that those who worshiped the holy God insisted that they had met this God in him? When the theological structures of antiquity, which were wrapped so tightly around him, collapse, as I believe they are doing in this generation, these questions will still force us to search amid the wreckage for the meaning of this Jesus. We will continue to look for that revelatory moment that people experienced in him, for that flash of wonder that drove them to their God language, and for that substance upon which the whole theistic theological superstructure of doctrine, dogma, and creeds would later be erected.

Even when the task of discerning what they found in him has been accomplished, we still must face an equally disturbing question: has their experience and ours been real, or have we all been deluded out of our primeval desire to discover that in this vast and impersonal world we are not alone? So into the Jesus story we now plunge.

We ultimately have only two places in which to look at the person of Jesus. One is in the Gospels themselves. Can we discern some things about his humanity underneath the supernatural frame of reference the Gospel writers applied to him? The second is to examine the impact of his life on history. It is, perhaps, harder to separate the person of Jesus from those interpretations of his life that compelled various responses throughout history. But we must try. Can we discern how it came about that this life has called, invited, or even compelled the human enterprise, or certain persons within it, to new levels of being?

The Johannine material in the New Testament suggested that love was but another name for God (1 John 4:8). Did Jesus bring that name to a new level of realization? He was certainly portrayed throughout the Gospel story as capable of reaching beyond the limits that have so frequently been placed on the meaning of love. So we seek first to understand how in the presence of this Jesus, the Gospel writers began to note that the barriers dividing one person from another seemed to fade.

In the world in which Jesus lived, a chasm of stereotypical prejudice separated the Jews from the Samaritans. They would not eat together, worship together, intermarry, or even share the same physical space if it could be avoided. Yet Jesus in the Gospels was said to have taught that the Samaritan was worthy of healing (Luke 17:11–19) and that a Samaritan who acted out the claims of the law in terms of showing mercy was more deeply a child of Abraham than even the Jewish priest or Levite (Luke 10:29–37). These were radical statements of barrier-breaking inclusion, which expanded rather dramatically and in a new way the meaning of love.

Beyond the barrier dividing the Jew from the Samaritan, there was the separation of the Jews from the gentiles, which also carried with it the force of a long and painful history. This separation had been part of the Jewish technique of survival through the centuries. It precluded any intermingling. In the service of this survival mentality, gentiles were even declared unclean by the Jews. They were known as the uncircumcised, as those not bound by the kosher dietary laws, and as those who were ignorant of the holy demands of the Torah. Association with gentiles, therefore, would corrupt the Jew and make him or her unclean and therefore equally unacceptable to the Jewish community and presumably to the Jewish God. It must be noted that gentiles were equally negative in their characterization of Jews.

Yet Jesus was portrayed in Mark's Gospel as going to the gentile side of the lake to repeat the feeding of the multitude in the wilderness story. This time seven loaves are said to have been adequate for four thousand people (Mark 8:1–10).[1]

He was also said to have reached out to the Syro-Phoenician woman, another gentile, and to have healed her daughter (Mark 7:24–30). The Gospels tell of Jesus healing the slave of a Roman centurion and even of commending his faith as greater than he had found in Israel (Matt. 8:5–10; Luke 7:1–10). Mark's Gospel concluded the crucifixion story with a gentile soldier standing before the cross and becoming the first one to understand the meaning of Jesus' death. "Truly this man was the Son of God," the centurion exclaimed (Mark 15:39).

Matthew, perhaps the most Jewish of the Gospel writers, wrapped his story of Jesus inside an interpretive envelope in which he suggested that at Jesus' birth gentiles, known as wise men or magi, had come to bring this Jewish messiah gifts. These magi, said Matthew, were led by a star, a heavenly sign visible to the whole world. Gentiles were thus intended to be drawn to the light of this Christ (Matt. 1, 2). After the death of Jesus Matthew completed this thesis by having the risen Christ commission his disciples to go into all the world—to go, that is, far beyond the boundaries which at that time separated Jew from gentile (Matt. 28:16–20).

In the second genealogy of Jesus to be included in the New Testament (Luke 3),[2] Luke said that Jesus himself was a descendant of Adam like every other human being. Thus, he was said to belong to all people, gentiles included. So in this Jesus no human barrier could finally separate one child of God from another. Luke made that point even more powerfully when he told the story of Pentecost (Acts 2), in which the Holy Spirit fell on representatives of all the nations of the earth, "Parthians, Medes, Elamites, and dwellers in Mesopotamia." In that same narrative, the Spirit was said to have removed the language barrier, which contributed greatly to divisions in the human family. In the presence of the Spirit, the human community was to be universal. That was a startling thesis in first-century Judea. There was something about this Jesus that propelled his followers from Jerusalem to the uttermost parts of the world.

Jesus also lived in a world where cultural barriers were drawn that defined women as subhuman and children as not worthy of God's concern. Yet Jesus was said to have spoken with the woman by the well, to have answered her questions, engaged her in dialogue, challenged her presuppositions, and even invited her into the worship of God "in spirit and in truth" (John 4:7–30). He was also portrayed as welcoming into discipleship a group of women, led by the remarkable Magdalene, who cared for the disciple band with their own resources (Luke 8:3). When the Church was born, women were present in the upper room to become numbered among the original recipients of the Spirit (Acts 1:14). Even Paul, responding to something in this Jesus, declared that in Christ "there is neither male nor female" (Gal. 3:28). This major cultural revolution seems to have been identified with Jesus, and it is so powerful that religious elements even today scurry to repress it.

When children were prohibited by his own disciples from coming to him, he was said to have rebuked those disciples and to have announced that the little children must come to him because "to such belongs the kingdom of God" (Mark 10:13–14). Indeed, he went so far as to say that unless we receive the kingdom like little children, we cannot enter it (Mark 10:15).

There were also cultic barriers in Jesus' time that served to exclude. Some people were declared to be ritualistically impure and thus not worthy of human contact. Menstruation was one source of this impurity according to the Torah (Lev. 12:2, 18:19). But if the menstrual cycle, which was complete in a few days, produced one who was for that brief span of time untouchable, how much more repelling would be a woman with a chronic menstrual discharge? Yet the Gospel record portrays Jesus as responding to such a person's defiling (as they thought) touch with acceptance, love, and healing (Mark 5:24–34). We also note that he actually touched the rotting flesh of the impure leper and brought him once again into human community (Mark 1:40, 41). Even cultic impurities seemed to fade before him.

Next, in a world that viewed mental illness as demon possession, Jesus was said to have confronted a deranged man who could not be bound with ropes and chains and who lived ostracized among the tombs of the dead. Jesus then called even this life back into wholeness (Mark 5:1–13).

Beneath the God claims made for this Jesus was a person who lived a message announcing that there was no status defined by religion, by tribe, by culture, by cult, by ritual, or by illness that could separate any person from the love of God. If love is a part of what God is or who God is, then it can surely be said of this Jesus that he lived the meaning of God. According to the Gospels, he lived it with a consistent intensity. It was as if his source of love lay beyond every human boundary. It was inexhaustible. It was life giving. Finally, when it was noticed, it was thought to be so deeply the meaning of God that the assumption was made that the love present in the life of this Jesus was the result of an external deity who had somehow entered into him.

When the story of his life was being chronicled in the early Gospel tradition, another aspect of his humanity also served to capture people's attention. He possessed an unearthly capacity to be present, totally present, to another person. People who entered his life experienced what Paul Tillich described many years later as "the eternal now."[3] It was as if time stood still inside the total attentiveness of this Jesus. He was able to give himself to others to a remarkable degree. This is what can be seen in his conversation with the rich young ruler (Mark 10:17–22; Matt. 19:16–22; Luke 18:18–23) and with the woman taken in adultery (John 8:1–11).[4] It was also present in the narrative of his conversation with Pontius Pilate after his arrest (Mark 15:1–5; Matt. 27:15–26; Luke 23:1–25), with the soldiers who tortured him (Mark 15:16–20; Luke 23:32–38), and even with the penitent thief on the cross (Luke 23:39–43). One has to possess himself or herself very powerfully in order to give one's being away to another so deeply and so totally. That was yet another aspect of his humanity that did not escape notice. It was a significant part of who Jesus was, and thus it had to be interpreted. In these interpretations people suggested that perhaps this quality of his life revealed that he somehow possessed the infinite depths of the life of God.

His humanity was also portrayed as able to manifest that essential, but rare, quality of true freedom, the freedom to be oneself under every set of circumstances. Another one of Paul's ecstatic utterances captured this aspect of Jesus' life, when the apostle wrote, "For freedom Christ has set us free" (Gal. 5:1). This portrait of freedom was painted in an especially unique way during the narratives of the last days of Jesus' life. The Gospels suggested that when Jesus came to Jerusalem at the time of the Passover, he was greeted as a king who came in the name of the Lord, and people spread their garments in his path (Mark 11:1–10; Matt. 21:1–9; Luke 19:29–38) and waved palm branches to hail his arrival. In that narrative we see his remarkable gift of freedom. It would have been so easy and so human for Jesus to have allowed those acclamations to fill up the needs of his ego, to turn his head from his destiny, and even to distort his humanity. The praise and cheers of human beings constitute a seductive drug that has been known to bring addiction to some very great people. But in the Gospel portrait, Jesus accepts this welcome and turns away from his purpose neither to the right nor to the left. This is a picture of one who knew who he was. He possessed the freedom of his own being. He did not need to incorporate the praise of the people into his self-definition.

This freedom was also revealed in the Gospel narrative from a different perspective just a week later. Now the cheers were silent. Jesus instead faced overt hostility. First he was on trial for his life. Then he was a condemned man without the ability to claim protection from cruelty or abuse. Finally, he was a dying man stretched out upon a cross from which there would be no escape.

When life is threatened, when it is being taken away from us violently, when we are the victim of another's aggression, when the verbal abuse of the crowd is heaped upon us, the overwhelming tendency in human beings is to resist, to defend, to attack, to curse, to plead, to whine, or to weep. Self-preservation, we have already noted, is located on perhaps the deepest level of the human psyche. But once again the picture painted of Jesus in the Gospels was that of a remarkably free man. He was free to forgive, free to endure, free to be, and free to die. His being was not distorted by his external circumstances. It was and is a startling portrait. It matters not whether any of these portrayals were literally accurate. They, in fact, recorded people's impressions of this person, and when the Gospel writers wrote them, they constituted riveting, unforgettable, rare glimpse into the depths of the humanity of this Jesus. There was clearly an enormous power present in his life.

Finally, look at the portrait drawn in the Gospels of his relationship with his disciples. They were, said one text, chosen by him out of a larger number after he had spent all night in prayer or meditation (Luke 6:12–16). He invested much of his life in this group of twelve. The Gospels portray him as turning away from the crowds to concentrate on this disciple band. When they did not grasp the meaning of a parable, he instructed them privately (Mark 4:10–20; Luke 8:9–15; Matt. 13:10–23). When they did not understand what his life was all about, he sought to enlighten them without berating them for their ignorance (Acts 1:7, 8; John 20:27; John 6:68).[5] When these disciples failed him, as they constantly seemed to do, he did not cease to reach out to them in love. The story of his life was drawn in the Gospels as if its purpose was to proclaim that nothing one could do and nothing one could be could separate any person from the love of God. When these disciples forsook him, he loved his forsakers. When one of them was said to have denied him, and another to have betrayed him, he loved the denier and the betrayer. When his enemies abused him, he loved his abusers. When they killed him, he loved his killers. What more can one do to live out the meaning of the God who is love?

As he died, the portrait painted in the Gospels was one of self-giving. He was the one condemned to die, but in the narratives he gave his life away even as they took it from him. He gave forgiveness to the soldiers (Luke 23:34). He gave comfort to those daughters of Jerusalem who were weeping for him (Luke 23:28). He gave assurance to the penitent thief (Luke 23:43), and he was even pictured from the cross as caring for his mother in her grief (John 19:26, 27). Again, it matters not how literally accurate any or all of these references are. When the community of faith wrote their accounts of the life of this Jesus, these were the human qualities that they discovered residing underneath the theistic interpretation of the meaning of Jesus of Nazareth. Here was a whole human being who lived fully, who loved wastefully, and who had the courage to be himself under every set of circumstances. He was thus a human portrait of the meaning of God, understood as the source of life, the source of love, and the ground of being.

Once we shed the theistic supernatural framework within which this life has been understood throughout the centuries, we are still left with a remarkable human portrait, indeed, with a humanity that seems to escape the boundaries of the human.

When one examines the way the meaning of his life moved through history, one finds that the impetus from this Jesus continues to compel the community that bears his name to journey forward beyond human barriers. The Church of Jesus Christ has constantly moved past the fences of prejudice in its drive to become a universal community. Gentiles did ultimately find welcome in the Church. Slavery was finally ended. Segregation and apartheid had their backs broken. Women did achieve ecclesiastical power and position. Mentally ill people were finally understood and treated as sick people, not crazy people. People whose depression led them to suicide were finally buried within the walls of the Church. Divorced people were finally not rejected but were offered a second chance at marriage and happiness. Left-handed people were finally understood and were accepted as they were, rather than being forced into an unnatural change and thus into the necessity of acting contrary to the way their brains were organized. Ultimately, gay and lesbian people are receiving the welcome of Christ into the Church without the barriers of either a willingness to "reform" or a guilt-laden celibacy being imposed upon them as the price of their admission. Also being removed is the limitation on the place that honest and open homosexual people can occupy in the life of the Church if they dare to live and love as a couple. Of course, throughout Christian history there have been difficult times, rejecting times, setbacks, and dark chapters, but ultimately the Christpower present in this community of believers has prevailed and the doors of the Church have been opened to those against whom they once were locked shut. That is the same mark that the Gospels found in the human Jesus of Nazareth, and it continues to break forth from the Church in generation after generation.

When we examine these data, we have to raise another question that in the theistic world of yesterday never would have emerged. Are those qualities that we call human and divine mutually exclusive? Or do they penetrate each other? Is the divine simply the depth dimension of the human? Or are these two entities perhaps two sides of the same coin? That is a new theological frontier and it is worth pursuing.

Some religious thinkers have suggested that all these modern attempts to reenvision the holy are finally nothing but the collapse of the transcendent otherness of God into a shallow sense of the immanence of God. This immanence is shallow because it is the only aspect of God, presumably, that human beings can embrace. That, however, is not my understanding of either transcendence or immanence.

Transcendence, as conservative thinkers tend to use the word, is, in my opinion, only an aspect of the theistic thinking of the past that has lost its primary meaning. I do not believe, for example, that transcendence is exhausted in the concept of a God external to this world who operates upon this world from a supernatural vantage point. I rather see transcendence as one additional dimension of the holy. The immanence of God might be identified with such human qualities as the presence of love, the quality of life, and the affirmation of being. One touches God first in that very human experience. But once we cross the barrier from the limitations of our humanity into the infinity of the source of being itself, then *transcendence* becomes the word that symbolizes the endless depths of life that are then available. Immanence stands for the point of contact between the human and the divine. Transcendence stands for the inexhaustible depths of the divine once the contact is made. Human life is capable of entering the infinity of God because the infinity of God can be found in the heart of every human life. The two are not distinct. Humanity and divinity flow together. That is what Tillich was trying to say when he called God "the infinite and inexhaustible ground of all being." That is also, I believe, what the Johannine writer was trying to say when he asserted that "God is love, and whoever abides in love, abides in God" (I John 4:16). That is what the mystics, from Meister Eckhart to John A. T. Robinson,[6] have sought to communicate when they have suggested that Jesus did not differ from you and me in kind. He differed only in degree, the degree to which the God-consciousness came to fullness in him. He was, in Robinson's words, both "the man for others" and "the human face of God."[7]

So, recalling our earlier attempt to speak of God in nonpersonal categories as the Ground of all Being, the Source of Life, and the Source of Love, we seek now to speak of Jesus in these categories.

In the being of Jesus we see a revelation of the Ground of Being. In his life we see a revelation of the Source of Life. In his love we see a revelation of the Source of Love. These were the aspects of his human presence that made his life so awesome and so compelling that people were driven to speak about him in terms of the theistic images of antiquity. So he was acclaimed "the Son of God," the incarnate one, and even the second person of the Holy Trinity. That was the only way that the Jewish Christian people of the first century who wrote the Bible and the later Christians of the fourth and fifth centuries who wrote the creeds could make sense out of their experience, given the frame of reference set for them by their presuppositions and their worldview.

Yes, God is real, intensely real, for me, but God is not a being—external, supernatural, or theistic—to whom I seek access. God is rather a presence discovered in the very depths of my life, in the capacity to live, in the ability to love, and in the courage to be. Jesus, the alive one, the loving one, the one who had the courage to be himself under every set of circumstances, was and is the life where God has been seen and can still be seen in a human form under the limitations of our finitude. If transcendence can be translated as infinite depth, if immanence can be seen as the point of access to those depths, and if the Christ figure can be interpreted as the life where transcendence and immanence come together, then we have a new way of understanding the meaning of the Trinity. The cross of Jesus revealed that one can give life away totally if one possesses it, or if one is in touch with or perhaps is at one with the source of life. The way of the cross becomes the way of constant vulnerability. It was the being of Jesus, the full humanity of Jesus, that ultimately revealed the meaning of God. It is the being of each of us, our full humanity, that also will finally connect us to the meaning of God.

So being a disciple of this Jesus does not require me to make literalized creedal affirmations in propositional form about the reality of the theistic God who supposedly invaded our world and who lived among us for a time in the person of Jesus. It only requires me to be empowered by him to imitate the presence of God in him by living fully, by loving wastefully, and by having the courage to be all that God created me to be. It does not mean that I must turn away from life to make contact with the holy, for the holy is within me. It does mean that I will commune with God only to the degree that I can give my life, my love, and my being away to others. One cannot be a worshiper of the God I am beginning to understand without being simultaneously an agent of life to another. This pathway to God also opens me to the truth of the wisdom of the ages, which suggested that it is in giving that we receive, it is in forgiving that we are forgiven, it is

istic believing past into our nontheistic, unknown,
ving future.

lways wanted to be a person of prayer. I have
ave that sense of immediate contact with the divine.
r than I have been willing to admit, even to myself,
essed to an external supreme being have had little
ng for me. My first presumption was that this repre-
ack of some essential aspect in my own spiritual
t and that all I needed to do was to work harder and
ercome this deficiency. So, like Jacob of old, I have
th this angel, the meaning of prayer, for a lifetime,
t willing even yet to let it go until it has blessed me
-32).

ourse of my life I have read every prayer manual or
ayer on which I could lay my hands. My personal
a shelf dedicated to once-beckoning, but now dis-
ks on prayer. I created a prayer corner in my study. I
with a prayer desk to remind me that this was a
e and so that I could quite literally kneel before God
ave organized my intercessions and special intentions
from various cycles of prayer. The clergy of the
Newark, their families, and their congregations have
rly before me during these prayer times. I once even
ross on my watch face so that every time I glanced to
e time of day I would be reminded to send a prayer
avenward to keep me connected with the God whom
ight be an external compass point by which my life
uided. My great ambition was to be one who lived in
nt awareness of the divine and could thus know the
comes from communing with God, the heavenly one. I
elieve that discipline and perseverance would lead me
als. My church encouraged that ambition with its easy
the centrality of prayer in the life of God's people.

in loving that we are loved, and, ultimately, it is through dying that we find the fullness of life.[8]

I cannot serve this nontheistic God or this revelatory Christ except by seeking to build a world in which all barriers to full humanity for every person have been removed. That is why, for me, no prejudice can ever be allowed to exist within that entity that has come to call itself "the body of Christ." For any prejudice, whether it be based on race, ethnicity, gender, sexual orientation, cult, or ritual purity, is finally nothing but a dagger aimed at the very heart of this gospel that rises from the life of Jesus.

Is this, then, a divine Christ? Is this a sufficient portrait of the meaning of Jesus to establish continuity with the historic tradition of Christianity? I believe it is, but that is, finally, not for me to say. It may not even prove to be terribly important. But for me at this moment in my life it is, at the very least, a glimpse of a way beyond the death of theism and into an understanding of Christianity and of the Christian life that might survive the exile. It is a vision, perhaps only a minimal vision, of a place to start in answering the question "Who is Christ for me?"

When I search for words to communicate this conviction in understandable concepts, I find myself driven again and again to the Johannine corpus to discover words that are usable. There Jesus was quoted as saying "I am the way, the truth and the life" (John 14:6). Jesus is for me the way into the heart of God, the Ground of Being. Jesus is for me the truth by which my life can be lived with theological and human integrity. Jesus is for me the life who has made known to us all what the meaning of life is. So I call him "Lord," I call him "Christ," and I assert that this is where God is met for me.

NINE

✳

The Meaning of Prayer in a World with No External Deity

"WITH WHAT SHALL I COME before the Lord and bow myself before God on high? Shall I come before him with burnt offerings, with calves a year old? Will the Lord be pleased with thousands of rams; with ten thousands of rivers of oil? Shall I give my first-born for my transgression, the fruit of my body for the sin of my soul?" (Mic. 6:6–7). These words of the prophet Micah were penned in the eighth century B.C.E.

"That night my husband and I did not sleep at all. We wept and wept. Privately we each pleaded with the universe to make the follow-up sonogram come out normal. We offered up our own body parts in exchange—eyes, arms, feet.

"The universe was deaf. The next day a doctor in a nearby university hospital concurred with the preliminary diagnosis of

clubfoot, subtle though the
Tuesday, November 26, 199
twentieth-century feature st
One Mother's Ordeal," by N

These two episodes, sep
reveal what has happened t
beings have moved from a pr
and magic into the postmod
edge, and scientific explanati
being, to whom sacrifices an
expectation that this divine or
tory. In the *Times* article Goo
impersonal universe, which
the offerings of a fragile petiti
a traditional faith perspective,
refrain from making their de
proposing a specific bargain w
These people, like their primit
modicum of control over their
that these tactics, borrowed
work. For people to embrace t
grips with a world over which
In the prayers that people have
can see the presence of human
can also see the loss of confide
coming into clear focus. I suspe
praying people just as deeply as
can we still pray if there is no
personally to our prayers? Car
exile? Will prayer be an activity
exile?

If my experience is typical, pr
will experience the most emotiona

from our the
and yet belie
I have a
yearned to h
Yet for long
prayers add
or no meani
sented the
developmen
harder to ov
wrestled wi
and I am no
(Gen. 32:22-
In the c
book on pr
library has
carded, boo
equipped i
prayer plac
on high. I h
with help
Diocese of
been regula
printed a c
establish th
darting he
I hoped m
would be g
a significa
peace that
really did
to these g
talk about

My attempts to achieve this ambition were quite public. When I was a theological student in the early 1950s, each senior was given one single opportunity to preach to the entire assembly of faculty and classmates. When my turn came, I chose the subject of intercessory prayer and laid my concerns and, I suspect, my somewhat immature convictions out before this not-always-supportive audience. That sermon represented my first formal and written attempt in a lifelong struggle to find meaning in the endeavor known as prayer.

Later, as a young priest, I regularly organized Lenten studies on prayer in my various congregations, thereby forcing myself to lead them. When I wrote my first book in the early 1970s, it reflected this constant internal struggle and was entitled *Honest Prayer*. My working title was even more revealing. I called it *Saying 'Our Father' in a Religionless World*. I revisited this theme in another book called *Into the Whirlwind,* written in the early 1980s, still seeking, still searching. Yet, despite this sometimes frenzied, but at least persistent, effort I could not make prayer, as it has been traditionally understood, have meaning for me. The real reason, I now believe, was not my spiritual ineptitude, but rather that the God to whom I had been taught to pray was in fact fading from my view. I suppose that I would not have been able to admit that even if I had been conscious of it. This was before I was ready to enter the exile. Perhaps there are many who will recognize this struggle in themselves and who will become aware that they have shared in a similar journey.

Before one is able to raise new theological questions, one must become convinced enough of the bankruptcy of old theological solutions. I, for example, had to come to the conclusion that I could never again pray in the same manner that my ancestors in faith believed they could pray. "Yet surely there must be another way," I would say to myself again and again.

"Lord, teach us to pray" is not a new request. It seems to rise in every generation. The temptation is to think that there is a method that will work for all time and that all we have to do is find it. There isn't, and even the words of Jesus can demonstrate that.

When the disciples of Jesus some two thousand years ago were reported to have said to him, "Lord, teach us to pray" (Luke 11:1), he responded, we are told, with the words, "When you pray, say 'Our Father, who art in heaven. Hallowed be thy name'" (Matt. 6:9; Luke 11:2). The depth of our separation from the God of the past becomes very apparent when we face the startling fact that we, in our time, cannot possibly begin in the same place where Jesus assumed that his disciples could begin.

Jesus' answer, for example, made assumptions that exile people are not capable of making. He assumed, first, that God was a person who could be addressed as "Father." He assumed, second, that this divine being was external to life, or "in heaven." Finally, he assumed that this male deity delighted in our recognition of the sacredness of his name. Those were all aspects of a theistic belief system that simply is no more. The concept of a personal deity who directs the affairs of individual human history from a vantage point above this earth, watching, intervening, rewarding, and punishing, has died. Human beings today fly through those demystified skies in airplanes and spacecraft. We chart the motion of the stars and planets with exactitude. We predict with precise accuracy eclipses of the sun and moon and even the exact year and exact place in which Halley's Comet will reappear in our atmosphere. Modern men and women have no working concept today of God as a supernatural heavenly Being.

If that were not enough to separate us from Jesus' answer about prayer, he continued with the suggestion that this theistic God enjoyed the flattery of his subjects. The first petition in what has come to be called the model prayer was that God desired above all else that the divine name be hallowed. It provides us with yet another insight into both the traditional content of our prayers and our dying theistic past.

We human beings learned quite early the social lesson that important people liked and coveted reverence and honor. So titles were invented to provide the means of giving respect to those people who were deemed to be authorities in our lives. "Your Honor," we learned to say to the one in whom the power to judge was vested. "Your Majesty," "Your Excellency," "the Führer," and "Your Lordship" have been titles that we have applied to our kings, our emperors, and our dictators. "Your Grace," "Your Holiness," "Your Beatitude," "Holy Father," and many other honorific titles have been accorded those who were presumed to speak for or to represent God. "Sir," "Lady," and "Esquire" are titles given even today in some societies to those who have achieved a recognized social status.

It was easy to turn that human practice into a major emphasis in the ancient patterns of prayer. If important human beings enjoyed and responded positively to honorific titles, how much more might the holy God who ruled the universe be moved to act toward us with kindness and mercy by similar designations of honor? So we filled our theistic prayers with flattering titles for the one whose name was to be hallowed. We called this God "divine," "almighty," "eternal," "everlasting," "most merciful," "loving," "righteous," and countless other complimentary words.

Human beings also wanted to make certain that this theistic God knew how much we respected that divine power. So we added to our prayers phrases designed to inform God of exactly what we thought, believed, wished, or hoped that God was like. "Gracious art thou and full of compassion," we said. God was "slow to anger and source of great kindness" or "more ready to hear than we to pray." One has only to turn the pages of the worship books of almost any Western religious tradition to find such concepts repeated almost endlessly. That seems a strange pattern of prayer to us now, especially when those phrases are lifted out of our worship moments and stated this boldly in a series of propositional statements. They just do not fit the world of our expectations.

So we face the fact that modern men and women cannot find help in our contemporary search for the meaning in prayer by following the answers Jesus was believed to have given. The guideposts, even of our Christian past, are not helpful in the exile. The definition of God implicit in the Lord's Prayer cannot be the operative definition for us today.

Our postmodern world has moved far beyond the supernatural assumptions of theism. We live inside a different understanding of reality, and we possess a different experience of both life and the universe. Inevitably, we will ask vastly different questions. When we cry out, "Lord, teach us to pray," we do so inside a world that has no reason to believe that any danger has ever subsided, any sickness been cured, any natural disaster averted, or any war won in response to the prayers of human beings. If we are to continue to engage in such an activity, we must learn to do so in a universe where the theistic view of God has become naive at best and unbelievable at worst. Can we then continue the activity of prayer if deep down we know that the skies are empty and that there is no divine protector to whom our words are directed? Those are the questions that we raise in exile.

I begin my attempt to reconstruct prayer for the exile dweller by placing into the coffin of theism one final nail. I do so in the conviction that only the absolute death of theism will enable us to move into a new pattern. Theism now, for me, not only is intellectually and theologically bankrupt, but also has become morally bankrupt as well. It is therefore unworthy of my continued struggle to be a prayer person in any traditional sense. This did not become apparent to me, however, until I lived through a deeply emotional period of my life and experienced the activity of prayer to a theistic God in that context.

In 1981 my wife, Joan, received a cancer diagnosis that was determined in all probability to be fatal. Because we were a well-known and publicly identified family in New Jersey, this news became public knowledge almost immediately. The religious resources of our people and our friends were quickly mobilized. Prayer groups throughout the diocese and even in ecumenical settings added my wife to their list of special intentions. Her name was spoken regularly during the prayers of the people in public worship in almost all of our churches. Concern, caring, and love were communicated to both of us by those actions, and we received that caring with deep appreciation. Remission did appear to have been achieved, and Joan lived for six and a half years from diagnosis to death. That was beyond anything that the doctors had led us to believe was possible. As this realization of a prolonged remission began to dawn, the people who were most concerned and whose prayers were the most intense began to take credit for her longevity. "Our prayers are working," they claimed. "God is using our prayers to keep this malevolent disease at bay." Perhaps there was present still that ancient but unspoken assumption that this sickness was the work of the devil and that this evil work was being thwarted by the power of God loosed through the prayers of God's people.

Despite my gratitude for the embracing love that these people demonstrated, both for me and for my wife, I could not help but be troubled at their explanations. Suppose, I queried to myself alone, that a sanitation worker in Newark, New Jersey, probably the city with the lowest per capita income in the United States, has a wife who had received the same diagnosis. Because he is not a high-profile person, well connected to a large network of people, socially prominent, or covered by the press, the sickness of his wife never comes to public attention. Suppose he is not a religiously oriented person and thus prayer groups and individual petitions in hundreds of churches are not offered on his wife's behalf. Would that affect the course of her sickness? Would she live less time from diagnosis to death, endure more obvious pain, or face a more difficult dying? If so, would that not be to attribute to God not only a capricious nature, but also a value system shaped by human importance and the worldly standards of social elitism? Would I be interested in worshiping a God who would treat my wife differently because we had had opportunities in life that the sanitation worker had not had? Do I want to attribute to the deity a behavior pattern based on human status? The answer to all of these questions is no, no, a thousand times no! If that was where praying to a theistic deity wound up, then dismissing so distorted a concept from organized religion was not a loss, but a positive gain.

I was at last free of the desire to pursue the meaning of prayer inside that traditional frame of reference. I would no longer struggle to make that pattern be my pattern. It was a painful moment, but it was also a moment of enormous relief. That remains my present conviction. If prayer is to continue to be part of my life, I must start in a new place that requires, first of all, a new way of envisioning God.

In my attempt to rebuild and to recreate the experience of prayer, I begin by asserting that there is something deep inside me, and I suspect deep inside every other person, that requires us to commune with the source of life. Perhaps that is what the hymn writer named the love "that will not let me go." Perhaps it is only an illusion, but illusion or real, we know its presence. It is like a mystical center of life that can neither be described nor denied. It is something beyond me, yet always it seeks to meet me in the depths of my own being. It is a presence that calls me into wholeness. It is something powerful that impinges on my consciousness and seems to invite me beyond the barriers of my security and even beyond the barriers of my humanity. It is something that nudges me into community and into caring for others. I address this presence as a Thou, not because it is a personal being, but because it seems always to call me into a deeper sense of personhood. When I try to speak meaningfully about this presence, I find myself almost wordless, and so I return once again to the Gospel portrait of Jesus of Nazareth. I do not seek there, however, his verbal instruction on prayer. I rather seek that aspect of his life that created his sense of living with what is holy. I seek to understand how that presence found expression in him.

I discover in these texts that Jesus was also a kind of first-century exile. He, too, apparently moved beyond, or at least outside, the religious formulas of his day. I hear him announcing to his world that somehow in his life the Kingdom of God is either coming or is actually present (Mark 1:15; Matt. 4:17; Luke 4:43). Later I hear him suggesting that this kingdom might even be within those of us who embody the principles of that kingdom (Luke 17:21). I see him pictured as teaching that the marks of the kingdom are not victory or righteousness, but rather the removal of those symptoms of human brokenness. In the Kingdom of God, he is reported to have said, the deaf will hear, the blind will see, and the lame will walk (Luke 7:18–23; Isa. 35:5–7).

This is a portrait of the presence of God in human life that manifests itself in wholeness. "This is what God is," I want to say, "and prayer is that experience of meeting God." Prayer is the conscious human intention to relate to the depths of life and love and thereby to be an agent of the creation of wholeness in another. Prayer is the offering of our life and our love through the simple action of sharing our friendship and our acceptance.

Prayer is my being calling to the being of another and thus giving that other the courage to dare, to risk, and to be in a whole new way, perhaps inside a whole new dimension of life. Prayer is also my active opposition to those prejudices and stereotypes that diminish the personhood and the being of another. Prayer is taking the proper political action to build a society in which opportunities can be equalized and no one will be forced to accept the status quo as his or her destiny. Prayer is the active recognition that there is a sacred core in every person that must not be violated. Prayer is the facing of life's exigencies, which involves us all in the realization that we live subject to a wide array of circumstances over which we have no control. Prayer is not cowering before these circumstances, but rather being willing to meet them with courage. Prayer is the ability to embrace the fragility of life and to transform it even as we are victimized or killed by it. Prayer involves shedding the delusion that we are the center of the universe or that our lives are so important to some external deity that this deity will intervene to protect us. Prayer is a call out of childish dependency into spiritual maturity.

So praying and living deeply, richly, and fully have become for me almost indistinguishable. Perhaps, I conclude, that is what the apostle Paul meant when he said, "Pray without ceasing" (1 Thess. 5:17 KJV) or "constantly" (RSV). We are to live as if everything we say and do is a prayer, calling others to life, to love, and to being.

I can only imagine, I could never guarantee, that when life is lived this way, an enormous amount of spiritual energy is loosed into the body politic of the whole society. I can imagine that this energy is an agent in bringing wholeness and even healing. But I do not trust anyone's effort to explain exactly how it works or to take credit for its effectiveness. All I know is that when I express my love, concern, and caring in thought, in word, and in deed, then somehow that expression has the opportunity to make a difference. I have seen examples of lives being turned around, and brokenness healed inside the power of a relationship. I have even seen the fear of death, if not death itself, dissipate when the dying person is able to receive the love of another into that fearful human experience. I have "prayed" beside hospital beds without ever addressing God because God was so deeply a part of the open, honest, and real conversations that I have shared with dying people. Prayer is being present, sharing love, opening life to transcendence. It is not necessarily words addressed heavenward. Perhaps that is the clue to what our ancestors thought were specific, answered prayers. Perhaps we human beings are more psychically connected than we have ever imagined. Perhaps positive thoughts and the release of the energy of concern does flow on networks we do not understand, affecting the life of another. These transformations seem to be miraculous only inside our limited knowledge. All I know is that it is natural to reach out, to love, and to care for others, and inevitably we feel compelled to give verbal expression to those aspects of our lives.

To be so alienated from another as to put that person deliberately out of our minds or to be so insensitive that we cease to care for anyone outside the orbit of our own lives is therefore nothing less than the very opposite of prayer. It is such an attitude that makes us unwilling to respond to the invitation to embrace a larger segment of life. In every experience of rejection or insensitivity, our lives close in and our being shrinks, and we live as if we are fractured, rather than whole, people. Every one of us has walked in that land of shadows.

When theism went unchallenged and God was perceived as a being external to life, then prayer became quite naturally an activity of withdrawal from this world so that we could concentrate on this unworldly God. We sang about this withdrawal in such hymns as "Take Time to Be Holy." The Church in time expanded these withdrawn moments and called them "quiet days," "pilgrimages," and "retreats." Each word revealed hidden assumptions. *Quiet days* assumed that God could not be found in the busyness of life but rather was discovered primarily in the experience of being quiet and still, and so we withdrew into silence. *Pilgrimages* assumed that one had to depart from the normal routines of life to visit a holy place, like the island of Iona, where God was supposed to be uniquely present. *Retreats* implied that one had to step back from life in order to meet the holy. Religious folk continue to promote these theistic activities as if they might still work. But a revolution in our prayer consciousness has occurred to match the revolution in theology that is symbolized by the death of theism. Ultimately these practices represent only the dying embers of the theistic point of view.

These activities never appealed to me even when I did not know why. Quiet days regularly bored me to the point of drowsiness. Pilgrimages were accompanied by the promise of some spiritual high that almost always disappointed. The very word *retreat* repelled me. I always wanted the Church to go on an "advance." A retreat was, in my mind, never the way to victory.

It was not until I laid theism aside that any experience of seeking God in solitude began to have any value for me. It was, however, a value almost totally reversed from the Church's traditional wisdom.

For years now I have spent the first two hours of the morning in my study. I once tried to claim that as my time of prayer. During that time I do sit self-consciously inside God's presence. I study the scriptures with the intensity of a seeker. I read constantly, and I write when I feel moved to do so. I anticipate my day, the opportunities that will come my way, the people that I will meet, the issues that I will engage. That time has always been and is now particularly valuable to me. But it was transformed when I finally stopped pretending that this was a holy time of prayer for me. I no longer think of this as prayer time at all. My life and my vocabulary have done a 180-degree turn. That time I now call focus time or preparation time. It is still essential, but it is not where I seek communion with God. My holy time, my commitment to be a praying person, comes later in the day. It comes in my living and in my engaging the lives of others. Prayer is that process of being open to all that life can be and then of acting to bring that fullness to pass. Prayer is entering into the pain or joy of another person. Prayer is what I am doing when I live wastefully, passionately, and wondrously and invite others to do so with me or even because of me.

Prayer is also the struggle for human justice. It is the fight to remove killing stereotypes, to hurl back the ignorance of prejudice, and to protect the holiness of God's creation. Prayer is the corporate, political act that serves to equalize opportunity so that privileged and underprivileged might have the same chance at the beauty of being made whole. Being made aware of these realities is the precondition of prayer.

So no longer do I privately make my prayer requests by storming the gates of heaven, where God supposedly dwells to direct the intimate affairs of my world. I do not begin by saying, "Our Father, who art in heaven."[1] I do not believe that there is a being, a supernatural deity, standing over against my world who seeks through some invasive process to imprint the divine will on the life of my world. The deity I worship is rather part of who I am individually and corporately. So praying can never be separated from acting.

It is when I walk into these dimensions and activities of life that I am praying. Prayer thus must never be a plea that I might be delivered from the task of being responsible for my world, from being mature, or from being a God bearer to all others.

Prayer is the recognition that holiness is found in the center of life and that it involves the deliberate decision to seek to live into that holiness by modeling it and by giving it away.

There is no magic here! There is no room for religious institutions or self-defined divine mediators to accrue power by pretending that this market can be cornered. There is no security, no putting your hand into the hand of the one who made the mountains. There are no everlasting arms underneath us waiting to catch us if we fall. There is only the call to be open to the depths of life and to live in such a way as to reveal those depths.

Is that enough to justify my self-identity as a person of prayer? I can respond only by saying that it is for me. I invite others to test it by trying it, living it, risking it, for that is the only way that I now know that one can learn how to pray. But my conviction is that holiness is there to be found. God is the presence in whom my being comes alive. My prayer is now honest, and it is an essential part of who I am.

TEN

✳

A New Basis for Ethics in a New Age

IF WE REMOVE from our worldview the external God of theism, who was thought to be the originator of the divine code of laws designed to shape human behavior; if we take away from our image of God the role of heavenly judge, complete with all-seeing eyes and a record book in which deeds and misdeeds are to be faithfully recorded; if we can no longer conceive of God as the one who, on the basis of the human deservings revealed in those records, metes out rewards and punishments either temporal or eternal, then does any basis for ethics remain? That is now my question.

The folklore of almost every ancient people contains a narrative that purports to record the moment when that nation received the laws by which its tribal life was organized. These laws were almost invariably said to have been dictated by, or in some way received from, the divine hand. Most of us are familiar to some degree with the Jewish version of this tradition. It was said to have occurred on Mount Sinai while the Jews were wandering in the wilderness toward their promised land, and it resulted in the divine gift of the Torah, which included the Ten Commandments.

That biblical story was recorded in the book of Exodus (19, 20). It was filled with dramatic details, all of which reflected the presuppositions of a theistic deity. First, the cloud of the heavenly God was said to have hovered over that sacred mountain as a sign of the divine presence. Next, violent and awesome signs of that presence were depicted as coming out of the sky—thunder, lightning, and even the shaking of the whole earth with volcanic tremors. Then the people were instructed in an exercise of ceremonial cleansing, which included a prohibition from coming too close to that special mountain. Distance was to lend enchantment to that occasion.

Finally, when the stage was fully set, Moses, God's chosen leader, was invited to approach the mountain, to climb it alone, and to enter into the cloud of God. It was inside this scene, these scriptures suggested, that God dictated to Moses the sacred laws that formed the Torah.

When Cecil B. DeMille created the motion picture entitled *The Ten Commandments,* first in 1923 and then again in 1956, he heightened these mysterious symbols with depictions of the presence of extraordinary miraculous power. In the 1956 version, God's very finger became a fiery divine drill capable of carving letters instantaneously into stone tablets held in the hands of Moses, who was played by Charlton Heston. It was an indelible scene, and, far more than people realize today, their mental image of Moses has been shaped by Heston. This film, however, captured accurately the primitive assumptions about the sacredness of the laws by which the Israelites lived. Almost all ancient people felt that they had to ground their governing rules in the absolute will of their deity. People appeared to know instinctively that godly power was essential if human obedience was to be achieved.

This mythology of a divine source of ethics enforced by the all-seeing God, however, has been revealed by the ancient codes themselves to be utter nonsense. A careful study of these codes reveals nothing less than the tribal prejudices, stereotypes, and limited knowledge of the people who created them. That is certainly true of the Torah and even more true of that part of the Torah we call the Ten Commandments. Within that familiar and honored code are found elements and attitudes that would be dismissed by most people today as unworthy of obedience. It is also apparent that these "divine laws" were not designed to reveal the will of a universal God, nor were they capable of lasting forever. The Ten Commandments, although still saluted by many religious people, have lost most of their ancient power. Many of those who still pay them lip service cannot tell you what commandments are included in the Ten or even which of the Ten they absolutely do not obey. Indeed, some aspects of the Ten Commandments need to be exposed immediately as immoral and to be removed from the ethical guidelines that any of us today would seek to follow.

The first clue in the Bible to the human rather than divine origin of these rules is seen in the fact that they were regularly violated when dealing with people outside the Jewish world. The Ten Commandments, for example, enjoined the people against bearing false witness. Moses, however, was depicted as being guilty of doing just that in his dealings with the Egyptians, and indeed his false witness was said to have come at the suggestion of God! (Exod. 3:18) Moses was portrayed in the text as trying to convince the Pharaoh that the slave people did not seek the freedom that God had promised at the burning bush (Exod. 3:7–12). They only desired, said Moses, a three-day sojourn in the wilderness to worship their God, after which, presumably, they would return to slavery. Neither Moses nor the Pharaoh believed this (Exod. 5:1–3). It was quite clearly a false witness and thus a violation of the sacred code.

The commandments said, "You shall not kill" or "You shall do no murder," but Joshua was said to have murdered five captured Canaanite kings (Josh. 10:22–27). Samuel was portrayed as "hewing into pieces with the sword" another king named Agag, who was kept in a cave to await his executioner (1 Sam 15:32–33). God was pictured as ordering Israel to go to war against two nations and, in those two wars, to kill "every man, woman, and child" of their enemies (1 Sam. 15:1–13; Judg. 21:8–13). Even the God of the Bible did not appear to take the commandment not to kill seriously when dealing with the non-Jewish world.

The one common thread in each of these morally embarrassing biblical episodes was that the recipients of these unethical behaviors were not Jewish. This law has little to justify its claim to be divine, if it was believed to govern only intratribal relations. Yet that is a limitation present in the Ten Commandments as they were lived out in biblical times. These commandments quite clearly did not affect Jewish activities toward the non-Jewish world. A universal or divine code these laws were not.

These laws also reflected the patriarchal mentality present among ancient people in that they assumed that a woman was the property of a man. This sexist attitude is overtly present in the last commandment, "You shall not covet," and by implication it is present in the commandment "You shall not commit adultery." The full text of that final commandment says, "You shall not covet your neighbor's house. You shall not covet your neighbor's wife, nor his manservant, nor his maidservant, nor his ox, nor his ass, nor anything that is your neighbor's" (Exod. 20:17). Please note there is no written prohibition anywhere in the Torah against coveting your neighbor's husband!

The reason for this was that a husband was not property, but a wife was. The neighbor was a male. His assets were listed in descending order of value. His house first, his wife second, his slaves third, and then his ox, his ass, and his other possessions. This strange view of a woman as the property of a man is still vestigially present today in many marriage ceremonies celebrated in Christian churches, where one man "gives the woman away" to another man as if she were a male possession.

The seventh commandment, against adultery, was enjoined in a culture that practiced polygamy, not monogamy. A man could possess as many women as he could afford. In its primary literal meaning, this commandment prohibited a man from violating the woman who was the property or possession of another man. The proof that this was the essential meaning of this law is found in that, according to this code of conduct, if a Jewish man had a sexual liaison with an unmarried woman, it was not adultery. It was rather a crime against the property of her father, for which the offender would be fined the amount necessary to make the father financially whole. The father had had his net worth devalued by this act, since he could not get the proper "bride price" for a daughter who was now "damaged goods." A code of law that treats human beings as if they are property needs to be pronounced immoral at once and forthwith abandoned. Parts of the Ten Commandments are surely in this category.

Furthermore, history has revealed that this supposedly divine code has been abandoned whenever it has become inconvenient. Few of the original Ten Commandments are still operative today no matter how much they are extolled by politicians and preachers alike as the ultimate basis for human ethics. Some of these abandoned laws are easy to identify. We have no prohibitions in law or in practice today against graven images, and our churches are filled with them, from crosses to crucifixes to tabernacles to ambreys to icons to stations of the cross. So the commandment against graven images has become irrelevant.

Our society no longer requires a civil contract to be sworn "in the name of the Lord," so that if broken, the offending party would be guilty of "taking the Lord's name in vain." Today contracts are signed into legal documents and enforced by the courts. Without that defining context, we have begun to suggest that this third commandment has something to do with profanity. Profanity may be either blasphemous or in poor taste, but it has nothing to do with "taking the name of the Lord in vain."

For 1900 years Christians, other than a small sect called the Seventh-Day Adventists, have not observed the Sabbath day, Saturday, or made any attempt to keep it holy. It is difficult to make excessive claims about the divine origin of commandments that have been so largely abandoned.

In still other cases, the God who supposedly authored these divine laws has been revealed as unable to anticipate the complexities of modern life. For example, is abortion murder? Some would argue that it is. But is it murder if the life of the mother is imperiled? Is it murder if it occurs in the first trimester, before life enters the fetus in that moment we call quickening? Is it murder if the pregnancy is the result of the violence of either rape or incest? Is it murder if the birth of the child will destroy the mental health of the mother or the economic well-being of the family? Is it murder if tests reveal that the fetus is malformed? Is it murder if it was an accidental pregnancy that has come to an older menopausal couple? Is it murder if proper birth control has prevented pregnancy in the first place? It is not my intention to debate these issues but simply to reveal how both modern medicine and medical technology have placed options before us that the ancient world in which the Ten Commandments were first composed could not have imagined. This ancient code of ethics is so clearly the product of its time. If we continue to suggest that somehow a theistic God was personally the author of these rules, then we have to face the fact that the God we postulate was not aware of the technological revolution that would someday overtake the world and render that God's divine and ancient laws radically incomplete.

When one turns to the other end of the life cycle, the questions are even more complicated. Before the advances of medicine, death came quickly in a wide variety of circumstances and sicknesses. Not so today. Modern medicine has pushed back the barriers of death to what sometimes seems to be absurd extremes. Bodies are kept breathing with respirators, hearts are kept beating on machines, and food is intravenously provided long after meaningful life has ceased to exist. Is a breathing cadaver the same as life? Is it murder to stop these processes? That conclusion is supported by some religious voices today, while others debate the possible morality of physician-assisted suicide. Once again, my agenda is not to seek to solve these issues, but to demonstrate how inadequate the ancient code we call the Ten Commandments has become amid the vagaries of ethical concerns today.

The ethical debate today is so complex, and the ancient religious codes are not capable of shedding light on that complexity. A major religious body opposes birth control and effective family planning. But overpopulation has led to massive starvation and death in those countries no longer able to feed their expanding populations. Is the absence of birth control in those circumstances even a moral option in our generation? Humanitarian relief efforts save lives today in starving countries, but these same efforts only guarantee the death of the next generation if the population is not limited, so the morality of such humanitarian activity also becomes questionable.

Throughout the world today the Christian Church is debating sexual ethics in a particularly vigorous way. At the core of this debate is an emerging understanding of homosexuality that challenges both the definitions and the stereotypes of the past. Yet in that debate defenders of the traditional mentality regularly appeal to something they call "the clear teaching of scripture." A recent study of this issue was published as a supplement to a major Florida newspaper.[1] Among the spicier quotations from a variety of religious leaders were these: "Homosexuality is an abomination to God. It is a dastardly sin that brings swift judgment." "The Levitical texts are blunt. . . . They simply prohibit homosexual behavior. It is unambiguous about what it is trying to say. . . . The early Church understood itself to preserve that prohibition of homosexual behavior." The Episcopal bishop serving Pensacola was not to be omitted from this exercise in questionable biblical analysis. He said, "I am still convinced that the basic scriptural teaching about sexuality is that all single Christians are called to celibacy . . . called to abstain from genital relations outside of Christian marriage." Trying to add a note of grace that would separate him from his gay-bashing colleagues and to be true to the broad tradition of his Anglican heritage, this church leader went on to say, "I make no distinction in that call to single Christians between heterosexuals and homosexuals."[2] It was a good try, but it did not save the good bishop from either his sexual naïveté or his biblical ignorance.

Other religious leaders at the highest levels in Catholic, evangelical, and even mainline traditions have weighed in with similar statements. They all seem to assume that there is a clear sexual ethic in holy scripture. The debate, however, rages on because, first, the sexual references in holy scripture are not consistent and, second, the authority of those texts which can be quoted literally has been seriously eroded. The Bible has been used in this way before, and it has not prevailed. Literal biblical texts were quoted in the past to uphold slavery, to battle against the way illnesses were treated, and to prevent women from being ordained, holding them in the status of second-class citizenship. We seem to forget that defenders of each of these archaic ideas also claimed to be acting according to "the clear teaching of scripture."

In a pamphlet that was as unusual as it was devastating to that attitude toward scripture, Professor Walter Wink, of the faculty of the Auburn Theological Seminary in New York City, documented the inconsistent biblical attitudes toward all human sexual practices.[3] The Bible, he wrote, condemned the following sexual activities, which we also condemn: incest, rape, adultery, and intercourse with animals. But the Bible also condemned, Dr. Wink continued, the following practices, which we today either generally allow or at least do not universally condemn: intercourse during menstruation, celibacy, marriage to non-Jews, naming sexual organs, nudity under certain conditions, masturbation, and birth control. Granted, some Christians today still condemn one or more of these things. The biblical voice of God, however, is regarded as uncertain on these matters today, whereas in the past the Bible was assumed to be quite clear and debate was, therefore, not allowed.

The Bible, Dr. Wink went on to say, also "regarded semen and menstrual blood as unclean, which most people living today do not." In this analysis we can see just where and how sexual attitudes have changed and that whenever these changes have occurred, the literal biblical attitudes are set aside.

Finally, Dr. Wink noted that the Bible permitted these behaviors that we today condemn: prostitution, polygamy, levirate marriage, sex with slaves, concubinage, treatment of women as property, and very early marriage (for the girl aged eleven to thirteen).

He went on to say that "while the Old Testament accepted divorce, Jesus forbade it." In conclusion, Dr. Wink observed that "of the sexual mores mentioned here, we only agree with the Bible on four of them and disagree with it on sixteen."

So when religious leaders claim the support of scripture for their own homophobia, it becomes quite clear that something besides truth is operating in them. The Bible is an ambiguous document about specific sexual practices. Perhaps that is what those who think of themselves as "Bible believers" have so much difficulty accepting. A real knowledge of scripture does not issue in certainty. Even one of the biblical instances that is quoted to demonstrate the Bible's clear denunciation of the "sin of homosexuality" (Rom. 1) confronts us with the strange idea that if we fail to worship God properly, God will punish us with homosexuality! That is an idea so bizarre as to merit immediate dismissal even if it does appear to have been uttered by the apostle, Paul. It is not, of course, the only Pauline utterance that we have rejected. He also insisted that women keep quiet in church, speak only to their husbands at night, and keep their heads covered.

The fact remains that these so-called laws of God, which God was supposed to have written on tablets of stone, or the excessive claims made for Holy Scripture in general, which involve the assertion that the Bible is somehow "the inerrant word of God," are today indefensible, regardless of who utters those claims or any variation on them.

In the traditions of the past, not only were the laws thought to have been written by the very hand of God, but these laws were also assumed to be the basis upon which this same God would carry out the divine role of the ultimate judge. Those who kept these rules would be rewarded fittingly. Those who broke these rules would be punished severely. This system exercised a powerful control over human behavior.

An ethical system, however, grounded in these presuppositions has become in our day quite obviously doomed. One cannot speak cogently to the ethical concerns of this generation by quoting two-thousand- to four-thousand-year-old authorities who claim to represent God's final word on these subjects. No longer is it deemed adequate to assert "but the Ten Commandments state" or "but the Bible teaches." Those claims settle no debate in our time. All they do today is to proclaim that the one who uses this tactic has nothing worthwhile to say to the current ethical dilemmas. There is no creditable external deity existing today on whose perceived will, spelled out in an ancient text, we can base our ethical decision making. No heavenly parent figure sets down and enforces the rules by which life is governed. No divine and eternal law has ever been written, either in the sky or on tablets of stone. The God who once was perceived as undergirding these primitive assumptions has been taken from us and destroyed by both the march of time and the explosion of knowledge.

The death of the God of theism, therefore, has removed from our world the traditional basis of ethics. That is the conclusion we are forced to draw. That is also why ethical issues are so widely debated in our society. It is frightening for many when they grasp the fact that we live in a morally neutral universe. Some respond with a panicked pursuit of pleasure. Some seek to escape their fears of moral meaninglessness in the world of alcohol and drugs. Some sink to the ultimate level of despair and fall into depression or even suicide. Some try to shield themselves from this unsettling sense of emptiness by becoming hysterically religious, as if shouting certain religious phrases with emotion and a feigned certainty might convince them that everything is still the way it has always been. These are but the signs that a loss of meaning has engulfed our world. We no longer know how to tell right from wrong, and above all else, our confusion reflects the death of the theistic God in whom all these things were once grounded.

To build a new basis for ethics, we must learn to look in a different place. We look, I believe, not outside of life for some external and objective authenticating authority, but rather at the very center and core of our humanity. We get to that core by asking a totally different series of questions. These are not God questions but human questions, such as: What gives us life? What lifts us into wholeness? What enhances our being? What introduces us to transcendence? What calls us beyond our limits? What do we ultimately value? These questions will force us to search, not the empty heavens, but the depths of our own being for answers. This search will lead us, hopefully, to some new possibilities. It will reveal, among other things, that any repression of our humanity can never be a doorway into life. Morality, in any area of life, will not be achieved by threats and negativity. The repression of sexual energy, for example, which marked traditional ethics for so long, did not lead to the fullness of life. It only created the backlash of an uninhibited exercise of sexual energy, which was also destructive to our essential humanity. When the value of human sexuality is repressed, it returns as pornography. When we try to take sex away from love, we succeed only in taking love away from sex.[4] Ethics and morality must go beyond this false dichotomy.

Surely human happiness is a desirable and even a coveted goal in life. But the search for a basis for ethics that is located in our humanity will reveal that fullness of life does not reside in seeking our own happiness. The data of human experience says instead that happiness is found when we seek the happiness and well-being of others. So in the process of pursuing the goal of happiness, I discover that my individualism is nothing less than a gift to me from the community in which I live. I cannot achieve my own destiny except as a part of the destiny of my interdependent world. I am thus both free and bound at the same time. I can seek my own well-being only in terms of the well-being of the community. The conclusion of this humanistic search for ethical norms is that something like ethical objectivity begins to emerge. There is an "objective" wrongness to seeking to cause or to increase the pain of another life. If I do that, I also inevitably become self-destructive. It goes against, if you will, the laws of the universe, which we have called the ultimate laws of God.

So the freedom to be myself is in dialogue with the need to enhance the being of others. Both of these values emerge from the core of our humanity. Both thrust us into an individual and corporate sense of interdependence. Both are seen as necessary and equal goals that our humanity requires us to take seriously. Such virtues do not come, however, from an external God. They come, rather, from our human depths, where I suggest the meaning of God must finally be sought.

A second ultimate but still human value emerges upon the heels of this freedom. It is the objective value of knowledge. A fully human person will use reason to enhance human well-being. When reason reveals, for example, that skin pigmentation is the result of an adaptive process that enables some people to survive well in climates exposed to the direct rays of the sun, then prejudice based on skin pigmentation becomes a manifestation of ignorance. It therefore becomes inhumane to use that ignorance as the basis of social and economic discrimination, and continuing to do so violates objective knowledge. When left-handedness is revealed to be the result of the way the brain has been structured in a minority of persons, it becomes inhumane to try to change a left-handed person. That, too, becomes a manifestation of ignorance.

When a homosexual orientation is revealed by the development of the science of the brain and its neurochemical processes to be a normal part of the sexual spectrum of human life, a given and not a chosen way of life, then it becomes inhumane to use a person's sexual orientation as the basis for a continuing prejudice. Therefore, the kind of judgment that compromises the worth and well-being of a homosexual person or places limits on the opportunities of that person becomes the activity of ignorance. Since that is so, then a third ultimate human value emerges. It is objectively wrong to act in such a way as to cause or to increase the ignorance that will issue in the diminishment or the destruction of another's humanity.

There is, therefore, an objective wrongness in seeking to cause or to increase pain in another life. There is an objective value in seeking knowledge. There is an objective wrongness in continuing to defend or to act on the basis of one's ignorance. Virtue is to be found in wisdom, in knowledge, and in openness to the nature of reality itself. These are the values that can be discerned when one probes the depths of life in search of a new basis for ethics.

If freedom, knowledge, and wisdom are recognized as objective values, then the extension of these values to all becomes an ethical imperative bordering on ultimacy. So all forms of restrictive tribalism, every attempt to increase or enhance human enmity, every effort to limit the increase of consciousness becomes recognized as overtly evil. Thus the highest value emerging out of the depths of our humanity is the expansion of the boundaries of the human experience. To enhance the being and deepen the life of every human being and to free the love that emanates from each person become part of the ultimate and objective standard for determining proper human behavior. These are the virtues arising from life itself. They are not external to life or vested in the authority of a being outside of life.[5]

Some years ago I addressed a group of Anglican clergy in the crypt of one of England's cathedrals. My subject was the changing patterns in human sexual behavior, including the issue of homo-sexuality. The bishop of that diocese at that time made it clear that he did not approve the discussion of this subject, and so he was not present. The clergy who did come were, with one or two exceptions, the most lifeless group of people I have ever encountered. They neither laughed nor got angry. They neither agreed with nor objected to this presentation that in many other places, I knew from personal experience, would have created a wide variety of emotional responses. These clergy reminded me of children who have been slapped both physically and mentally so often by parents, teachers, or authority figures that they no longer respond to anything, unless given permission to do so.

Under the guise of promoting family values, many "Christian" groups support corporal punishment as a way of breaking a child's rebellious spirit, or curbing the child's "original sin." In my mind that is not a family value at all but an attempt to impose a control system to insure conformity at the expense of life and creativity. It is also from my perspective a violation of the God presence in each person.

I encountered an adult version of that same syndrome in an ecumenical clergy gathering in Auckland, New Zealand. I was addressing this group on the subject of effective leadership. In the discussion that followed, a young New Zealand pastor related an experience he had had in another part of the world, where he heard a bishop publicly praise a young priest. Commending this priest for effective leadership, the bishop predicted a bright future for this young man, concluding his remarks by saying, "I hope I live long enough to see you as a bishop of this church!"

"That would never happen in New Zealand," this pastor continued. "And if it did it would absolutely kill any chance that priest had for future success and leadership."

"Why is that?" I asked.

"Because in New Zealand we are infected by the 'tall poppy syndrome.'"

"What is that" I inquired.

"In this country," he went on, "it is considered inappropriate to shine, to stick one's head above the crowd. A herd instinct, not leadership, is rewarded. When one poppy grows taller than the others in the field, it regularly has its head cut off."

There are those I'm sure who would name such attitudes Christian. I would not. For they are deeply at odds with my understanding of an ethical system that is based on the conviction that God is present in every life, calling that life to the fullness of its own unique being. It is ultimately and objectively right, I believe, to expand and enhance life. It is ultimately wrong, I believe, to act in such a way as to distort life or to shrink a human being's potential.

When the basis for determining right and wrong becomes hazy and confused, as I think is the case today, when traditional standards that once were thought to reflect the revealed will of a supernatural deity begin to fade, when one wonders if there are any objective values left by which to judge behavior, then I suggest we look into the depths of our humanity and identify the behaviors that enhance life and call them good and those that diminish life and call them evil. We might even read that part of the gospel story that says that life and behavior are to be judged only by the fruit that they produce.

Does this position give us only a humanistic ethical system? I do not think so. If we can only begin to grasp the possibility that the Holy God is not external to life but is rather the Ground of life itself, the Being in which all being is rooted, then these ostensibly human values can be seen to be eternal and rooted in the ultimacy of God. Such a God is, however, not a theistic God. It is a God whose Being emerges as all being is enhanced, whose Life is revealed as all life is lived, whose Love is manifested as all love is shared, and whose identity is revealed when barriers are broken and community is formed.

The reward that such an ethical system contains, however, is not a motivating bliss or a desire to escape eternal punishment. It is, rather, simply the reward of doing what is right. It is the reward of a life that is enhanced, a humanity that is affirmed, a being that is deepened, and a love that always flows back to enhance the being of the giver. Radical English theologian Don Cupitt calls this "solar ethics." Solar ethics means committing oneself to live as the sun lives, that is, to do what you were created to do without regard for recognition, permanence, or reward.[6] There is something clean about the sun being the sun even as it burns itself out in the process. There is something clean about human life being all that it was created to be, both in life and in death. Surely, the ethics of the exile must also embrace this clean principle. Ethics must be freed from the tactic of controlling human behavior by imposing on it the will of some external deity. Christian ethics in the future must be directly linked to the right to explore selfhood, to the courage to live, to love, and to be simply for the sake of living, loving, and being.

One final ethical question before us in the exile remains unanswered, and it is a profound one. Is what I and others have called the depth of Being a reality, or is it an illusion? Is that power out of which our being emerges real? Is it personal? Since it is not separate from us, manipulative or invasive, can it be called God? Does God have to be understood as a person to be God? Does God have to be "a person" to be called "personal"? Or can it be said that the more deeply we live, the more passionately we love, and the more we discover the courage to be, the more we become revelatory of God—a God now understood as the ultimate reality, the essence of life? Can that process of becoming our true and real selves now be seen as a new way of understanding what the Bible was trying to say when it suggested that we were created in the image of God? Was it not these very qualities of selfhood—the ability to live, to love, and to be—which were observed in the life of Jesus, that caused people to see the presence of God in him? Is this not what the disciples were trying to say about him when they said, "You are the Christ, the son of the living God"?

If we can grasp these possibilities or at least be willing to explore these tiny cracks leading to a different way of thinking about God, and if the Holy God can be understood not as a person, but as the depth and ground of life itself, then the ethical task of the Church becomes quite different. Christian ethics are not found in a system of behavior control. They are rather found in a call to the fullness of life. The business of the Church is, therefore, not to judge life, but to enhance consciousness, to expose ignorance and prejudice, and to remove the barriers to life in all of its fullness. The Church's task is to assist its people in plumbing the depths of their own humanity, where transcendence, mystery, being, and even love are discovered, and to bring those qualities found in the center of life into the world. I name that center of life God.

This God is not a parent who will reward or punish me for my virtues or shortcomings. This God is rather a power, a presence that calls me into responsibility, into adulthood, into self- reliance, into living for others, and into contributing to the well-being of all humanity. This Infinite Beyond in the midst of my life invites me again and again to abandon my fears, to enter infinity, and to walk into the timelessness of God. So I worship at this shrine, and at the same time I take responsibility for my life and, to the degree that I am able, for the life of this world. That is where ethics emerge. So long as I possess life, I will live it deeply, richly, and fully. I will expect no reward for my commitment to these ethical principles save the reward of a life well lived. I will not blame my failures or my shortcomings on some external God, for God is part of who I am. Is that so novel an idea as to be unacceptable? Not to me it isn't, for I have entered the exile. The theistic God whose will constituted the ethics of the past is dead. So my search for the basis of ethics to guide me beyond the exile drives me back to the same arena where a non-theistic God was found and where Christ was redefined. My journey through the exile is beginning to take shape.

ELEVEN

✳

The Emerging Church:
Reading the Signs Present Today

Dotting the landscape of the Christian world, from densely populated urban areas to remote villages, are buildings that people call churches. *Church* is a funny word, being derived from the same word that gives the Scottish people their word *kirk*. The great Danish philosopher Søren Kierkegaard had a last name that literally meant "church yard." This single word *church* is used in our language to describe an enormous variety of structures, from a magnificent medieval cathedral to a simple wooden frame building. Churches can be decorated with the finest and most expensive works of art, or they can be as plain as an unpainted wall. Some inspire gasps of wonder at their beauty, and some are covered by the handiwork of an urban graffiti artist. Churches can have exquisite stained glass through which to filter the light of the world, or they can have clear glass panes to allow the reality of God's creation to be seen as it is. In the course of my life, I have lectured in a church in Galilee, Nevada, whose open back wall allowed its worshipers to stare out on Lake Tahoe and the Sierra Nevada mountains of California, as well as in a church whose clear windows allowed the mighty and sometimes raging Mississippi River to be viewed as it flowed past Memphis, Tennessee.

Some of these church structures are automatically heated and cooled for the comfort of the worshipers, while in others people gather around a potbellied stove in winter and battle the heat of summer by fluttering hand fans featuring an advertisement for the local funeral home. Some churches boast cushioned theater seats and are lighted with indirect and rheostat-controlled fixtures, while others offer hard wooden benches and illumine their worship space with naked bulbs suspended on drop cords. Yet, regardless of the age, size, shape, or affluence of these buildings, each structure is instantly recognized as a church. Its ecclesiastical identity is somehow self-evident.[1]

Perhaps the identifying mark is a steeple pointing to the heavens. Perhaps it is a tower that proclaims that our God is "a mighty fortress." Perhaps it is the slant of the roof, the pointedness of the windows, or even a burial plot nestled around the building that proclaims it as a church. But whatever announces its identity, the structure has been so deeply part of our world that the presence of a church hardly registers upon our minds as we pass by it. It is, in fact, part of our social scenery, familiar furniture in our cultural household.

Two primary functions are housed in these church structures. The first and probably the most important is the gathering of the people week after week on Sunday for divine worship. The liturgical form followed at these weekly occasions of worship will vary from tradition to tradition. But most of them will include such familiar elements as singing hymns, reading scripture, reading scripture, preaching a sermon, and saying prayers. In the more liturgical churches, that Sunday service will also normally include the sacramental observance known as the Mass, the Eucharist, Holy Communion, or the Lord's Supper.

In each of these activities the unspoken assumption is that divine worship in some form is the means by which human beings below are related to the God above. The upward sweep of the buildings is designed to lift people's consciousness almost physically to this external God. The hymns that worshipers sing tell about the coming of this external God into this world, the life of this God figure while in this world, and the departure of the visiting God from this world. One has only to scan any hymnal to discover such titles as "O Come, O Come Emmanuel,"[2] "Joy to the World, the Lord Is Come," "Forty days and forty nights, thou wast fasting in the wild," or "Hail the day that sees him rise, glorious to his native skies." The words of these hymns invade our minds, chart our convictions, and shape our understanding of God far more deeply than we think. Such words as "Veiled in flesh, the Godhead see, hail the incarnate deity" or "Manhood to deliver, manhood did put on" portray Jesus as a divine visitor from another realm who only appeared to be human. When the hymns are not about an invasive supernatural deity, they might express our desires for divine companionship and speak to our fear of cosmic loneliness: "What a friend we have in Jesus, all our pain and grief to bear" is a good example.[3] Others will speak to our fear of alienation by expressing our plea for forgiveness and restoration: "Dear Lord and Father of mankind, forgive our foolish ways." In the more evangelical tradition the note of victory enters as we sing to the God whose "love lifted me" or who has planted "our feet on higher ground."[4] These hymns also incorporate and continue that activity of divine flattery that we noted earlier: "Immortal, invisible,

God only wise" or "How great thou art."[5] Sometimes one of the great theological controversies in the history of the Church will get "perfumed" and then be allowed to sneak into the hymnal. One thinks of Martin Luther's words, originally written about the pope, "The Prince of Darkness grim, we tremble not for him. His rage we can endure, for lo his doom is sure. One little word will fell him." That one little word for Luther was *alone*. For him, salvation was by faith "alone," not by works, on which the whole indulgence system of the Vatican, against which Luther struggled, had been built. But today these words are said to be referring to Satan, and so this hymn is sung lustily, even in Roman Catholic churches. Mariolatry, denied theologically by Anglicans in the days of the Reformation, nonetheless found its way into Anglican worship in the second verse of the hymn entitled "Ye Watchers and Ye Holy Ones," where the words suggest that Mary is higher than the angels: "O higher than the cherubim, more glorious than the Seraphim, lead their praises, thou bearer of the eternal word, most gracious magnify the Lord." Anglican Catholics must have smiled at their coup. But today even Protestants sing these words with no qualms. The Church usually incorporates in some form the things it once excluded, even those things excluded violently.

The scriptures that are read in church services are also filled with the concepts of a theistic supernatural deity who invades the world and is actively engaged in its affairs. Indeed, the primary purpose in gathering for worship historically has been to enable worshipers to learn something of the nature of this God who was believed to control all aspects of our human destiny. The worshipers call these scriptures "the word of the Lord," and the sermon, which was designed to expound on and to make clear "the word of the Lord," filled that need week after week.

The eucharistic liturgy, we have previously noted, was said to reenact the drama of the cross, where the price of sin was said to have been paid by Jesus, the rescuer, to secure our salvation. The liturgy was and is filled with symbols that to our modern ears sound strange indeed. Echoes of eating flesh and drinking blood are still heard. It presents the concept of a sacrifice being offered to God on our behalf. Sometimes such phrases fill our minds with great discomfort when we stop to embrace their meaning. The otherworldly setting tends, however, to mute these literal images and thus to compromise their horror.

Church attendance at these regular Sunday morning services is declining in every tradition around the Christian world today. Explanations of this decline tend to serve the vested interest of the one explaining. It must be noted that individual exceptions exist, where a charismatic clergy person will promise heaven, security, and the lack of a need to think (you simply have faith) sufficient to create excitement and growth for a period of time, but that kind of activity seldom can be passed on to the clergy successor, and the number of people who leave those churches soon begins to equal the number who are attracted to them. But in spite of overall declining attendance, this pattern of regular Sunday worship in the churches of the land still has power. It still attracts. It still is a recognized part of life. It still plays a vital social role, though that is today true more in small towns than in city settings.

The second activity that draws people into these church structures has been the worship services attached to the critical points in the life cycle of an individual. The experience of a birth, for example, has been met with the liturgy of a baptism. Maturation has been celebrated with some kind of ecclesiastical puberty rite. The instinct to love and mate has been incorporated into marriage and commitment ceremonies. Sickness is marked with various visitation rites, including extreme unction, and death is followed by a funeral service, sometimes called a requiem and sometimes just known as the burial of the dead.

Long after the Church has lost its appeal as a place to gather on Sundays for regular worship, it still attracts people for ceremonies marking individual rites of passage, which are humorously named the "hatching, matching, and dispatching" functions of church life.

But will these functions continue, and will there be a church for people to attend on Sundays beyond the exile? Can this institution survive? Does it have any purpose once the idea of a theistic, intervening God has disappeared? Surely it cannot go on as if its operative presuppositions are still intact. If the Church does walk into life beyond the exile, then what changes will be required? How will its liturgy be designed and its buildings be restructured or used? If our destiny is to live in a world where people can no longer pretend to relate themselves liturgically to a heavenly parent figure who fixes anything or who rewards and punishes worshipers according to their deservings, then is there a future for those structures we call churches or for those worship activities and liturgical observances that have been conducted inside those structures?

I must begin by speaking to these questions with my own witness. Worship, both private and corporate, continues to be a major part of my life, even as I walk deeper and deeper into the exile. I do not think this can be explained simply by saying that worship is the habit of my lifetime. As a bishop I engage in, indeed I lead, corporate worship services with great regularity, on average two hundred to three hundred occasions a year. In those services I still use the traditional prayers of my faith community, despite their strange, archaic, and sometimes even unbelievable literal content. I still confess my sins. I make my deepest desires known to God in my petitions and intercessions. I still express my profound sense of thanksgiving. I still listen to the readings from the sacred scriptures, which continue to intrigue me even though some of the passages are absolutely bizarre and even offensive. Ezra tells me, for example, that all foreign wives must be divorced (Ezra 9, 10). My own wife is a naturalized citizen of the United States. Paul tells me how slavery can be made kinder and gentler (Col. 3:22, 4:1). Many members of the diocese I serve are the descendants of slaves, whose scars are still apparent in their psyches. The author of the pastoral epistle called 1 Timothy tells me that women are to be submissive. They are forbidden to teach or have authority over men and are to be saved by bearing children. I cannot imagine the women I know responding to those images. The Torah tells me that homosexuals are to be executed (Lev. 20:13), that children who are disobedient to their parents are to be stoned (Deut. 21:18–21), and that people who worship a false God shall be made to perish (Deut. 6:14, 15, 8:19, 30:17, 8). The Gospels tell me that sickness is the result of a demon that must be rebuked (Luke 4:35, 39; Mark 2:1–12). The historian who wrote the book of Kings informs me that military defeat is the direct consequence of not keeping God's commandments (2 Kings 24:3). Some of the words, practices, and traditions of worship bend my mind into contorted shapes, as I try to fit these words into the world that I inhabit. Yet I continue to worship.

Honesty compels me to admit that most of my difficulties with the words and concepts of worship arise from the fact that these words assume the truth of the theistic definition of God. In the traditional understanding of that word, I am not a theist. I do not believe that I have been a theist since the time that my theological life first began to be shaped by the aforementioned Christian scholar named Paul Tillich in the early fifties. Tillich and his fellow academicians trained a generation of clergy, but they themselves remained in the theological centers of learning, where they talked about this theological revolution only to one another. They did not worry about how their concepts affected the ordinary believer, the person in the pew, or even the ordained one who interacted daily with the people of the pews.

My life, however, was to be one of those that confronted the people. I was a parish priest first and a bishop second. I faced the people of my congregations and preached to them Sunday after Sunday as their worship leader. I baptized, confirmed, married, buried, and counseled the people who were assumed to be my responsibility. My life has thus been spent processing Tillich's nontheistic thinking as it interacted with the received theistic tradition of the Christian faith. Most of the bridge building between the theistic past and the nontheistic future has occurred in the minds of those pastors who have been willing to do as I have done, to live their lives on this cutting edge, this narrow divide. We have spent our lives seeking honesty in worship, rethinking and reinterpreting our liturgical words and symbols daily, and trying to call the church we served and loved into a possible and realistic future. I suspect that for many of us it has sometimes been a lonely vocation.

But today this revolution has entered the life of the people who still come to worship. Its signs are scattered chaotically through every denomination and are finding expression in a variety of practices.

My task is to assemble these clues, to bring their meaning to consciousness, to stand them side by side, and then to read the message to which they point so provocatively.

The first sign that confronts us is that over the past fifty years the altars in the more liturgical churches of the world have come out from against the walls and the priests celebrating the Eucharist or offering the Mass have been turned around so that they now face the people. This has been a quiet, but almost universal, change. Younger clergy today absolutely insist on it. People have explained and justified this change from a wide variety of perspectives. Some have sought to demonstrate that it is nothing more than a return to the primitive practice of the early Church. Others have developed a more complex theological reasoning process to explain and to justify this transition.

The facts are, however, that the same theological shift that has caused the religious leaders of this century to stop thinking of God in theistic supernatural categories has now entered the thought processes of ordinary church people in this subtle way. The God who was "up there" or "out there" has so clearly faded. Hence, a worship pattern designed to face or even to embody that external deity is also in decline. So altars have come out from the walls and have been placed in the center of the people. Priests who led worship by facing God have turned around to face the people in whom this God is increasingly perceived to be present. The Kingdom of God, which was once thought to be destined to descend out of the skies, is now assumed to be present in the midst of the people. The transition toward a worship pattern appropriate to the exile has begun.

A second symbol of change is found in the fact that people engaged in worship are beginning to rise from their knees. The posture of kneeling thought to be appropriate for a worshiper approaching an external deity came originally out of the relationship of a subject to a king. It was the approach of a serf to the lord of the manor or of a beggar to the source of the next meal. It was also the posture of an Uncle Tom to his master. It reeks of the supernatural images of theism. But, once again, without quite knowing why, slowly and yet quite deliberately the practice of kneeling is beginning to disappear. Increasingly worshipers stand to pray, stand to receive the bread and wine of communion, and stand to acknowledge and even to confess their sins. Most of these worshipers are not conscious of what impels this change. They only know it feels right. I suggest that this is simply one more dawning response to the realization that there is no God out there and that we must thus begin to look for God within ourselves. Does it not quickly become inappropriate behavior to kneel before something that is part of each of us? So kneeling is declining in liturgical churches everywhere.

A third symbol of this shift in consciousness shows up in the compelling need to alter liturgies that is apparent everywhere today. A standard form of worship has long since departed from almost every church. In many congregations worshipers are presented with so many liturgical aids when they arrive at the church door that a loose-leaf notebook is required to keep order. Experimental liturgies are proliferating. Word changes in old liturgical forms have become so routine as to be standard. We are even beginning to question the meaning of some of the words that in the past we simply recited. Traditionally we invited people to worship with the words "the Lord be with you," as if the divine one, who was external to our life, could not be present until the request was uttered. Now, however, experimental liturgies are beginning to substitute the words "the Lord is with you," as a statement of fact simply being called to consciousness. Once the ancient kyrie eleison invoked God to have mercy, as if it might be the divine prerogative of a capricious deity not to do so unless we asked. Now we are beginning to substitute a prayer of thanksgiving that the very nature of God is to be merciful and that we live continuously inside this depth of a divine caring expressed through our caring for others and their caring for us. Once we included in our burial office and in many of our prayers of intercession a petition for God "to remember" the departed one or the one for whom our intercessions were being offered. It was language that, if literalized, suggested that perhaps without our petitions God might be forgetful, as if the divine mind, having lived to such a ripe old age, was afflicted with the early stages of senility. Now those words are slowly but surely being discarded as a new awareness of God as the very ground of our lives, an inescapable presence, the Being underneath our emergence as people begins to be recognized. Thus a new vocabulary is forced onto our lips in worship.

A fourth symbol of this shift in consciousness comes when we take a longer view of history and trace the revisions in worship found in the various editions of our prayer books. Gone from contemporary prayer books are prayers that suggested that the weather patterns could be changed by human petitions, that sickness was God's punishment for sin, that the woman needed to be ceremonially cleansed after childbirth, and even that God and our particular nation were so deeply entwined that the success of one was the will of the other. This is not to say that the purging of our prayer books is complete. Far from it! The vestiges of these ancient tribal and theistic attitudes are still present, but the gross and overt forms of their claims from the past have been muted significantly. Our official revisions in the books used in worship reveal that God increasingly is not conceived of by us as an external power capable of being manipulated by the prayers of the faithful.

A fifth symbol becomes apparent when we recognize what has happened to the life of the ordained ones in this generation. We note, first, that the parental words once used for both the church and the clergy are fading away. "Mother" church is no longer referred to as a benign institutional symbol. Indeed, "mother" church is not without her severe critics, not the least of whom are women enraged at what "mother" church has done to them over the centuries. The sacred mother, to whom all were said to belong, is clearly under attack for its prejudice.

At the same time, the authority that once lay behind the title of "Father" for priests is also rapidly eroding. The austere sound of the word has shifted first to the folksy sounds of "Father Bill" or "Father Joe." In traditions that have begun to ordain women to this priesthood, titles like "Mother Lauren" or "Mother Carol" are being heard. They are an intimate form of greeting, and yet they seek to hold onto the parental priestly power of antiquity. Inevitably, they will not succeed.

We noted earlier that this priestly power was born in that unique but primitive claim that the designated holy person could somehow stand between the theistic God above and the fragile life of a human being below. The priestly person claimed the ability and the right of interpreting the ways of God to human life. The designated holy person explained the meaning of sickness and the message found in the forces of nature, both of which were said to be expressions of the divine will. To protect people from the dangers inherent in these difficult moments of life, the priest sought to enable the people to know God's will so as not to offend the divine sensitivities and thereby risk tragedy from one of these sources. So the priest claimed the power to decide how God was properly to be worshiped and what God required in terms of the people's ethical behavior. In a believing age, the people accepted this claim with remarkable acquiescence.

As the power of the professional holy person grew, it began to be assumed that the priest also had the ability to forgive sins and to convey blessings. In time this power meant that the priest was thought to be able to determine one's eternal destiny. Thus the priest was assumed to be the ultimate arbiter of what occurred at the moment of death. The confessed and forgiven sinner might receive the reward of bliss, while the unrepentant and thus unforgiven sinner might be assigned to the realm of punishment and even eternal torment.

In the heyday of this priestly power, claims were made that the only way such a theistic God could operate was through the authorized sacraments of the established Church. These sacraments were the solitary means of grace for all people, but only the legitimately authorized and ordained priest could administer them. Outside the Church, it was claimed, there was thus no salvation, because outside the Church there could be no priestly absolution and so no forgiveness, no sacramental grace, and no priestly blessing. It was a powerful and closed system. The heavenly Father God was represented by the ordained father figure. Theism was incarnate in the male priesthood.

The capstone in this impressive ecclesiastical structure was added in the nineteenth century when the pope, called the vicar of Christ and thought of as the ultimate priest, validating everyone else's priestly ministry, was declared by the Roman Church to be infallible when speaking ex cathedra on faith and morals. All of this structure represented the evolution of that original claim that the tribal holy person alone had the ability to interpret the will and the desires of the theistic deity to the believing world.

Today that superstructure of ecclesiastical privilege is tottering before our eyes. Its fall is inevitable, for it was built on the theistic premise that in our day has been eroded to the point of nonexistence. It will take the ecclesiastical structure about a century to recognize that the validating principle of its life no longer exists. But the signs of that demise are already present. The loss of priestly authority and priestly respect, so rampant in our society, is but one of them. That power and respect have been diminished everywhere except among the most docile, the most superstitious, and the most premodern of believers. No one, however, is more aware of the departure of that power than are the ordained ones in the Church's life today.

This reality has produced a major contemporary crisis in priestly identity, which has spread from Catholic priests to Protestant pastors. It manifests itself in clergy persons seeking justification for their very being in ancillary definitions and occupations. In the thirteenth century a priest who needed to justify the priestly role was all but inconceivable. But today we see priests and pastors casting themselves in the roles of social workers, psychotherapists, or spiritual directors. We see a rapid rise in the number of nonstipendiary clergy who work in secular jobs. To me these are but increasingly obvious symbols of the fact that, far more than the religious establishment recognizes, the patterns of worship and the structure of church life founded on belief in the theistic God of yesterday are simply being dismantled. Worship beyond the exile will surely reflect the loss of priestly power and priestly privilege. I suspect, for example, that a lay person will preside at the Eucharist during the next century, even in Catholic circles. It is inevitable. The channels of grace for a nontheistic God cannot be closed or controlled by the designated holy person.

A sixth symbol of the Church's shift away from theism is seen in that this loss of priestly power is now affecting the haberdashery worn by the ordained, especially the vestments worn by the hierarchy. In 1996 the Anglican primate of the Scottish Episcopal Church[6] took a long look at the vestments worn by the Church's bishops and raised to consciousness their medieval and royal content. He went so far as to propose that his fellow bishops join him in a prophetic act at the next meeting of the Anglican bishops of the world, which convenes at the invitation of the Archbishop of Canterbury once a decade in England. "Why not gather on the banks of the river Thames," he suggested, "and hurl our medieval mitres[7] into its dark waters and be done with them forever?" That was perhaps the first shot fired across the bow of yet another dying church custom. The bishop's mitre is indeed a thinly disguised crown. The bishop's cope, which accompanies the mitre, is an ecclesiastical version of the king's royal cape. The bishop's ring is reminiscent of the royal signet ring with which the king sealed his official documents. The bishop's crosier (pastoral staff) is a replica of the king's royal staff. The bishop's chair, like the king's chair, is called "the throne," and people kneel at the feet of the bishop, seated on his throne, when they are confirmed. Finally, the bishop's house is called "the palace." All of these symbols represent traditions out of the past! One wonders who the bishops are fooling. Perhaps those were appropriate symbols in an era of ecclesiastical dominance. At least they fitted the landscape created by the theistic God. Today, however, the bishops of the Church do not rule the world from their episcopal thrones as the vicars of a deity who sits on a heavenly throne beyond the sky. Indeed, the opinions of bishops on most subjects are widely ignored. Yet our costumes seek to disguise the fact that we are engaged in a massively irrelevant charade of enormous pretension. An English divine in Oxford said to me on one occasion, "Part of our duty is simply to dress up and walk around." That may be so, but perhaps costume balls are a more appropriate place for that than churches. Royal vestments will surely be discarded if a new church capable of living beyond the exile is to be born.

So the symbols of a Church in radical transition are present, waiting to be observed and interpreted. Free-standing altars have turned the priest around to face the God in the midst of the people. Worshipers are rising from their knees as if in response to a divine call. A variety of experimental liturgies are forcing changes in the use of ancient set words. Prayer books delete the most galling concepts of the theism of yesterday. Parental names and priestly power both are under siege. A lay presidency of the Eucharist is being debated. New vestments, the dismissal of royal vestments, or no vestments at all are being contemplated. These are the signs even in the midst of the present religious world that a new consciousness is being born and a new concept of God is evolving. Surely the evidence points to one conclusion: the driving force behind all these changes is the dawning recognition that the theistic God of the past is dying, and with that death, the way human beings relate in worship to that supernatural, invasive, transcendent deity is collapsing. If there are no changes in worship, then worship dedicated to a theistic God will cease. If there is no other purpose for the Church than to point people to the external God above, then churches will finally disappear from our landscapes.

When these changes in consciousness are raised and the driving factors understood, then a clear choice stands before believers in exile. We can give up the struggle and abandon hope for a God presence and a church purpose beyond the exile. Or we can peer into the future and see a new kind of worship and a new purpose for the church rising to confront us. I suspect that both the liturgy and the structure of that emerging Church will have a very different look—so different, in fact, that I wonder if we will see continuity between the Church of yesterday and the Church of tomorrow.

I turn now to peer into that future and to sketch out a vision of how the Church will look and act in that future. It is speculation based on what is known now. Only time will tell if it is a speculation that can move us forward toward that future. All I am convinced of now is that the alternative is no Christian future at all.

TWELVE

❋

The Future Church: A Speculative Dream

C AN ONE REALLY WORSHIP in a meaningful way if there is no concept of a theistic deity to receive that worship? Can one confess, give thanks, offer petitions, or sing praises if there is no personal being to whom these acts of worship are directed? Those are crucial questions and demand a serious answer. Some in the religious community are sure that traveling this path will result only in the death of the religious past with no hope of a religious future. I do not agree with that judgment, and I am prepared now to demonstrate why.

I begin with a story that a Buddhist monk and mystic named Thich Nhat Hanh told about himself in his book *Living Buddha, Living Christ*. A Protestant pastor came up to this monk and rather aggressively asked him, "Are you a grateful person?"

Taken back by this question for a moment, Thich Nhat Hanh took a moment to respond. This allowed his adversary to press on, which he did in a quite revealing way. "If you are really grateful, how can you not believe in God? God has created everything we enjoy, including the food we eat. Since you do not believe in God," he concluded with a flourish, "you are not grateful for anything!" The judgment out of which the question arose was now fully revealed.

Thich Nhat Hanh is a holy man, known and respected the world over. He has been praised by a fellow mystic from another tradition, the Roman Catholic monk Thomas Merton. He has been acclaimed as a spiritual giant by the great civil rights leader and Protestant pastor, Martin Luther King, Jr. Popular theological writer Elaine Pagels has publicly expressed her debt to his spiritual leadership. Thich Nhat Hanh prays and meditates every day of his life. He lives inside a God-consciousness that is apparent in everything he says, does, and writes. How could this Protestant pastor and Western religious critic make the assumption that Thich Nhat Hanh could not be a grateful person because he did not believe in God?

That question arose because Thich Nhat Hanh's Christian adversary, like so many fearful religious people in a fast-changing world, made his judgment based upon the assumptions present in his own theological definitions. This Buddhist mystic has moved, in fact, beyond the God of theism. Yet that was the only definition of God that his questioner understood. The questioner was therefore blind to anything that did not lie within his own limited theological parameters. He had defined the reality of God quite narrowly, and thus he had dismissed anything beyond his vision as not real. That is not an uncommon attitude in religious circles. Anyone who tries to redefine worship in nontheistic categories or to reshape institutional Christianity for a new age will surely confront a similar response.

Indeed, Andrew Brown, the former religion editor of one of the United Kingdom's finest major dailies, *The Independent,* has already made such a charge about me in print. In a personal profile entitled "All Gas and Gaiters," published in the magazine supplement of the Sunday *Independent,*[1] Brown wrote, "It seems to me that if you remove from God all power to make any difference in the world, you are not a heretic, but an atheist, no matter how well you perform as a bishop." Perhaps disturbed by that conclusion, Brown then added his own more humble disclaimer, "but then I too am . . . not a theologian." Brown, like so many others, cannot envision God save as an intervening, personal, supernatural presence who can invade history to make a specific difference.

But my contention is that once the holy has been redefined in nontheistic terms, a revolution in the meaning of worship will be inevitable. Worship to me is not a peripheral activity. It is, rather, central to the meaning of our humanity. To be human is to see ourselves self-consciously in terms of what is ultimately real. Worship is the name of the way we practice that self-definition. So worship may well have to be defined anew in every age, but worship must always be an aspect of our humanity. Since worship must be located somewhere, then something like a church as a center or place of worship must always be a part of our future. Both the activity of worship and the structure of the church may be very different, but my conviction is that we cannot be fully human without them. The question for our time is, can worship and the Church escape its theistic understandings, which will guarantee the deaths of both as we know them? Can both move from where they are today to where they must be tomorrow without a complete break with yesterday? Must a death to the past be a prerequisite to life in the future for these aspects of our humanity?

We have looked at the signs of change already apparent in

the activity called worship. Now let me try to sketch the future, first in broad brush strokes and later in more specific details.

Worship beyond the exile will not be marked with chanted words to an external deity. Liturgical activity will not be a repetitious living out of a remembered tradition that celebrated the perceived activity of the theistic God. Worship in the future will be marked, rather, by the self-conscious awareness that all of us are or can be God bearers and life givers and that our deepest religious task is to give ourselves away. It will involve a call to that state of being where giving one's life away is both natural and desirable. Worship beyond the exile will not be oriented toward an external God but toward the world of our human community. That, however, will not result in a shallow humanism but in a recognition that the place where God is ultimately found is in the depths of our own humanity. So there will be no attempt in our future worship to escape life, but every attempt to expand life.

Since God will be seen as a presence at the heart of life, available to everyone and not as the special possession of the religious institution, then surely worship in the future will be less and less hierarchical and more and more circular. It will inevitably shed its denominational agenda and its territorial wars. It will lay down its royal images and its pretensions. It will cease to pretend that it speaks for God or that it is the sole channel of divine grace. It will dedicate itself to the search for truth, universal truth, rather than expending its energies in seeking to defend its narrow version of truth. It will treasure its sacred scriptures as the record of its ancestors in faith as they sought to worship God. But it will not be bound by either the cultural or the cultic limitations of those scriptures. It will recognize that the revelations of the Holy One did not cease when the canon of scripture was closed. It will call people into the fullness of life. It will not exist to support that specialized activity called religion. Those few whose being has been affirmed by the theistic patterns of the past will find themselves stripped bare. But those who hunger for God, who thirst for righteousness, and who believe that worship issues in an enhanced being for all will rejoice.

These changes are upon us at this moment. The world is taking part in a spiritual quest, but many citizens of this century no longer believe that the Church is an asset to their quest. Institutional religion today is tearing itself apart externally as it collapses internally. The choices are clear. Religion moves into the future and beyond the exile, or it dies. Worshipers have already noticed that the traditional words of worship are no longer capable of embodying literal truth. Some have already begun their exodus from Church life. Next, those who remain will struggle to translate these archaic forms into usable concepts. At this task they will ultimately fail. Finally, out of this practice of muttering nonsensical concepts in worship will be created the life-or-death scenario. Substantive changes will be irresistible when the alternative is death. Then the forces of change will cascade as if falling off a cliff, and the Church of the future, with liturgical forms for the future, will come into being.

The liturgical changes will begin by focusing on the God experience itself, not on the explanations of the God experience that rise out of yesterday's consciousness. A new liturgical awareness will include acknowledging that the God experience carries us into a sense of awe and wonder, into a state of life beyond limits or time. It can never be bound by rationality, nor will it always be fully responsive to human inquiry.

Those believers in exile who, like me, grew up in a Christian worldview will need to find a way to journey through that Christian system to what lies beyond all systems. We will wonder what, if anything, from our Christian past we can appropriately carry with us. Can the theistic symbols be viewed nontheistically? Can the Christ figure still be a doorway for us into the divine? Can we move beyond the definitions of the past in order to get to something new? Exploring that tactic will, I believe, offer more promise than most have suspected.

If I am still to be able to claim the Christ as a doorway, I will be compelled first to remove from that Christ all of the exclusionary and imperialistic claims that have been placed upon him by a power-conscious Church of the past. This Christ will have no part in the division between Protestants and Catholics that historically has torn the Western world and still divides Ireland. Nor can this Christ ever be used again to denigrate or to judge the adequacy of any of the world's other great religious traditions, which surely have been the doorway into the holy for countless numbers of people. The Church beyond the exile will seek a Christ who is not the arbiter at the gate determining who is worthy of entering but rather an inviting presence who says to all, "Come unto me and discover the infinite dimensions of transcendent wonder." When that occurs, then that Church will be able to claim whatever treasures it can from the wisdom of its own religious heritage. So purging and opening will be the dual foci of future worship. Those who embark upon this journey will require not only courage but also spiritual maturity.

How does one purge and open simultaneously? One does it by clinging to the essence while allowing the forms to wither away. Christian worship historically has been dominated and shaped by the life of this Jesus. The church year starts with his birth and journeys through to his ascension. It is theistic to its core. Can we transform that sacred calendar and those holy days so that they will be celebrated beyond the exile? I believe we can.

The birth of Jesus was the moment when Christians recognized that the Holy God had now emerged in human history in a self-conscious way. In the birth of Jesus, Christians celebrated the recognition that the God who had been perceived as holy and other now was revealed to be present in the heart of human life. That is why angels were said to have sung and stars were said to have appeared in the eastern sky as a sign of that birth. That is why wise men and shepherds were said to have journeyed from near and far to worship this moment of revelation. The God met in this Jesus was not to be a limited God, the revelation of a national or tribal deity. This birth was a sign that the infinite could be known in the finite, that the eternal could be met in that which is transitory, and that the divine and human could not be separated. These are the realities that lie underneath the Christmas stories, and they can be celebrated and observed fully. Their truth extends far beyond the literalized symbols of the birth narratives. Thus, purged and opened, these symbols can join our journey into and beyond the exile. Christmas was indeed a moment of light that was able to shine in our darkness. That light can still draw the searchers to itself.

Easter with its story of the resurrection can also be transformed, I believe, and carried with us into a postexilic future. Yet before that is possible, the miracles of physical resuscitation, the angels who roll stones away from tombs, and the bodies that appear out of nothing and disappear into thin air must be dismissed for the developed legends that they are. But life that transcends every human limit is a powerful portrait. Death, which opens all things to new possibilities; love, which triumphs over hatred; being, which overcomes nonbeing—those are the truths to which Easter points, and those are the truths that emerge when God is met on the edges and at the limits of our finite humanity. That is what the stories of the resurrection are all about. So it is that purged and opened Easter can also accompany us beyond the exile.

Ascension, the story of Jesus rising into God, and Pentecost, the story of Jesus dispensing the God Spirit to all people, are perhaps the easiest of all the Christian celebrations to transform. We dismiss once again the literal accounts of angelic beings who come out of the sky to interpret the event in the biblical text. We make no attempt to preserve the gravity-defying cosmic levitation or the language-defying unity said to have been found in the new Church. Those are once again the legends of our theistic past. But we concentrate on the nontheistic aspects of these narratives, which suggest that the human has entered into the divine, that God and human life are not divided, that humanity ultimately empties into divinity, and that we are called to an expanded life in the Holy Spirit of God. Once again, purged and opened, Ascension and Pentecost can walk with us beyond the exile.

Next, the Church of the future must examine those liturgical moments that traditionally have been wrapped around the major transition points of human life. If they are to survive the exile, they, too, will have to be rethought in nontheistic categories.

The baptism service of entry into the life of the Christian Church has been a liturgy so filled with the theistic language of a supernatural deity as to be repugnant to an increasing number of believers today. It speaks of a cosmic fall requiring a cosmic act of redemption. In any developing liturgical rite, we must journey beyond those offensive assumptions which assert that the child was born in sin and that without this act of baptism that life is doomed. We must discover a deeper and more profound experience and meaning behind the act of baptism, or it cannot continue to be part of the Church of the future.

When we look at baptism nontheistically, we discover that the question implicit in the moment of every person's birth is "Who am I?" In this postmodern world the process of reproduction is not nearly so magical or mystical as it was when the faith and practice of the Christian Church were being developed. We now know, for example, that the fertilization that created each of us genetically was a random chance meeting of one of millions of sperm from our fathers with the ripened ovum of our mothers. Yet that chance meeting determined our genetic coding. The level of one's parents' personal security is a second chance factor shaping the mental health and emotional well-being of the newborn life. Whether or not our mothers got proper prenatal care or consumed alcohol and caffeine during their pregnancies is still another chance factor that will help to determine the baby's limits of development. Whether we are the first, middle, or last child in our particular family will shape much of our psychic makeup. All of these chance qualities raise deep and significant questions about our ultimate identity, our self-definition, and our being.

Without understanding the dynamics of birth, yet aware of its mystery and wonder, our ancestors in faith developed a liturgy whereby parents would take their newborn child to a place of worship and symbolically incorporate that child into the life of the community. Through the process of worship and Church life, that child then learned something about who he or she was and indeed where the parenting skills of the mother and father might be augmented by the whole community. This process also connected the child to a group of people who were self-consciously pointed beyond themselves to that which they called holy. So the Church became the place where life was first touched by the opportunity to participate in transcendence. The child was to be called beyond his or her limits. The child began to learn that he or she was a part of what God is. These are the places in which the nontheistic meanings of Holy Baptism are to be found.

Baptism in the postexilic Church becomes, then, not a ritual that purifies us of the sin of Adam, but rather a ritual that calls each candidate to be all that that person was created to be. It becomes a powerful starting point for entry into nontheistic worship.

The same can also be true for the other rites of passage that the Church has incorporated into its worship, if we can only enter their deeper meaning. The various puberty rites of our religious traditions were designed to acknowledge a powerful change in human status from childhood to maturity. They mark a transition when identity is confused, when glands are active, when hormones are colliding, and when one seeks clarification of one's very being. The primary message of the Christian Church to the emerging adolescent in the Church's rites of passage is "You share in eternity. You are holy. Your life reveals the presence of God." Once we travel beneath the rhetoric of our worship, the need for the image of an external deity begins to disappear. The reality of God and the potential of human life are not identical, but neither are they different or even separate. The puberty rites simply call us back to our deepest definition of selfhood.

We move on liturgically through the rituals of adulthood, such as marriage and childbirth, to that part of life in which we experience the decline of our human powers in both sickness and in the aging process and finally arrive at the moment of death. The various liturgies of the Church surrounding those defining moments continue to call believers to recognize themselves as sharing in the Being of God. We are God bearers, the revealers of the God who is present in all of life. That is the meaning behind the words we hear proclaimed in services of holy matrimony, in thanksgiving after childbirth, in sickness, and even in death. Once we refocus these services designed to mark the turning points of life, we will discover that much of their meaning can be preserved. The Church might well come out of the exile with its rites of passage intact, even if they have been redefined.

Moving on to the primary liturgical act that has defined Christian worship for centuries, we ask if the common meal of the Church, the Mass, the Eucharist, the Communion Service, or the Lord's Supper, can be retained in any form. The answer to this query is surely negative so long as it remains caught up in the magical, supernatural power of the ages. A ceremony in which ordained hands transform ordinary elements from the tables of life into the supernatural realities of the body and blood of Jesus is not going to survive.

Tracing the roots of medieval eucharistic theology is not easy. Some of its antecedents are probably the primitive practices of prehistory, in which worshipers tried to capture for themselves the strength and courage first of their enemies and later of their gods by eating their flesh and drinking their blood. These cannibalistic rites, wrapped in more acceptable words, probably entered Christianity through the various cults of the Mediterranean mystery religions like Mithraism, with which Christianity competed for dominance in the first centuries of its non-Jewish life, though that connection is not universally agreed. In those traditions the liturgical practice of feeding on the symbolic flesh of the god figure was thought to enable the worshiper to share in that god's divinity. Such practices were certainly not present in the Jewish womb, which birthed Christianity. The Jews might eat the sacrificed animal, but to identify the sacrificial animal with the one to whom it was offered was inconceivable to them. The Christ was identified both as the priest offering the sacrifice and the victim who was sacrificed, but only much later was he seen also to be the God to whom the sacrifice was offered. Even the biblical accounts of the Last Supper are highly stylized liturgical creations of the early Church. They are not the literal words of a moment in history when this liturgical observance was born. Furthermore, the words attributed to Jesus by the tenth-decade Gospel of John about "eating his flesh and drinking his blood" are clearly a reading back into the Jewish Jesus of the late-developing practice in the Christian community, in which the Church's worship incorporated mystical moments of identification between worshiper and the deity (see John 6). Yes, surely there was a meal shared on the night before the crucifixion, and surely that meal, in retrospect, was invested with significant meaning. The last meal that this group ever ate together, like all last meals, became a point of reference to be recalled again and again until it was incorporated fully into the group's worship life. It was, however, probably not a Passover meal, though that interpretation was laid upon it very early.[2] In this liturgical context, as the Christian story developed, that meal was used, first, to interpret Jesus' death and, second, to communicate the continued risen presence of Jesus with his disciples. Finally, that presence was interpreted theologically in terms of the traditional theistic understanding of God. This service bears all of these marks to this day.

The essential element of eucharistic worship can survive once we understand the tremendous and almost mystical power present in the act of feeding. The sharing of food in human experience is the very basis of all human community. Our language reveals that time and again. The word *companion,* for example, literally means the sharing of bread with another.[3] In the act of breast-feeding, the life of the newborn infant was not only saved but sustained and enabled to grow. In the ancient world, the death of the mother in childbirth almost always guaranteed the death of the child. Feeding another is the experience in which life, love, and being are first shared. So inevitably in our social order the deepest symbol of love has always been located in the act of feeding. That is why eating together is the primary way that relationships grow and are nurtured. It is the means by which love is shared. If love is ultimately a gift of God, and if love itself is finally the creator of our life and our being, then eating must always be seen as a holy act, an act in which God, newly understood, can enter our lives. This is not, however, the God identified with the external, supernatural language of classical theism. It is rather the God defined as the presence that is over, under, around, and through the very fabric of life, the God who is not a personal being but who is made known in the personal being of the whole creation. Here we encounter the God who calls the created order into self-consciousness in that one creature who has the ability to escape the boundaries of nature and to commune with his or her creator. So the people beyond the exile who gather to celebrate the God in whom they live and move and have their being must build community around a common meal, for there is no better way to acknowledge the God who can be met, indeed revealed, in the life of the world. As we enter into that meaning of the Eucharist, we who are worshipers find ourselves not just transformed, but also enabled to be transformers and redeemers of the whole creation. The mission of the Christian Church is not to convert the world, but to call all who are also part of the creation into the fullness of life. This was, I believe, also the experience that was seeking expression in the original shapers of the theology of the Eucharist. They were certain that God was met in the breaking of bread, but the only God they knew how to speak about was the God who lived beyond the world. So they placed upon the Eucharist the magic of theism and the rules of their value system. They decreed who could celebrate the Eucharist and even who could receive it. The only prerequisite that will remain beyond the exile for coming to the table of the Lord is that the worshiper must be hungry.

Once we have a new frame of reference into which we can place our traditional liturgical and sacramental symbols, then worship itself begins to take on a new meaning. What, for example, does the activity called confession symbolize? Is that not a liturgical way in which we human beings, over the centuries, have tried to come to grips with a sense of our barriers, our boundaries, and our limitations? In our evolutionary history we had to battle to prove ourselves fit enough to survive. Our survival instincts made us cling to our fears, to defend ourselves against all foes, and to seek our own advantage at the cost of denigrating others. Yet in worship we catch a vision of life's potential and, from that perspective, look anew at life's actuality. Confession arises out of our recognition that we human beings are not what we were created to be. It comes from an awareness of our unwillingness to risk our frail security systems for the chance to enter an expanded world. It is an expression of a humanity so desperate to receive that we act as if we have nothing that we can freely give. It proclaims a human nature so deeply a prisoner of its own limits that it believes it can capture God inside religious power systems. It is seeing that we have defined our life out of our evolutionary past instead of our expanding and potential future. To grasp this is nothing less than an act of confession. Confession is not a peasant sinner groveling before the king, begging for forgiveness in order to escape punishment. This is only the warping of our reality with the images of a theistic god. Confession is my being confronting the Ground of all Being, and forgiveness is my moving beyond my limits into something more real, more whole, more life giving than I can now contemplate. It is in this sense that confession and absolution, as liturgical acts interpreting profound human experiences, can be carried by the corporate worship of the Church living beyond the exile.

Thanksgiving is the gracious recognition of the gifts we have received. It is an attempt to acknowledge those people who called us into being and those moments in which we were able to respond to that call. So thanksgiving can also accompany us into the liturgical life of the Church beyond the exile. We are eucharistic people. That is, we live out of gratitude. The Protestant pastor who challenged Thich Nhat Hanh, the Buddhist mystic, could not have been more wrong. Gratitude is not only possible, it is necessary to be the full human beings that life in a nontheistic exile calls us to become.

The emphasis of corporate worship will surely shift dramatically as the theistic patterns of yesterday continue to decline and a nontheistic way of approaching the holy begins to beckon us in worship. But worship will endure, for it is through worship that we begin to glimpse who we are. It is an intensely human activity.

The Church that worships in this way will also be a Church that will create new architectural forms, new organizational structures, and new identifying marks. I suspect its arches and steeples will shrink until they are but vestigial remains of the inner need to point to the God beyond the sky. I suspect its stained glass windows will no longer seek to capture ancient truths in these timeless, otherworldly forms. I suspect the music of the Church will no longer sing of Jesus as a divine visitor but as a revelation of all that is true about life, love, and being. The affirmation of this postexilic Church will be that Jesus revealed this God through his humanity and thus that he was the God bearer, perhaps even the ultimate God bearer for those of us who see God inside this particular family of faith. The faith of the postexilic Church will be expressed in the conviction that we, too, will reveal this God when the Ground of Being draws each of us beyond our limits into fuller living, wasteful loving, and courageous being. Since form always follows function, Church architectural forms inevitably will begin to express the new understanding of God that is being born among us.

Clearly change in both liturgy and structure is inevitable, and this change will probably be radical, if not total. Those whose lives are dedicated to serving the Church of the past will resist these suggestions with a vehemence that always emerges from threatened hierarchies and dying institutions. Yet the forms the Church assumed in the past inevitably must die. Those forms and their defenders simply cannot evolve fast enough to prevent institutional, ecclesiastical death from becoming a reality. But the seeds of resurrection are present in the exile, and in time those seeds will sprout and bloom. When they do, we will once again be able to see continuity between the Church of the past and the purged and opened Church of the future. Just as the Church of the high Middle Ages, which built massive Gothic cathedrals, was able to recognize the earliest Church, which worshiped in the catacombs, as its ancestor, so in time the Church of today will recognize the postexilic structures of tomorrow as its descendants. When that connection is seen, the reformation that we are now entering will be complete. I am able to see just enough of those seeds beginning to bloom to be excited about letting the process of death and resurrection proceed.

THIRTEEN

✳

*Eternal Life
Apart from Heaven and Hell*

WILL THIS NONTHEISTIC VIEW of God, the promise of a new spirituality based upon the building of a life that is full, free, and whole, motivate human beings to a journey into the transcending mystery of God in the future? Will pilgrims in the exile seek God in the ground and depth of their own being if there is no perceived and obvious reward? Is it enough to suggest that a life lived fully, marked with an expansive love, called into a new being is its own reward? Is there hope for life beyond this world apart from the images of our theistic past?

In past eras it was that hope for life after this world that fueled the religious passions of human beings. People lived with not just the promise but the conviction that there was life after death. That is what enabled the frailty of human life, beset as it is with trauma and chance, to seem meaningful. Can any part of that conviction survive the exile? Can a case for life after death be made that is devoid of self-centered hopes that our goodness will be rewarded? Those are the questions that inevitably emerge out of this attempt to rethink the Christian symbols for a new day.

I begin this ultimate chapter in an unusual way by stating my conclusions first. I do believe that there is an eternity that lies beyond the limits of my human finitude and in which I can participate. To say it traditionally, I do believe that there is life after death. I want that to be clear, but before the defenders of traditional piety begin to feel affirmed in their uncritical faith assertions, let me state my second conclusion. The content of this reality of life beyond the boundaries of death is so radically different from anything that has been proposed by the religious systems of the past that it is all but unrecognizable. Now, with the conclusions stated, let me build my case.

Sometimes a television commercial can be more perceptive and more true than its creator imagined. Such was the case, in my opinion, when the punch line of a beer commercial in the United States stated, "It doesn't get much better than this!" The words were spoken amid a picture of vibrant and happy young adults, male and female, sitting before a crackling open fire on the shore of a gorgeous lake or river with a beautiful moon above. On the fire delicacies were being roasted, and of course the brand-name beer was in everyone's hand. It was a compelling, indeed even an enchanting, scene, freeing the imaginations of the viewers to contemplate both what had come before this scene and what might well come after. "It doesn't get much better than this" was not unlike the statement of an article of faith or perhaps even a creedal assertion of the ultimate goal of life in a postmodern world.

I doubt if such a sentiment could have been articulated by, much less have found a resting place in the minds and hearts of, the citizens of western Europe in the thirteenth century. They were not eager to drink deeply of the joys of this world. Rather, they thought of themselves primarily as pilgrims in a valley of tears destined for what they hoped was the bliss of a better world in an eternal heaven. Never would they have imagined that any scene native to this world could elicit such words as "It doesn't get much better than this." Those thirteenth-century inhabitants, in which faith was supreme, dreamed of beatific visions and of a final destination where the joy of their relationships would not be ended either by parting or by death. For them the image of a group of young adults in robust health would always have been tempered by the very real fear and anxiety that came in a world where disease, pain, suffering, and even early and sudden death were so prevalent as to be subliminally present at every moment. In that era a sense of joy in this world was fleeting at best, a mirage at worst. Thirteenth-century citizens were sustained not by the conviction that "It doesn't get much better than this," but by the hope that someday when they entered the Kingdom of God, it would in fact be better than anything they could imagine.

That hope had a powerful influence upon everything they did. To strive to build a just society here and now was to concentrate on what was transitory and perhaps even illusory. Besides, justice was God's business and would be tended to in the Kingdom of Heaven, where it was an unquestioned article of faith that the good would be rewarded and the evil punished. That promise removed any necessity for reform movements. It contributed mightily to a relatively stagnant social order. People were taught to accept and to live within the status into which they had been born. It was argued that this life was so short and, compared with heaven, so meaningless that energy should be used only within the limits of one's station to do the best one could do with the circumstances one faced. The reality of both the heavenly reward for the righteous and the feared punishment that would await the condemned in the pits of hell was so intense that it provided an enormous bulwark in building a stable society. The intermediate state of purgatory filled the gap between those destined for heaven and those destined for hell, and its time-limited, but nonetheless very real, punishments became almost an equal motivator of positive behavior. To shorten one's time in purgatory before one entered the realm of bliss was not an insignificant desire.

The contrast between the faith of thirteenth-century people, as expressed in their vision of heaven, and the faith of this current generation, expressed in the words of a beer commercial, is but another consciousness-raising symbol of the fact that the theological consensus of yesterday has died. The age of faith is no more. If believing in God requires acquiescence to the convictions of the past, then believing in God will disappear. Postmodern people might pretend to believe for another generation or so because the fear of living in a godless world over which neither the individual nor God has any control is too traumatic to embrace except in small doses. But ultimately such fear will not recreate faith.

Time, America's foremost news magazine, ran a recent cover story on heaven, entitled "Does Heaven Exist?" That question itself is one that our ancient forebears would never have raised. Interestingly enough, *Time*'s reporters sought in vain to find any robust conviction about heaven, even among traditional believers. "It is a boring place or a silly myth or something people invent or all of the above," *Time* quoted theologian Jeffrey Burton Russell as saying. Even David Wells, a conservative theologian from the faculty of the evangelical Gordon-Conwell Seminary in Massachusetts, had this to say about heaven: "We would expect to hear of it in the evangelical churches, but I don't hear it at all. I don't think heaven is even a blip on the Christian screen from one end of the denominational spectrum to the other. The more perplexing question is, 'What explains this?'"[1]

A contemporary evangelical professor thus admits to being mystified by this phenomenon. The fact is that his evangelical credentials mean that he could not possibly embrace the answer for which his own question yearns. The demise of heaven is a direct result of the death of the theistic image of God on which the evangelical tradition, with its personalistic view of heaven, rests. People who understand heaven as the reward given for a life of faith and work must also understand God as a personal deity who hands out rewards and punishments based on personal deservings. Such a God is a thinly disguised parent figure who controls the child's behavior with a series of threats and promises. This God was perceived as keeping intimate and copious notes on human behavior. He—and the theistic God was almost always a he—was not unlike another supernatural figure that we allow to enter our consciousness every December. Does it not occur to us to see the similarities between this theistic God image and Santa Claus? We are told that Santa Claus has an all-seeing capacity: "He's making a list and checking it twice. Going to find out who's naughty and nice." Does that not sound like the all-seeing record-keeping theistic deity? This Santa figure also comes out of the infinite skies, accompanied not by a heavenly host but by magical reindeer. He brings presents to the good children as their reward and ashes and switches to the bad children as their punishment. Santa is but one more icon of the theistic deity who, as the personal judge, gives the ultimate reward of heavenly bliss through all eternity to the deserving or the fiery punishment of hell through all eternity to the unworthy. Such a deity would inspire exactly the kind of worship we have offered. It is worship filled with praise and breast-beating confessions of our unworthiness, accompanied by pleas for mercy.

But that theistic deity, we now suspect, is nothing more than a projection of a human need into the sky. From those same skies modern knowledge has removed the mystery and the intrigue. There appears to be no place in our universe for heaven. It has been radically dislocated from its ancient spot just beyond the clouds. If heaven is no longer a locatable concept, then we have to recognize that neither is God, since heaven was God's abode. We can and do rationalize this by saying that heaven is not a place and God cannot be thought of spatially. That is of course true, but a God who cannot be located or envisioned begins to fade into an oblong blur. Once God had been removed from the position beyond the sky from where divine judgment, to say nothing of personal intervention, was believed to occur, then the major pillars upholding the concept of heaven were removed and the believability of heaven collapsed. That is why heaven is not spoken of today. Evangelical Christians do not speak of it, for it no longer makes sense even to them. Neither does the theistic God who reigned from that same heaven, but they have not yet come to that awareness.

Beyond this spatial problem, other understandings traditionally undergirding both heaven and hell are also collapsing. Indeed, these understandings were bringing about the collapse of our images of the afterlife even before we began to deal with our growing awareness of the size and shape of the universe. When the Western world first began to temper its understanding of individualism with a sense of the radical interdependence of human life, then in an instant the basis for divine judgment was compromised, perhaps irrevocably. Individualism itself, we need to recognize, has been the unspoken prerequisite to every concept of life after death in the Western world. It is the very basis for positing divine judgment.

Most people do not recognize that even among our spiritual ancestors, the Jews, the concept of life after death is a relatively modern one. It does not receive a mention until the sixth century B.C.E., and, not coincidentally, it was born with the rise of a concept of individualism. Ezekiel appears to be the first figure in Jewish religious history to articulate a sense of individual responsibility on the basis of which individual reward and punishment might be assigned. "What do you mean," Ezekiel wrote, "by repeating this proverb concerning the land of Israel, 'The fathers have eaten sour grapes and the children's teeth are set on edge'? As I live, says the Lord God, this proverb shall no more be used by you in Israel. Behold all souls are mine, the soul of the father, as well as the soul of the son is mine: The soul that sins shall die" (Ezek. 18:2–4).

Ezekiel then went on to spell out his understanding of righteous behavior. It involved avoiding idolatry, adultery, indebtedness, and oppressing one's neighbor, among other things. The one who avoids these things, he asserted, "shall surely live," said the Lord God (Ezek. 18:5–9). Next Ezekiel spelled out his understanding of evil behavior. It involved robbery, oppression, adultery, and producing children who did evil things. Ezekiel concluded by stating emphatically of the one who does these things, "He shall not live. . . . he shall surely die" (Ezek. 18:10–13).

Just to make sure that his point was clear, Ezekiel repeated himself in his conclusion: "The son shall not suffer for the iniquity of the father nor the father for the iniquity of the son; the righteousness of the righteous shall be upon himself and the wickedness of the wicked shall be upon himself" (Ezek. 18:20).

We have lived with the idea of individualism for so long we are not able to embrace the radical power this new insight of Ezekiel must have had on the thinking of the people of Israel. In the ancient world the tribe was the basic social unit. The tribe would be punished corporately for the sins of a single member. The people of Egypt were afflicted with dreadful plagues, according to the book of Exodus, for the hardness of the Pharaoh's heart. The nation of Israel would be crushed by its enemies because of the idolatrous behavior of its king, who was the symbol of the nation. The overwhelming value and chief good in that era was the survival of the tribe, not the survival of the individual. It was a quantum leap in consciousness to begin to think individualistically. But no concept of life after death could emerge until the concept of individualism had arisen, for individualism is a prerequisite to every concept of life after death that has thrived in the Western world.

But individualism has been compromised significantly by the sociological thinking of the nineteenth century and the psychological thinking of the twentieth century. These compromises were the primary places in which the Western confidence in life after death began to erode, long before an awareness of the infinite dimensions of space entered the common mind.

In some sense these issues were posed sociologically by such nineteenth-century voices as novelists Victor Hugo and Charles Dickens.[2] Is one who steals committing a punishable offense? Is stealing a sin for which the individual is to be condemned? Of course it is, the Church replied, and both the human and the divine punishment for stealing were said to be rigorous. But what if that act of theft was necessitated by the fear of starvation for the thief or for his family? What if the forces of the industrial revolution had reduced the options for some by making wealth for a few, but joblessness for many, a fact of life? If the supply of food is ample, should any human being be allowed to starve? Can the world be divided morally into the dieters and the hungry? Is there not something evil about a system in which some people die of hunger in the midst of plenty? If so, then upon whom does the judgment fall when one is reduced to theft as the price of survival? Suddenly the judgment on which our eternal reward was to be based became murky.

Is murder wrong? Yes, of course it is, said the Church, and capital punishment for capital crimes has been the earthly punishment for murderers in most of the nations of the Christian West and for most of the years of Christian history. The anticipation of eternal punishment in hell has certainly been used to enhance the horror of that person's presumed destiny.

But what makes a murderer a murderer? Extensive psychological studies in modern times have given us abundant new insights. We now know that an abused child quite frequently will grow into being an abusive adult. The sins of the parents are, in fact, visited upon the children to the third and fourth generation, as the Ten Commandments suggested. How then can we judge the guilt present in any individual act? When politicians defend their decision to support capital punishment, it is based on the ability of the threat of execution to serve as a deterrent. But if the murderer is obsessed with that strange desire to achieve fame, to be written about and pictured on the front pages of the newspapers of the land, and if the public's own ambivalence about capital punishment is fed with a public countdown-to-execution mentality, then is deterrence achieved? Could it not also be argued that murder, as a doorway to momentary notoriety, is actually encouraged? Beyond that, deterrence, even if it worked, is one thing, while assigning blame is quite another. When one takes away from one's view of final things the twin defenses of individual reward for one's good deeds and individual punishment for one's evil deeds, the concept of life after death fades visibly. But reward and punishment have both been compromised so totally that they are gone. Heaven and hell have departed with them.

Hell is in our society little more than a mild oath, often used quite inappropriately. What does "Oh, hell!" mean? What does it mean when one muses about "a cold day in hell"? When one says "my life is a living hell," it has nothing to do with life after death. Hell, as a concept, has been incorporated into life here and now. Heaven is not much different. Heaven has become only a synonym for fulfillment, for that quintessential moment when we can say, "It's like heaven to be with you," or "It really doesn't get much better than this."

But is a system of reward and punishment essential to life after death? Will religion survive without heaven as the ultimate reward or hell as the ultimate punishment? Is there any motivation for righteousness if no personal reward accompanies that righteousness? Is there any reason not to indulge the pleasures of the flesh if no punishment follows such indulgence? If the theistic parent deity in the sky can no longer be the content of the meaning of God, if heaven and hell are dismissed as mechanisms of medieval behavior control, can any religious value that was based upon those assumptions endure? Can a believer in exile hope for the permanence of his or her being amid the finite and transitory life that we have come to experience in our secular generation? Can the faith that emerges beyond the exile have a credible concept of life after death attached to it? Because of the enormous power this idea of immortality has had on our deepest sense of who we are, the believer in exile must explore this question. Can any of us with any degree of honesty continue to say the words, "I believe in the resurrection of the body and the life everlasting"? If we cannot, can we make any credible claim to being linked still to the faith story inaugurated by Jesus of Nazareth and called Christianity? If this book does not address these issues, it will have no credibility!

Yet addressing these issues means that I must begin by dismissing the supernatural, external God of theism in favor of an understanding of God as the Ground of all Being, the source of life, and the source of love. It means that I must dismiss the theistic concepts of God that traditionally have been used to interpret Jesus of Nazareth. We are driven to find another way to talk about the God presence that he so powerfully made manifest. It means that I must dismiss the idea of God as a record-keeping deity before whom I shall appear on the day of judgment to have my eternal destination announced. My heart will never worship that which my mind has rejected. To try to force me to do so not only would be dishonest, but also would mean living in spiritual denial. But, as I have tried to state in these pages, I do believe in God. I do enter God through the person of Jesus, whom I acknowledge as the ultimate revelation of God for me. I do find both a meaning in prayer and a basis for ethics inside this emerging belief system I am groping to describe.

Now, finally, I want to make it clear that it is out of this same understanding of both God and Christ that I can state that I believe I do now, and will forever, share in that ultimate gift of life that is both transcendent and eternal. It is my responsibility, therefore, to seek the words to talk about this aspect of my faith as a believer in exile. It is at this point that I have to speak in an intensely personal way.

I have lived long and well. I have not yet reached that biblical norm of threescore years and ten, but I am not far removed. In the course of those years, I have known heights and depths, community and loneliness, love and despair, life and death. I have entered expanded horizons and seen things beyond my ability to imagine or to articulate. I have also been driven into the contracted stance of a meager survival mentality in which my life was reduced to an existence so bare that it was hardly worth enduring. It is out of both the richness and the poverty of those experiences that I have come to think about, and even to place my hope in, a concept of eternal life.

I accept as a valid starting place most of those liberal efforts to capture some shred of credibility from the traditional view of life after death. I do not denigrate them because they are not enough. They add bits, even if tiny bits, to an unfolding pattern.

For example, I do think that we live through our children, our friends, and our associates far more powerfully than most of us can perceive or admit. I carry within myself, in ways I cannot conceive, not only the heritage of the gene pool that created me, but also the cultural and emotional history that shaped me. My venturesome great-great-grandfather, who left the County of Kent in the United Kingdom, where his family had moved after generations of farming the spongy bottom land (and hence the family name) of that flat and marshy part of England called East Anglia, surely found expression in me as I ventured out of the safety of the traditional ways of thinking to explore the anxieties of the unknown and the unfamiliar. My mother, who was removed from school six weeks into the ninth grade to help support her family, who was married at twenty to a man eighteen years her senior, who was widowed at thirty-five with three small children, who lacked both financial resources or marketable skills, gave me more than I can now quantify. She not only survived her circumstances, she also achieved aspects of life far beyond that which she or those who knew her might have been led to expect. Surely these qualities are still present deep in my own survival struggles and in those inner demands that drive me to achievement. This mother surely still lives in me. That is, at least, one tiny aspect of eternal life. It is not enough, however, and so I press on.

There is also some level of immortality in those whose lives each of us has shaped in relationships both professional and personal. In the course of my life I have been able to live inside the treasure of a mutual friendship with a number of people, both male and female. I have found these friendships to be incredibly life-giving. Not all of these friendships lasted for a lifetime. Not all of them were free of pain.

Perhaps six times or so in my life I have reached levels of pastoral intensity with a person living with a fatal diagnosis. Once two people step across the barrier of death emotionally and begin to engage with each other in that mysterious and feared place, a whole new landscape for sharing is discovered. In those circumstances one enters deeply into the very being of another. Those few people with whom I have had this privilege are still living as part of who I am. I remember especially a forty-four-year-old doctor who died of leukemia and a young mother of three who battled heroically a malignancy that threatened and finally destroyed her ability to raise those children.

I have had people living in the center of my life, sharing the realities of who I am, but my relationships with them ended in fracture, leaving me, and I suspect them, wounded emotionally for years. Yet I recognize that these friendships carried me in dark moments of my journey, and I am still grateful for that even as the pain of the fracture remains real. I can never remove those people from my life, for they have entered my being and they will always live in some way in me.

Sometimes the friendship has even been with a child. I remember especially a little girl, perhaps seven or eight years of age, when I first met her on a Sunday church visitation in Chatham, New Jersey. She was absolutely adorable in her long socks, pleated jumper skirt, and pigtails. I went down on one knee to speak to her eye to eye. Out of my experience as the father of three very special daughters, I said, "I bet your daddy really loves you." She replied, "My father is dead." I almost died at my insensitive assumption, but from that rocky beginning grew a friendship with a child who became special to me, and in some tiny way I suspect I helped to fill that enormous void where once a father stood in her life. She is today grown, married, and deeply invested in her practice of medicine. My contact with her has been minimal, almost nonexistent, during the past ten years. She did write when she was accepted at medical school in Kansas, and I received an invitation to her wedding, but the contact is very slight. Yet she is still a part of who I am, and I suspect I am a part of who she is. I will be part of who her children are, too, when they are born, though they may never hear my name spoken. Some piece of immortality resides in the depths of our relationships, and I do not for a moment minimize it. This is one more tiny element in my quest to understand eternal life. But eternal life is still more than this to me.

I have lived in the world of thought and ideas more than most, I suspect. In my profession, one learns what it is to enter another's mind, to be enriched by another's thinking, to feel partnered on another person's journey. I have taken other people intellectually into myself so that their thoughts have been able to live again. I think of John A. T. Robinson, with whom I have shared not only the bishop's office, but also the marginalization that comes to those ecclesiastical figures who refuse to be bound by the thought forms of the religious past. I think of John E. Hines, the presiding bishop of my church from 1964 to 1973, whose courage was matched only by his integrity and whose boldness to confront issues is surely part of who I am. I think of Michael Goulder, my English atheist friend, whose New Testament scholarship clicked so totally with the dawning insights of my study into the Jewishness of the Gospel narratives that reading his work was like having my entire mind mysteriously illumined. Two of these personal heroes and life-giving mentors have finished their course on this earth, but so deeply are they now a part of me that at times I still sense them conversing with me and entering my brain anew. To some degree I will also pass them on in life. There is just a bit of immortality in that. Yet all of these aspects of an interdependent immortality put together still constitute but the tiniest speck of what I mean by eternal life. If there is not more than this, there is no lasting power, no ultimate truth in the concept itself. So I press on.

I see every life as existing somewhere on the being-becoming spectrum. That is a deceiving spectrum, for we cannot know the depth of our own being until we can embrace the totality of our potential being. Apart from that vision, we are tempted to accept what is and to call it all that shall be. That would not be unlike a prepubescent twelve year old thinking that he or she has experienced all that life has to offer, only to live into the postpubescent experiences that no twelve year old could possibly contemplate. It would be like the brand new Oxford University graduate whom I heard speaking to the college porter while I was a visiting scholar in that great university. With degree in hand, she announced, "Now I've learned everything there is to know." I think the four most exciting and expansive years of my life were my first year at the university, my first year in graduate school at the theological seminary, my first year as an ordained priest, and my first year as a bishop. The common reality throughout these four experiences was that I could not have imagined them before I entered them. I was the first member of my family to attend a university. The incredible sweep of knowledge present in the university setting, the vastness of the library, the open doors into aspects of life that I had no previous way of imagining separated me forever from my past. The same was true when I embraced the experience of graduate school, where the scope of knowledge is actually limited but the depth of knowledge becomes limitless. My first year as a priest plunged me into a world I had observed often and talked about frequently but had never known and would never know from outside it. One who has not walked in the shoes of the ordained pastor will never understand what it means to be wrapped in the images of antiquity, to be related to by others out of experiences that you did not shape, to be loved and trusted far beyond any deserving on your part, and to be hated and feared beyond any cause to which you have contributed. People invest their lives in their designated spiritual leader, and the responsibility is awesome. My first year as a bishop multiplied that experience a hundredfold. I discovered that I lived inside God-sized expectations that I could never fulfill, and simultaneously I recognized that no one else could deal with those realities but me, for that is the nature of the episcopal office.

Each of these four expanding experiences made me aware that I do not know much about the ultimate size and shape of life and that frequently when I think I have approached life's limits, I am shocked to discover that I have simply reached another security barrier beyond which I must journey in a new and seemingly limitless expanse. I suppose my hope for and confidence in life after death or eternal life is nudged into reality and then fed by this realization.

My conviction about eternal life, however, is not just a pious dream standing in hope at what seems to be the ultimate barrier of death. It is also attached to my understanding of God as the Ground of all Being. I know what it means to have my life and my grasp on being shrink in the face of hostility, fear, and abuse. I also know what it means to have my life and my being expand to the place where hostility, fear, and abuse become so insignificant as to be dismissed as nothing. I will never forget the day on which I buried my first wife in St. Paul's Church in Richmond, Virginia. Seated beside her casket in the first pew with my three daughters prior to the start of the service, I was amazed to feel myself struck from behind across the shoulders by an elderly woman wielding an umbrella and to hear her say in words audible to all who were near, "You son of a bitch." She continued her strange journey out the side door of the church, where she walked through the waiting pallbearers. To these somewhat amazed persons, all but one of whom were clergy from the Diocese of Newark,[3] she said, "I've been wanting to tell that bastard what I think of him for years, and I finally got the chance."

She then disappeared out of my life, to remain unknown forever.

Following that service, I approached a young man in his early thirties who had served as the crucifer for the funeral. Since the service was on a Wednesday afternoon, I assumed that he must have taken off from his work to be part of that service, so I wanted to thank him. "Bishop," he said, "you don't know me, but I know you. I am a gay man. Most of the members of the choir today are members of Integrity. We would do anything for you because you have done so much for us." Integrity was the national Episcopal organization for gay and lesbian people. The experience of the woman with her umbrella paled when placed beside the words of this young man, whose name I also never knew. The expansion of life can be so incredible that those who would diminish another lose all ability to do so. That is part, a bigger part if you will, of what life is all about, life that is eternal.

I have but one other illustration. I am a person who knows what it means to be loved. I live inside the love of a wonderful wife, a supportive family, and a host of friends. I live with the appreciation of those who seem to feel that both the person I am and the words I speak and write have been a source of love and/or acceptance for them. As I receive affirmation and love from these sources, I discover that a new ability is born within me to be loving. I grasp a new dimension of life. I lay a new claim on what it means to be. This love emboldens me to press life's edges, to touch those dimensions of life that we call transcendence, to be introduced to that which is both infinite and beyond but that also seems to dwell in the heart of life. As I am empowered, affirmed, and called by the life-giving power of love to venture nearer and nearer to that ultimate core of being, I discover myself shedding limits, abandoning my security walls, and being freed to give more of my life and my being away. Remarkably, this giving experience is not accompanied by any sense of loss. I also discover an ability to accept and even to love what at an earlier and less secure time in my life I could not or would not have been able even to tolerate. This insight enables me to become newly aware of the infinite quality of that ultimate truth that I grasp only at its edges. It also makes me conscious of the infinite and sometimes even contradictory forms that this truth assumes when it journeys far from its source to the edges of life. This experience must not be reduced to something so fatuous as a recognition of the relativity of all propositional truths, nor does it lead to sacrificing truth for the sake of peace. Rather, this is a vision of truth that lies beyond every human manifestation. It is a call beyond the limits to which human judgment is attached, a call into the realm where truth is not bound, even by those who would dare to speak of it. It is a mystical experience of escaping boundaries. The God that I define as the Ground of Being seems to meet me in this place, and finitude fades into infinity. My quest to embrace a sense of eternity takes a quantum leap forward in this realization. But once again, that is not the end of my exploration.

I move next to explore my human experience that love is the power giving birth to life. Love enables being to emerge in each of us. When that love is total, or when it reaches toward totality, the journey into being can and does occur. That journey for me also becomes a journey into a life without limits because it is a journey into God, who is without limits. This God is not even bound by the limits of my words about God that I am using at this moment.

This sense of God as a presence, expansive, mysterious, and calling, is what gives meaning to the holiness that the biblical record suggests was the secret to the meaning of the life of Jesus of Nazareth. Jesus is portrayed as having the capacity to live, the ability to love, and the courage to be to such a degree that people found it easy to record him as saying, "He who has seen me has seen the father" (John 14:9). This is also why others could say of him, "In Christ God was reconciling" (2 Cor. 5:19).

The being of Jesus touched, opened, and revealed the Ground of Being. When my being is enhanced by love, called to a new reality by love, introduced through love to limitless freedom, then I believe that I have touched that which is timeless, eternal, and real. My confidence in eternal life, life beyond the limits of finitude and death, is found in that experience, and my doorway into that experience is still the one who, for me, seems to have embodied it, Jesus whom I call Christ. In the community of people who constitute themselves as disciples of this Jesus, I still experience, above all else, the call of this Christ to live, to love, and to be. That is what it means to me to live "in Christ," a phrase Paul used constantly. So my doorway into and my hope for life that is transcendent and eternal is located at this point. I stand here convinced that there is something real beyond my ultimate limits. I have but tasted it. So I embrace this vision and live in this hope.

I also dismiss as all but meaningless the traditional content that the religious institutions of the West have imposed upon the concept of life after death. I have no interest in a system of rewards and punishments. I do not see the purpose of life after death to be that of motivating behavior in the here and now. I can live without any sense of heaven as a place of reward or hell as a place of punishment. But I do believe that life is infinite, and I do believe that we are called to explore its depths and to drink deeply of its sweetness. I do believe that life here is but a limited and finite image of full life, which is limitless and infinite. I do assert that one prepares for eternity not by being religious and keeping the rules, but by living fully, loving wastefully, and daring to be all that each of us has the capacity to be. I also assert that making it possible for everyone else to live, to love, and to be is the only mission that Christian people possess. Our task is not to convert; our task is to call people into the depths of their own capacity to be. I discover that I, as a believer in exile, must leave behind most of the baggage of heaven and hell, all of the theistic understandings of God, and, most especially, those legendary and fanciful attempts to interpret Jesus as the incarnation of a theistic external deity. But I will journey as a Christian beyond the exile. I will do so as a believer who lives in the being of God, who loves with the love of God, and who anticipates some sense of eternity in which my being, differentiated and defined by the power of love, is joined with the being of others who are at one with the Ground of all Being. The God I meet in my depths becomes the God who is infinite, boundless, transcendent, immanent, and real. To the degree that I know this God, I know the meaning of life. In that faith I believe that I discover life that is eternal. Is that sufficient to say that Christianity redefined, freed from many of its supernatural claims of the past, but still recognizable, will survive the exile? I think it is. But time alone will conclude whether or not my judgment is correct. I, however, will live my life as if it is.

Epilogue: A Final Word

So our journey into a new way of understanding our faith comes to its conclusion. I summarize that journey by looking again at the words of the creed, and I state the conclusions to which this study has led me.

I believe that there is a transcending reality present in the very heart of life. I name that reality God.

I believe that this reality has a bias toward life and wholeness and that its presence is experienced as that which calls us beyond all of our fearful and fragile human limits.

I believe that this reality can be found in all that is but that it reaches self-consciousness and the capability of being named, communed with, and recognized only in human life.

I believe that heaven, the domain in which this reality has traditionally been domiciled, is not a place but a symbol standing for the limitlessness of Being itself.

I believe that this realm of heaven is entered whenever the barriers that seem to bind human life into something less than that for which it is capable are set aside.

I believe in Jesus, called Messiah, or Christ.

I believe that in his life this transcendent reality has been revealed so completely that it caused people to refer to him as God's son, even God's *only* son. The burning God intensity was so real in him that I look at his life and say, "In you I see the meaning of God, so for me you are both Lord and Christ."

I believe that Jesus was a God presence, a powerful experience of the reality of that Ground of Being undergirding us all at the very depths of life. That is why the earliest Christians interpreted this Christ experience in the language of theism. That was the only language in which they knew how to speak of God.

Since their assumption was that Jesus was God in a human form, they attributed to him the ability to do whatever they believed God alone was able to do. He could create out of nothing, so they wrote that he could feed the multitude with only five loaves. He could command the forces of nature to obey him, and so the storm was stilled. He had power over demonic forces, and so he exorcised demons. He could teach with divine authority, and so it was said of him that he did not teach like the scribes. Since God's presence on earth was a sign that God's rule or realm was being established, they attributed to Jesus the treasured signs of that kingdom. So it was that people touched by this Jesus described his life in terms of the ancient expectations of what would mark the coming of God and God's kingdom. Their narratives depicting the signs of God were attached to the remembered life of Jesus of Nazareth.

When this life came to its violent conclusion, it was said of him that this was but the prelude to the full establishment of God's kingdom. So his death on the cross was portrayed as his living out that final conflict between good and evil that would be fought at the battle of Armageddon. There the goodness of God was snuffed out by the evil of humanity. The forces of evil were destined to prevail momentarily, and so after the battle was over, it was said in their sacred sources that darkness must reign over the whole earth for three days. Then at the dawn after the third day, proclaimed these Jewish legends, the heavens would open and the Kingdom of God would emerge anew. The power of death and evil would be broken forever. That day on which God's kingdom dawned would be called the first day of the new creation.

So it was that these traditions were wrapped around the written life of Jesus, and it was said of him that when he died, darkness covered the whole earth. Then, at the crack of dawn, after three days, the tomb of death was opened and the risen Christ came forth, and that day was called the first day of the new creation and was observed on the first day of every week. The Kingdom of God had dawned in Jesus, or at least the first-fruits of that kingdom had been experienced. The reality being proclaimed was that the being of God could not be terminated and that Jesus, in some way, brought this God to us. So it was said of him that Jesus triumphed over death, and that story was told in terms of ancient Jewish symbols.

All of this was but the interpretative framework in which the God experience in Jesus of Nazareth came to be understood. It was an interpretation based upon the theistic concepts of God present in that era of human history. This language employed the vocabulary of a premodern, nonscientific world. There was no other alternative for processing the God experience in the first century of this common era. That interpretive language was then incorporated into our creeds, our liturgies, our prayers, and our theological concepts. It is this language that has become all but nonsensical. The frame of reference that produced those under-standings of reality has disintegrated. The words, the concepts, and the theological reasoning by which they interpreted their experiences have all become empty and meaningless. To reject that interpretive language was inevitable, but to reject the interpretive language is not to deny the power of the experience. So I have sought to achieve this separation, to discern the God presence met in Jesus, and to talk about it outside the theistic language of the past.

Jesus was said to have called the egotistical Peter into wholeness; a corrupt tax collector, Levi Matthew, into generosity; the short Zacchaeus into an expanded life; the mysterious Mary Magdalene into the apostleship of sharing in the resurrection; the doubting Thomas into a life of faith; the angry John, whose nickname meant "Son of Thunder," into being the apostle of love. It was as if the being of Jesus was limitless. The more he gave his being away, the more he had being to give. So the endless depths of being, the being of God, if you will, appeared to be present in him.

The limits that defined human life also fell before him. At the end of his life even the barrier dividing the finite from the infinite seemed to disappear. Death is the name for this ultimate symbol of human limitation. The Ground of Being entered the tomb and emerged with alleluias ringing, for death was conquered. The final limit on human life was broken.

Yet this Jesus had his roots in human history, a fact that was validated by linking his death to a specific time when Judea was governed by a specific procurator and the Temple of Jerusalem was ruled by a specific high priest. His full humanity was affirmed in that he died. Christian theology was born in the attempt to make sense of his death. His access to God was asserted when it was said of him that, when he ascended, he sent the Holy Spirit to abide with his followers forever. The universality of that Spirit was symbolized when the story recounted how this Spirit fell upon Jews and Gentiles, men and women.

The Spirit became a sign of the intrinsic unity of all human life, creating a community beyond every human difference. The defining marks of the past—tribe, language, race, gender, or even sexual orientation—faded. Inevitably, so will the most difficult and painful of all aspects of human behavior, namely, those barriers erected by the religious convictions of human beings. For a brief reading of human history will reveal that the religious systems of human beings, more often than not, have set the members of the human family against one another in a fratricidal, killing struggle.

So it needs to be said clearly that the God presence of this Jesus will lead us ultimately beyond every religious definition. Indeed, it will lead beyond Jesus himself. That becomes essential to human development whenever our idolatrous convictions identify the messenger of God with God. So the Ground of Being will finally be worshiped apart from any system of religious thought. It is a startling but real insight into the future of worship.

I believe in that gift of the Spirit who was called "the giver of life." Once we located God only externally and called this God the Father Almighty. Next, we located this God in Jesus, and we called him the Son Incarnate. Now we locate God in every person, and we call this God the Holy Spirit. I believe that this Spirit inevitably creates a community of faith that will come, in time, to open this world to God as the very Ground of its life and Being. We call that community "one" because the source of life is one. We call it "holy" because the holy God is seen through it. We call it "catholic" because it is universal and must embrace the whole creation and all the families of faith. We call it "apostolic" because it was recognized as present in Jesus, and it flowed to us through the witness of his apostles and disciples. That is our point of entry. It will not be our conclusion.

But we also name it as inclusive because nothing can separate us from the Ground of Being or from those whose lives share in the Being of God. Not even the name of Jesus must be allowed to do that.

I believe, therefore, that being in touch with the Ground of Being creates the universal communion of saints, the forgiveness of sins, the reality of resurrection, and the doorway into the life that is everlasting. Those may not be the words I would now choose to use to describe the reality to which they point, but once they have escaped their idolatrous literalization, those words will do. The experience of God as the Ground of Being has a way of breaking open every human word and making it usable again. Human language is so inadequate. All it can do is to describe human experience, but the God who is the source of life constantly breaks into human experience. Human experience can never be exhausted by language. Language can never do more than point to that which it seeks to describe. It can never capture truth. Religion is, therefore, not what we have always thought it to be. Religion is not a system of belief. It is not a catalogue of revealed truth. It is not an activity designed to control behavior, to reward virtue, and to punish vice. Religion is, rather, a human attempt to process the God experience, which breaks forth from our own depths and wells up constantly within us. We must lay down, therefore, the primitive claims we have made for our religious traditions. None of them is drawn from otherworldly revelations. None of them is inerrant or infallible. None of them represents the only way to God. None of them can be used legitimately to coerce or compel another to belief. All evangelical and missionary activities designed to convert the heathen are base born. They are the expressions of our sense of superiority and our hostility toward those who are different. The only divine mission in life that the Church of the future could possibly have is to open people to a recognition that the ground of their very being is holy and that when they are in touch with that holy Ground of Being, they can share in God's creation by giving life, love, and being to others. That is the task of those who claim to be God bearers. The Christians of the world are not here to build institutions, to convert other people, or even to claim that we can speak for God. Those aspects of our religious heritage must be sacrificed as the premodern misunderstandings of our primitive history. We are now exile people.

So what the exile has done is to free us from the killing, idolatrous limits of the religions of the world, including our own Christianity. The gods of those religious systems have also died. The god of church, synagogue, and temple is no more. The magical, personalistic, manipulative, supernatural, and sometimes vindictive power of these deities has been used historically not to enhance life but to bless the status quo, to increase priestly power, and to support those claims of state that have expanded the wealth and power of the ruling classes.

The God who is the Ground of Being cannot be so owned. God is a universal presence undergirding all of life. God does not bless and curse individuals according to an imposed prescription of conduct. God, the source of life, calls us all to live fully. God, the source of love, calls us all to love wastefully. God, the Ground of Being, calls us all to have the courage to be ourselves. So when we live, love, and have the courage to be, we are engaged in worship, we are expanding our humanity, we are breaking out of our barriers.

That is the call of the God who lives beyond the exile. It is that God to whom or to which all religious institutions must point. It is the call of this God that will carry us into a living worship in the postmodern world. That will be the basis of the faith that will sustain me as I live in my postmodern world.

Those who think that Christianity consists of a supernatural deity who invades the world periodically, who works through a virgin birth, a physical resuscitation, and a cosmic ascension, will find all that I say a threat to their faith. Those who believe that creeds are literally true, Bibles are inerrant, or popes are infallible will find me a challenge to their presuppositions. Those who have made the consensus of yesterday their only understanding of truth will call this heresy. Those who cannot think of God outside the categories of theism will call me an a-theist. I expect to hear such charges as these more than once.

But that religious understanding is doomed to die, no matter how frantically or hysterically people seek to defend it. It will not survive. For countless numbers who live in the Christian world, it ceased long ago to be compelling. I write for those for whom it has died already. I write to call those who are in exile from the ancient understandings of faith into some new possibilities. If they can hear the call, respond to it, claim it anew, and walk as believers beyond the exile, then my purpose will have been achieved.

Is my reformulation of Christianity adequate for our new world? I would be surprised if it is judged to be so. It is at least the best I know how to offer at this moment, given when I live and how far into the future I can see. But if I were asked to bet on what will happen tomorrow, my best guess would be that my approach will prove to be not too radical, as my critics will claim, but rather not nearly radical enough. I suspect that the next generation might even dismiss me as an old-fashioned religious man who could not quite cut the umbilicus to the past in order to enter the future.

In less than a hundred years I am certain that the shape of religion in general and Christianity in particular will be clear. The new role and purpose of the Church and the continuing meaning of liturgy will be apparent. Then the world can judge my contribution as to whether it destroyed the old or created the new. That will not be up to me to say. I am content to let the passage of time make that determination.

If there are those who do not believe that the Church of yesterday can any longer contain those of us who carry within ourselves the Church of tomorrow, then I am ready to engage in that debate in any public arena that they choose. I prefer, however, simply to be a bit of leaven in the lump that will help the Church to evolve into its future shape.

I am first, last, and always a believer. I define myself theologically as a believer who lives in exile. I have lived and worshiped as a believer. I shall continue to do so and to be so until the day I die. When that moment comes, I expect to enter even more deeply into the reality of the God in whom I have lived and moved and had my being.

I am therefore at peace.

Shalom.

Notes

PREFACE

1. *This Hebrew Lord: A Bishop's Search for the Authentic Jesus* (San Francisco: Harper & Row, 1974). This book was reissued by Harper San Francisco in 1988 and again in 1993 and as of this date is still in print.
2. Monophysitism held that in the incarnate Christ there was but a single nature, and that a divine one. In popular Christianity the assumption is that Jesus was divine and not human. Classical theology tried to hold the two natures, divine and human, in a tension that has not always been successful.
3. The text is translated "anointed one," which was, of course, the meaning of *mashiach*.

4. This book is out of print today except in Australia and New Zealand, where it has been republished in an updated version by Desbooks, Thornberry, Australia (1992), with a foreword by the former primate of the Anglican Church in New Zealand, the Right Reverend Sir Paul Reeves. Copies are available in the United States from Christianity for the Third Millennium, Inc., P.O. Box 69, Morristown, NJ 07963–0069.

5. Matthew implied a physically resuscitated body only in his story about the risen Christ appearing to the women in the garden. That, however, is a deliberate change in Mark's meaning that Matthew was copying. Luke also copied the Marcan story but the women did not see Jesus in Luke's account. Matthew's other story of the resurrected Jesus meeting the disciples on the mountain in Galilee referred not to a physical Jesus but a Jesus who appeared out of heaven, transformed.

6. All five of these books are still in print and are listed in the bibliography.

7. The Protestant Episcopal Theological Seminary in Alexandria, Virginia. Dr. Stanley taught theology there for over twenty years.

8. These videos are available through Christianity for the Third Millennium, Inc.

CHAPTER ONE

1. Psalm 139, especially verses 7–12.

2. It needs to be said that in its day the image of God as Father in the Bible carried with it the positive attributes of caring, loving unconditionally, and reliability. That is not enough, however, to save it from its patriarchal overlay.

3. From the play *J. B.* by Archibald MacLeish. See bibliography.

4. Although leukemia is technically also a tumor, in the public mind it is distinct from a malignant or a benign mass, and therefore I refer to it separately.

5. Quoted from the *Selected Lectures of Robert G. Ingersoll*. Details in bibliography.

6. The book of Acts suggests that Jesus was buried by those who crucified him (Acts 13:29). If that is so, his body might have been dumped into the Valley of Hinnom and would have been allowed either to burn or to decay. If this is true, it might have provided the kernel of truth behind the creedal phrase "he descended into hell." For the Valley of Hinnom (called Gehenna) was the analogy by which Sheol or the place of departed spirits and later hell with its fires was understood, or at least these definitions interpenetrated one another. In 1 Peter the idea that Jesus preached to the departed spirits in Sheol entered the Christian tradition (1 Peter 4:6). Interestingly, most of the New Testament references to the fires of hell are in Matthew's Gospel.

7. In *Resurrection: Myth or Reality?* I documented these internal contradictions in part 2, particularly chapter 9.

8. This council determined the boundaries of the theological debate over the nature of the Christ "complete in Godhead, complete in manhood, truly God, truly man, of one substance with the father as regards his godhead and at the same time of one substance with us as regards his manhood." The entire text of the Chalecedonian formula is printed in the 1979 Book of Common Prayer on p. 864.

9. Arius argued that Christ was of *like* substance with God; Athanasius that Christ was of *the same* substance with God. On that definition creedal orthodoxy turned.

CHAPTER TWO

1. Hipparchus died ca. 127 B.C.E. He is thought to have done his work between 146 and 127 B.C.E. Ptolemy died ca. 151 C.E. and did his work between ca. 127 and 151 C.E.

2. Karen Armstrong, *A History of God,* p. 19. This phrase is sometimes rendered "Lord of Hosts." It refers, however, to a divine military force. See bibliography.

3. From *Conversation at Midnight,* by Edna St. Vincent Millay (1892–1950), pt. 4, sec. 1. Spoken by Ricardo. The exact quotation is "Man has never been the same since God died. He has taken it very hard. . . . He gets along pretty well, as long as it is daylight, . . . but it's all no use. The moment it begins to get dark, as soon as it is night, he goes out and howls over the grave of God." See bibliography.

4. If the human being is defined as a creature capable of language, then the later date is appropriate. If Homo erectus can be called human, then the earlier date is more likely to be correct.

5. *The Demon-Haunted World: Science as a Candle in the Dark* (1995). See Sagan in the bibliography.

6. To the degree that western thought has now permeated the entire world, this is now the reality of thinking people the world over.

CHAPTER THREE

1. *Midrash and Lection in Matthew*, and *Luke: A New Paradigm* (2 vols.) are my favorite Goulder texts. See bibliography.

2. Richard Swinburne, *Coherence of Theism*, p. 1. See bibliography.

CHAPTER FOUR

1. Socrates was executed ca. 399 B.C.E.

2. The publication of *Leben Jesu* by David Frederich Strauss in 1835–36 brought the mythical and legendary aspects of the Gospel stories to public attention. This book was published in English in 1846 under the title *The Life of Jesus Critically Revealed*. See bibliography. Julius Wellhausen (1844–1918) pushed this study forward with his four-document theory of the formation of the Torah.

3. Bultmann's major works advancing this thesis were *Die Geschichte der Synoptischen Tradition* (1921), published in English as *The History of the Synoptic Tradition* (1968), and *Jesu* (1926). *Jesus Christ and Mythology* was its English title (1960). His Gifford Lectures of 1955 were published under the title *History and Eschatology*. He lived from 1884 to 1976.

4. See especially Whitehead's books *Religion in the Making* (1926) and *Process and Reality* (1929).

5. See *Letters and Papers from Prison* by Dietrich Bonhoeffer, edited by Eberhard Bethge. See especially letters from 16 July onward.

6. Regius Professor of Divinity at Oxford Dr. Keith Ward has made the point (in conversation) that these Tillichian concepts can be found substantially in the writings of Thomas Aquinas. He emphasizes that in the world of academic theology, even the supposedly modern concepts have been around for quite a while.

7. This concept permeates the writings of Tillich, but it is best expressed in his three-volume *Systematic Theology,* published between 1953 and 1964. See bibliography.

8. Gen. 1:27 RSV, with masculine words for God changed.

CHAPTER FIVE

1. In *Liberating the Gospels,* I documented the dependence of Matthew on Paul (see chapter 7) and the dependence of Luke on the book of Deuteronomy (see chapter 9).

2. See *Born of a Woman* for documentation. No birth account appears in either Paul or Mark, the only parts of the New Testament written before the ninth decade.

3. See *Resurrection: Myth or Reality?* for documentation. The first account of a physical body associated with the resurrection is in Matthew 28 (the story of the women grasping Jesus' feet in the garden). Both Mark, on whom Matthew is dependent, and Luke, who was also dependent on Mark, disagree with this Matthean expansion of Mark's story. If that is discounted, then Luke, in the late 80s at the earliest, would be the first New Testament story of a physical resuscitation as the meaning of Easter.

4. See Jaroslav Pelikan, *The Emergence of the Catholic Tradition, 100–600.*

5. I will provide textual support for this claim later in this chapter. See endnote 9.

6. Some early manuscripts omit the words "Son of God," but, whether stated or not, this was Mark's operating conviction, as his text reveals time after time.

7. The fourth Gospel portrays two of John's disciples, one of whom he identified as Andrew, Simon Peter's brother, leaving John and following Jesus as a result of the baptism and John's witness as to Jesus' identity (see John 1:29–42). There was a clear connection between John's movement and Jesus' movement, which would seem to indicate that the baptism of Jesus was known in both camps.

8. Many New Testament scholars do not affirm the Pauline authorship of Colossians.

9. See Rom. 4:24, 8:11, 10:9; 1 Cor. 6:14, 15:15; Gal. 1:1; 1 Thess. 1:10 for the use of the word *raised*. See Rom. 8:34; Phil. 2:9; Col. 3:1 for Paul's sense that resurrection was into God, not back to life on this earth. The reader needs to be aware that when these verses were written by Paul, there was no tradition of the ascension as separate from the resurrection. That would not develop until the ninth decade. Note also that Paul says (1 Cor. 15:1–6) that the appearance of the risen Lord to him was like every other appearance save that it was the last. I know of no one who argues that Paul saw a physically resuscitated Jesus.

10. I develop this thought process much more fully in my book *Resurrection: Myth or Reality?*

CHAPTER SIX

1. This is the burden of the argument in Paul's epistle to the Galatians and the principal argument of Romans 1–8.

2. Paul had started this process by declaring that Christ, our paschal lamb, has been sacrificed for us (1 Cor. 5:7). Paul, however, did not spell out the narrative details of his death as occurring during the Passover celebration.

3. Peter Brown of Princeton University, in his book *The Body and Society: Men, Women, and Sexual Renunciation in Early Christianity,* makes the point that Augustine's concept of the "fall of man" was his way of individualizing the catastrophe through which he lived—the fall of the Roman Empire. The symbol of human perfection as the sexless woman or the nonpenetrated woman was an individualized symbol of the redeemed or nonpenetrated empire.

4. Karen Armstrong, in her book *A History of God*, contends that this was the particular emphasis only of the Western Church, not of the Eastern tradition. I do not argue with

that, but since we are the recipients of Western Christianity, this has been our inheritance.

5. From *The Confessions*, bk. 1, chap. 1.

6. *The Selfish Gene* by Richard Dawkins. See bibliography.

CHAPTER SEVEN

1. When Paul wrote I Thessalonians he did not use capital letters since they were used nowhere at that time. When we capitalize these words today we do it in the service of a doctrinal development that Paul never knew. To seek to capture Paul's original sense I have left spirit in the lowercase.

2. Most scholars believe that 1 Corinthians is a composite of more than one original letter written by Paul.

3. By the time Luke wrote Acts circa 95 C.E., Holy Spirit had become distinct. I will capitalize it in those instances.

4. Many scholars believe that Philippians was Paul's last epistle. It is usually dated around 62–63 C.E.

5. Midrash or midrashic writing was the Jewish practice of retelling sacred stories of the past to illumine a sacred experience in the present. For a much fuller exposition of these themes, see my books *Born of a Woman: A Bishop Rethinks the Virgin Birth and the Role of Women in a Male-Dominated Church* and *Liberating the Gospels: Reading the Bible with Jewish Eyes*.

6. For a fuller explanation of the relationship between the forty days Jesus spent in the wilderness and the forty years Moses spent in the wilderness, see my *Liberating the Gospels,* especially the chapter on Matthew.

CHAPTER EIGHT

1. The story of the feeding of the four thousand is told also in Matthew, but it is omitted from the narratives of Luke and

John. Some New Testament professors suggest that Mark duplicated the story so that a eucharistic type of celebration could be provided for gentiles as well as for Jews—a speculative, theory, I suggest.

2. The first genealogy was in Matthew 1:2–16. The two genealogies are quite inconsistent at a number of points. See my analysis of these differences in *Born of a Woman*.

3. *The Eternal Now* was the title of Tillich's third book in a *Trilogy of Sermons*. See bibliography.

4. This is a disputed text and may well not be original. It does not, in fact, occur in the earliest texts of John. It seems to have been a free-floating story. In some ancient manuscripts it appears in John after 7:36 or after 21:25. In others it follows the text of Luke 21:38.

5. I suppose one could say that his words to Peter, "Get thee behind me, Satan," were berating. But they are presented in the Gospel as a rebuke to enable Peter to grow. Peter's subsequent behavior does not reveal a berated or diminished disciple (Mark 8:33–34).

6. Many will be surprised to see John A. T. Robinson described as a mystic. That was, however, my primary impression of him, both in our personal contact and through his books. He struggled, as I do, with words because words are so inadequate to grasp the infinite quality of his God-filled experience.

7. "The man for others" is from *Honest to God;* "the human face of God" is from his book by that title.

8. From a prayer attributed to St. Francis (1181–1226).

CHAPTER NINE

1. The Lord's Prayer can be transformed when its words are understood symbolically rather than literally. That is what I

sought to do so many years ago when I wrote *Honest Prayer* (New York: Seabury Press, 1973).

CHAPTER TEN

1. *The Pensacola New Journal*, May 16, 1997, written by Alice Crann.

2. Those quoted, in order, are the Reverend John Kilpatrick, pastor of Brownsville Assembly of God, Pensacola; the Reverend Marion L. Soards, professor of New Testament Studies at Louisville (KY) Seminary and a minister of the Presbyterian Church, U.S.A.; and the Right Reverend Charles Duvall, Episcopal bishop of the Diocese of the Central Gulf Coast.

3. *Homosexuality and the Bible* (1997) by Dr. Walter Wink, professor of biblical interpretation, Auburn Theological Seminary, New York (published independently).

4. These concepts were first stated in a public lecture by the Right Reverend Michael Ingham, Bishop of Westminster, in British Columbia.

5. The initial impetus to explore this line of thinking came from Professor Keith Ward of Oxford. I commend his book, *A Vision to Pursue* (London: SCM Press, 1991), for his explication of the way these principles might be employed.

6. Don Cupitt, *Solar Ethics* (London: Xpress, 1993). Don Cupitt and I might disagree on the ultimate value that we assign to the human experience of being, living, loving, and giving, but we both are able to avoid the negativity of an ethical system based on reward and punishment.

CHAPTER ELEVEN

1. The word *ecclesiastical* comes from the Greek word ἐκκλησία, or *ecclesia,* which means "called out."

2. Unless otherwise noted, all hymns and lyrics are from Anglican hymnals published in the 1980s.

3. From the Anglican hymnal of 1940.

4. "Love Lifted Me" begins with the self-deprecating words "I was sinking deep in sin." "Higher Ground" begins, "Lord, lift me up and let me stand by faith on heaven's tableland." Both are found in most Protestant evangelical hymnals.

5. This was the theme song of George Beverly Shea of the Billy Graham Evangelistic Association.

6. The Most Reverend Richard Holloway.

7. Sometimes spelled miters.

CHAPTER TWELVE

1. March 19, 1994.

2. I discussed the reasons for this removal of the Passover meal from the Last Supper in *Liberating the Gospels: Reading the Bible with Jewish Eyes.* I note, further, that the fourth Gospel, John, also argues against that identification.

3. According to the *Shorter Oxford Dictionary* (1976), *com* means "with" and *panis* is "bread."

CHAPTER THIRTEEN

1. *Time,* March 24, 1997, 70–78.

2. I think especially of *Les Miserables, A Tale of Two Cities,* and *David Copperfield.*

3. That one was the Reverend Loren Mead, D.D.

Bibliography

Altizer, Thomas J. J. *Radical Theology and the Death of God.* New York, 1966.

———. *The Gospel of Christian Atheism.* London: Collins, 1967.

Armstrong, Karen. *A History of God.* New York: Ballantine Books, 1993.

Augustine, Bishop of Hippo. *The Confessions of St. Augustine.* Translated by Rex Warner. New York: New American Library, 1963.

Barbour, Ian. *Religion in the Age of Science.* San Francisco: HarperSanFrancisco, 1990.

Barth, Karl. *The Epistle to the Romans.* Translated by E. C. Hoskyns. Oxford: Oxford Univ. Press, 1938.

Bonhoeffer, Dietrich. *Letters and Papers from Prison.* Edited by E. Bethge. New York: Macmillan, 1972.

Borg, Marcus. *Meeting Jesus Again for the First Time*. San Francisco: HarperSanFrancisco, 1994.

Bornkamm, Gunther. *Jesus of Nazareth*. London: Hodder & Stoughton, 1973.

Brown, Peter. *The Body and Society: Men, Women, and Sexual Renunciation in Early Christianity*. New York: Columbia Univ. Press, 1988.

Bultmann, Rudolf K. *History and Eschatology*. Edinburgh: Univ. of Edinburgh Press, 1957.

———. *The History of the Synoptic Tradition*. London: Blackwell, 1968.

———. *Jesus Christ and Mythology*. London: SCM, 1960.

———. *New Testament and Mythology*. London: SCM, 1985.

Campbell, Joseph. *The Hero with a Thousand Faces*. Princeton: Princeton Univ. Press, 1949.

———. *The Power of Myth with Bill Moyers*. New York: Doubleday, 1989.

Chadwick, Henry. *The Early Church*. 1967. Reprint, London: Penguin, 1993.

Crossan, John Dominic. *Jesus: A Revolutionary Biography*. San Francisco: HarperSanFrancisco, 1994.

———. *Who Killed Jesus?* San Francisco: HarperSanFrancisco, 1995.

Cupitt, Don. *The New Christian Ethics*. London: SCM, 1988.

———. *The Sea of Faith*. London: BBC, 1984.

———. *What Is a Story?* London: SCM, 1995.

———. *Solar Ethics*. London: London Xpress, 1993.

———. *Taking Leave of God*. London: SCM, 1980.

Darwin, Charles R. *The Origin of Species by Means of Natural Selection*. 1859. Reprint, London: Harmondsworth/Penguin, 1988.

Davies, Paul. *God and the New Physics*. London: Dent, 1984.

———. *The Mind of God*. New York: Simon & Schuster, 1992.

Dawkins, Richard. *The Blind Watchmaker*. London: Harmondsworth, 1991.

———. *The Selfish Gene*. London: Granada, 1978.

Dickens, Charles. *Tale of Two Cities*. New York: J. H. Seares, 1925.

———. *David Copperfield*. Oxford: Oxford Univ. Press, 1955.

Freud, Sigmund. *The Future of an Illusion*. Translated by W. D. Robson-Scott. 1927. Reprint, London: Hogarth, 1962.

Funk, Robert W. *Honest to Jesus*. San Francisco: HarperSanFrancisco, 1996.

Geering, Lloyd G. *Creating the New Ethic*. Wellington, New Zealand: St. Andrews Trust, 1991.

Goulder, Michael D. *Luke, a New Paradigm*. 2 vols. Sheffield: Sheffield Academic Press, 1989.

———. *Midrash and Lection in Matthew*. London: SPCK, 1974.

Goulder, Michael D., and John Hick. *Why Believe in God?* London: SCM, 1983.

Hampson, Daphne. *After Christianity*. London: SCM, 1996.

Hanh, Thich Nhat. *Living Buddha, Living Christ*. New York: Riverhead Books, 1995.

Hart, David. *Faith in Doubt*. London: SPCK, 1993.

Hartshorne, Charles. *Aquinas to Whitehead: Seven Centuries of Metaphysics of Religion*. Marquette WI: Marquette Univ. Press, 1976.

———. *Man's Vision of God and the Logic of Theism*. New York: Harper & Brothers, 1941.

Hawking, Stephen. *A Brief History of Time*. London: Bantham, 1989.

Hefner, Philip. "Biblical Perspectives on the Fall and Original Sin." *Zygon: A Journal of Religion and Science* 28, no. 1 (March 1993).

Hick, John. *Death and Eternal Life*. Basingstoke: Macmillan, 1985.

———. *The Myth of Christian Uniqueness*. London: SCM Press, 1988.

Hugo, Victor. *Les Miserables*. New York: Penguin Classics, 1976.

Ingersoll, Robert G. *The Selected Lectures of Robert G. Ingersoll*. New York: Wiley, 1938.

James, William. *The Varieties of Religious Experience*. 1902. Reprint, with introduction by Martin Marty, New York and London: Penguin, 1985.

Jung, Carl G. *The Archetypes of the Collective Unconscious*. London: Routledge, 1990.

———. *Man and His Symbols*. London: Arkana, 1990.

———. *Modern Man in Search of a Soul*. London: Routledge and Kegan Paul, 1961.

———. *Memories, Dreams and Reflections*. New York: Vintage Books, 1965.

———. *Psychology and Religion*. New Haven: Yale Univ. Press, 1938.

Kant, Immanuel. *Religion within the Limits of Reason*. New York: Harper, 1960.

Keck, Leander E. "Wanted: Theological Renewal and Reform." *Circuit Rider* (April 1993).

Küng, Hans. *Does God Exist?* London: Collins, 1980.

———. *On Being a Christian*. New York: Doubleday, 1976.

MacLeish, Archibald. *J. B.: A Play in Verse*. New York and London: Samuel French, 1956.

MacQuarrie, John. *Thinking About God*. London: SCM, 1975.

———. *Principles of Christian Theology*. New York: Charles Scribner & Sons, 1966.

Millay, Edna St. Vincent. *Conversation at Midnight*. New York and London: Harper & Brothers, 1937.

Moore, George F. *Judaism in the First Centuries of the Christian Era*. 3 vols. Cambridge: Harvard Univ. Press, 1927–1930.

Moule, Charles F. D. *The Origins of Christology*. Cambridge: Cambridge Univ. Press, 1977.

Niebuhr, Reinhold. *The Nature and Destiny of Man*. Vol. 1, *Human Nature*. Vol. 2, *Human Destiny*. New York: Scribners, 1941, 1943.

Nock, Arthur D. *Early Gentile Christianity and Its Hellenistic Background*. 1904. Reprint, New York: Harper, 1964.

Ogden, Schubert M. *Christ without Myth*. New York: Harper & Brothers, 1961.

Otto, Rudolf. *The Idea of the Holy*. Oxford: Oxford Univ. Press, 1923.

Pagels, Elaine. *The Gnostic Gospels*. New York: Random House, 1979.

————. *Adam, Eve and the Serpent*. New York: Random House, 1988.

Pannenberg, Wolfhart. *The Apostle's Creed*. London: SCM, 1972.

Peacocke, Arthur. *A Theology for a Scientific Life*. London: SCM, 1993.

Pelikan, Jaroslav. *A History of the Development of Doctrine*. Vol. 1, *The Emergence of the Catholic Tradition 100–600*. Vol. 2, *The Growth of Medieval Theology 600–1300*. Chicago and London: Univ. of Chicago Press, 1971, 1978.

Pike, James A. *A Time for Christian Candor*. New York: Harper & Row, 1964.

Polkinghorne, John. *Science and Creation*. London: SPCK, 1988.

Robinson, John A. T. *Explorations into God*. London: SCM, 1962.

————. *Honest to God*. London: SCM, 1963.

————. *The Human Face of God*. Philadelphia: Westminster, 1974.

Sagan, Carl. *The Demon-Haunted World: Science as a Candle in the Dark*. New York: Random House, 1995.

Sandmel, Samuel. *Judaism and Christian Beginnings*. Oxford: Oxford Univ. Press, 1978.

Sanders, E. P. *Jesus and Judaism*. London: SCM, 1985.

Schillebeeckx, Edward. *On Christian Faith: The Spiritual, Ethical and Political Dimensions*. New York: Crossroad, 1987.

Scholem, Gershom G. *Major Trends in Jewish Mysticism*. 1954. Reprint, New York: Schocken Books, 1995.

Sheehan, Thomas. *The First Coming: How the Kingdom of God Became Christianity*. New York: Random House, 1986.

Smart, Ninian. *The Philosophy of Religion*. London: Sheldon, 1979.

Smith, John MacDonald. *On Doing Without God*. Oxford: Emissary, 1993.

Smith, Wilfred Cantwell. *Toward a World Theology: A Faith in the Comparative History of Religion*. London: Macmillan, 1981, 1989.

Spong, John Shelby. *Born of a Woman: A Bishop Rethinks the Virgin Birth and the Place of Women in a Male-Dominated Church*. San Francisco: HarperSanFrancisco, 1992.

———. *Into the Whirlwind*. New York: Winston Press, 1983. Desbooks, Australia 1992.

———. *Liberating the Gospels: Reading the Bible with Jewish Eyes*. San Francisco: HarperSanFrancisco, 1996.

———. *Living in Sin? A Bishop Rethinks Human Sexuality*. San Francisco: HarperSanFrancisco, 1988.

———. *Rescuing the Bible from Fundamentalism: A Bishop Rethinks the Meaning of Scripture*. San Francisco: Harper SanFrancisco, 1991.

———. *Resurrection: Myth or Reality? A Bishop's Search for the Origins of Christianity*. San Francisco: HarperSanFrancisco, 1994.

———. *This Hebrew Lord: A Bishop's Search for an Authentic Jesus*. San Francisco: Harper & Row, 1974, 1988, 1993.

Strauss, David Frederich. *The Life of Jesus Critically Reviewed*. 1846. Reprint, London: SCM, 1973.

Swinburne, Richard. *The Coherence of Theism*. Oxford: Oxford Univ. Press, 1977.

Teilhard de Chardin, Pierre. *The Phenomenon of Man*. New York: 1959.

———. *The Appearance of Man*. London: Collins, 1965.

———. *The Future of Man*. London: Collins, 1964.

———. *Hymn of the Universe*. New York: Harper & Row, 1961.

Tillich, Paul. *The Courage to Be*. London: Collins, 1962.

———. *The Eternal Now*. New York: Scribner, 1963.

———. *Systematic Theology*. Vols. 1–3. London: Nisbit, 1953–1964.

Vermes, Geza. *Jesus, The Jew*. London: SCM, 1994.

Ward, Keith. *God, Chance and Necessity*. Oxford: One World, 1996.

———. *Religion and Creation*. Oxford: Clarendon, 1996.

———. *A Vision to Pursue*. London: SCM, 1991.

Whitehead, Alfred North. *Process and Reality*. 1929. Reprint, New York: Free Press, 1978.

———. *Religion in the Making*. Cambridge: Cambridge Univ. Press, 1927.

Index

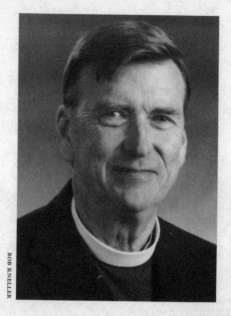

ROB KNELLER

JOHN SHELBY SPONG "has been surrounded by controversy as he has labored on the leading edge of movements
to bring blacks, women, and homosexuals into the full
life of his church" *(New York Times)*. The Episcopal
(Anglican) Bishop of Newark in New Jersey, Spong is
the author of fifteen books, including *Rescuing the Bible
from Fundamentalism*, and more than one hundred arti-
cles. He will retire as bishop after more than twenty
years and become a lecturer at Harvard University in
the year 2000.